Ethics

HARPERCOLLINS COLLEGE OUTLINE

Ethics

Peter K. McInerney
Oberlin College
George W. Rainbolt
Georgia State University

HarperPerennial
A Division of HarperCollinsPublishers

Produced by American BookWorks Corporation
Project Manager: Mary Mooney
Editor: Thomas H. Quinn

Library of Congress Cataloging-in-Publication Data
McInerney, Peter K.
  Ethics / Peter K. McInerney, George W. Rainbolt.
     p.   cm.
  Includes bibliographical references and index.
  ISBN 0-06-467166-6
  1. Ethics. 2. Ethical problems. 3. United states—Moral conditions.   I. Rainbolt,
George W.   II. Title
BJ1012.M416   1994
170—dc20   93-50930

94 95 96 97 98 ◆/RRD 10 9 8 7 6 5 4 3 2 1

Contents

Preface

Ethics is designed to help students to understand the major issues and arguments of ethics, including both ethical theory and topics in applied ethics. It systematically examines all the issues that are normally taught in a first course in ethics at the college level. The book summarizes all the major positions on each issue and provides all the basic arguments for and against each position. We have selected the topics in applied ethics that are most frequently discussed, and have attempted to give all the major positions a fair treatment. We want to encourage students to think about the reasons for a position and to draw their own conclusions based on the arguments.

Ethics is intended to serve as a study guide for students, to supplement introductory readings, and to introduce the general public to contemporary ethical thinking. It would be a valuable supplement to primary sources, because it outlines the major issues and arguments. It could also be used as a main text in an issue-oriented introductory course.

1

Ethics and Morality

All of us sometimes think about what we should do. Should we try to make more money, to get in better shape, to develop better friendships, to "look out for number one," to be more charitable, or to promote justice? Parents, friends, religious leaders, and public figures may tell us very different things. One friend may tell us that it is most important to get ahead at any cost, while another may tell us that it is our moral obligation to promote the welfare of all people. How do we figure out what we should do? Ethics and moral philosophy are the branches of philosophy that rationally investigate questions about the best way to live.

THE SUBJECT MATTER OF ETHICS AND MORAL PHILOSOPHY

Ethics and moral philosophy are about the best way to live. They are concerned with the sort of goals a person should have and with how we should treat other people. Every society has its customs and normal ways of life. The society teaches its children to act according to its customs, and people in the society expect and require that other people behave according to these customs and standards. These customs can be considered to be the unreflective ethics of the society at large. The customs tell people how to live, what to do, what sort of person to be, and how to evaluate other people. Acting and living in these ways is considered within the society to be the best way of life.

Why We Consider Ethical Issues

If a person learns how to live and what to do from her society, why do ethical and moral issues ever arise? Why does anyone ever think about questions of ethics? There are many factors that lead people to think about the best way to live.

Individual Resistance For many different reasons individuals may not want to adopt some of the customs of their society. As an example, children may not want to eat only what they are supposed to eat, or teenagers may want to engage in sexual activities that are not allowed, or adults may not want to obey the authorities in the society. Customs and morals always place restrictions on satisfying desires. Hence, it is inevitable that people ask why they should follow the societal customs and standards rather than do something else.

Conflicts and Balancing People have many different social roles in any society. The requirements of one social role may conflict with those of another. What a woman should do as a mother of her children may conflict with what she should do as a member of a state or as a partner in a business. For example, in ancient Greek theater, Antigone experiences the conflict between her family obligation to bury her dead brother and the king's command that her brother not be buried. Even when a direct conflict has not already occurred, people have to think about how to balance their roles. A person has to determine which goals and requirements should take precedence over other goals and requirements, and in which circumstances. She has to combine and balance all the customs that apply to her. For example, a person will have to decide how much time and energy to devote to her career, and how much time and energy to devote to personal relationships. To combine and balance customs and to resolve conflicts, people have to think about which combinations and alternatives would be best.

Choice Among Societal Ways of Life In many traditional societies, a person has no choice about his occupation or way of life. Authorities or his circumstances decide these issues for him. However, in our society people can and usually must choose the occupation and way of life that they will pursue. It is part of our cultural way of life that people have to decide whether to join the military, become a salesperson, pursue a medical or business career, and so on. People also must decide whether to get married, be involved in a religious group, and perform community service. To make these decisions, people have to think about the best way of life.

Social Change The customs and values of any society may change over time. In our society there have been major changes in the last thirty years concerning acceptable sexual behavior and woman's work outside the home. Many factors contribute to societal change, but ultimately people in the society must accept and live by the new standards if any change is to occur. To decide whether to continue the traditional ways of life or to adopt changes, people have to think about the best way to live.

Societal Pluralism Our current society does not have one uniform set of customs and values. There are many different standards, and some of these standards contradict others. For example, some people emphasize individual success even if it requires abandoning one's background to move ahead. Others insist on the importance of family or group identity and on conserving a traditional culture. Individuals have to think about ethical issues in deciding which customs and standards to follow and how to evaluate people who follow other standards.

Being Responsible for Standards Some people want to be responsible for themselves. They think that they ought to decide actively on their own standards and ways of life. Just to absorb standards and ways of life passively from one's society is not enough. They feel that the customs and values that an individual receives from society are not really their own until they have explicitly chosen them. To make standards their own in the fullest sense requires that they think about them and have reasons for living by one set of standards rather than another. This is what the ancient Greek philosopher Socrates (470–399 B.C.) meant when he taught that "the unexamined life is not worth living."

Having True Standards Most people think that there is an objective good. They think that some goals and some ways of treating other people are objectively good and others are objectively bad. Morality is not a matter of personal opinion or societal tradition. Personal and societal views can be true or false. If one believes in objective goodness, she has reason to want to be sure that the standards by which she lives are the true ones. She should be ready to revise her standards and moral positions to make them agree with what is objectively good, if that is necessary. In order to determine that their standards are true, people have to think about ethical questions.

Major and General Issues

Any question about what to do is an ethical question in the most general sense. However, many everyday decisions are not very important, and many decisions depend upon very specific circumstances and on facts about individual people. Studies in ethics cannot consider everything that we do and all of the specific facts and circumstances that affect our everyday actions. Studies in ethics focus on major issues about what goals to pursue and how to treat other people. Studies in ethics focus on general standards that apply to many people and to large parts of their lives. Differences between types of people, such as between men and women and between more capable and less capable people, are included in some theories about the good life and the right way to treat people, but many ethical positions say little about differences between individual people. They do not deny that there are many individual differences, but they think that differences do not affect general ethical claims. Differences make a difference only in the application of more general ethical positions to individual cases.

Ethics, Morality, and Political Philosophy

Ethics tries to figure out both how an individual can live a good life and how people should treat one another in a good society. Most ethical thinkers consider these issues to be interconnected, but some focus on one or the other of them. There are disagreements about whether what makes an individual's life go well would also agree with the rules for treating other people well. Different conceptions of the good life for an individual give different priorities to individual self-interest and treating people morally. Moral philosophers consider treating everyone morally to be what is most important, so that the good life for an individual includes always treating other people morally. Other conceptions of the good life for an individual, such as egoistic hedonism or selfish self-development (see chapter 2), are basically immoral. According to such nonmoral conceptions of the good life, an individual person will be better off by sometimes violating the rules for treating other people well.

Moral Philosophy The terms "ethics" and "moral philosophy" are frequently used interchangeably. Many people consider them to mean basically the same thing. Particularly those who consider being moral to be the best way of life for an individual are likely to equate the two. However, there is also a narrower conception of moral philosophy. Moral philosophy in the narrower sense is an investigation of the basic principles and underlying ideas of Western morality. In this narrower sense moral philosophy would never advise someone to do something that is immoral, whereas some conceptions of the good life do advise people sometimes to act immorally. Most studies in "applied ethics," such as medical ethics or business ethics, assume this narrower conception. Most studies in applied ethics focus on the moral dimensions of specific issues such as abortion or affirmative action. This book considers both questions about the good life and questions about the right way to treat people.

Ethics is usually distinguished from social and political philosophy. Both ethics and social and political philosophy examine what makes a society good, but they focus on different features of a good society. Ethics considers the rules for how individuals should treat one another. Social and political philosophy consider which form of government and what economic and institutional systems are best. The features of a good society that are examined by ethics and by social and political philosophy are not always completely separable from each other. Many moral theorists think that morality shows that certain economic and social arrangements ought to exist.

Ethical Theory and Applied Ethics

Ethics includes both reasoning *about* basic and general principles and reasoning *from* those principles to what someone should do in a specific situation. Ethical theory attempts to state basic and general principles for acting and judging, and attempts to find a basis for having one set of principles rather than another. Applied ethics is the study of specific ethical issues that are controversial, such as whether abortion or euthanasia are good things.

If everyone knew in every case which course of action was morally right, there would be no practical need for ethical theory. People would already be sure what morality required of them, and ethical theory would be interesting only to intellectuals. However, there are many specific moral issues, such as those of applied ethics, about which people are unsure. They may have conflicting ideas about which course of action is moral, and they do not know how to go on from there. An ethical theory tries to defend explicit standards that can be applied to difficult cases, as well as to easier ones. The explicit standards would tell people what characteristics make an action, a state of affairs, or a life moral, so that they would know what to look for. Moral theories tell people what type of facts are relevant for determining what is moral. People can then seek out these facts in specific cases.

Not all attempts to state clearly the basic and general standards for acting and judging are ethical theory. Religions, political parties, and other organizations may want a clear and consistent statement of their standards, or of what they take to be the revealed word of God, or of the teaching of some prophet or leader. Ethical theory does more than formulate explicit statements of basic and general principles for acting and judging. It tries to justify the standards, rather than simply accepting them as dogma. Ethical theory tries to show that some set of standards is better than any other set.

Ethics is supposed to help people decide what to do. Basic and general principles have to be applied to specific issues and to the very specific situations in which we find ourselves. Applied ethics is the study of specific issues that are ethically controversial. Applied ethics tries to figure out for these specific issues what features are morally relevant and what general ethical principles apply to them. The study of applied ethics develops a person's judgment. The practice that is gained by considering what features are morally relevant and what general ethical principles apply may help us to decide similar questions about our own unique situations.

ETHICS AS PHILOSOPHY

The term "ethics" refers both to a subject matter—the best way to live and moral behavior—and to a way of investigating that subject matter. Ethics as a way of investigating is a branch of philosophy. Ethics is the part of philosophy that rationally studies how to live, what sort of person to be, how to treat other people, and how to judge other people. Ethics seeks reasons that support one position over another. All people already have views about these questions, and they regularly act from these views. Hence, people are likely to be strongly emotionally attached to some specific views. However, having strong feelings about an ethical issue is not an argument or justification for one's position. People have had strong feelings about many mistaken views, such as that the earth is flat or that members of other races are intrinsically inferior. The study of ethics requires that we develop objective reasons for the views that guide our acting and judging. It requires that we step back from our already established commitments in order to consider and evaluate the reasons for and against the alternative positions. The study of ethics does not require that we abandon our previous positions, but only that we consider alternatives to it with an open mind.

Rational Support

Ethics seeks rational reasons that support one position over another. Rational reasons for a position indicate or show that that position is true or better than any of the alternative positions. They lend support to that position or are evidence for it. Ethics seeks objective evidence for the truth of claims about the good life and the right way to treat people. Such evidence should hold for anyone who can comprehend it and will consider it with an open mind. Thus, although some people may be more intellectually capable than others, ethical and other philosophical positions are in principle available to anyone. No special revelation or social position is necessary to understand them; we have only to be able to think and reason about the evidence.

Ethics is ultimately about what *should* be, but the justification for what should be lies in *what is* or the facts. Ethical positions are supposed to be supported by facts. Ethical positions usually depend upon some combination of facts about the circumstances for acting or judging, about human nature, about the individual agent and his society, and about what is intrinsically good or moral. Different ethical positions make different claims about what really exists. For example, some ethical theories claim that goodness depends entirely on what makes people happy, while other theories claim that there is a standard of goodness by which people should act whether it makes them happy or not. Some applied ethical positions claim that a fetus has a soul that gives it a right to life, while other positions deny this. Figuring out what the facts are and taking all the relevant facts into account are important parts of ethical thinking.

Clarity

In thinking about ultimate questions, ethicists and other philosophers try to make concepts and positions as clear as possible. This is in order to understand exactly what is meant by the concepts and positions. Probably everyone has had the experience of finding that they actually agreed with someone with whom they had been arguing. The apparent disagreement turns out to be the result of meaning different things by the same words. Being clear about what we mean allows us to understand what the real differences are and what evidence would support one position rather than another. The analysis of concepts and clarification of positions helps to show how they are logically and conceptually connected with each other. Philosophers investigate whether two ethical positions are consistent with each other, whether one presupposes or requires the other, whether one makes the other more or less probable, and whether one type of action, such as abortion, is an instance of a more general type, such as murder.

Considering Alternative Positions

In seeking the best supported position on an ethical issue, philosophers have to consider all the reasonable alternatives and provide strong reasons why one position is better than any of its competitors. For this reason many ethical discussions are like a debate between alternative positions. Each side is trying both to defend its own position and to attack the other positions. Defenders of different ethical positions are each trying to show that there is more and better evidence for their position than for any of the alternatives.

Disputed Issues

You will notice that ethics and other branches of philosophy are different from most other subjects that you study. The study of history, psychology, mathematics, or chemistry involves learning established truths and how the truths were determined. Philosophy focuses on fundamental issues concerning which there are disputes. Significant ethical issues cannot be directly settled by sense perception or experimentation, so that it is much more difficult to settle them conclusively. For this reason, even introductory works in ethics discuss the reasons for and against alternative positions, rather than teaching established ethical truths.

However, it would be a serious error to conclude that ethical positions are just different personal opinions and that any position is as good as any other. There have to be good rational reasons for any ethical position, so that philosophers argue about only those alternatives for which they can make a reasonable case. Furthermore, at any given time the evidence for one position may be stronger than the evidence for any of the alternatives. Over a period of time, new distinctions, new arguments, and accumulating empirical evidence make some positions very implausible. Those ethical positions that lose most of their support drop out of consideration. They are no longer among the reasonable alternatives.

Ethics is concerned with the sort of goals a person should have and with how we should treat other people. Many factors lead people to think about the best way to live. Individual resistance to the restrictions that customs and morals place on desires, the resolution of conflicts between what different customs demand of people, the balancing of different requirements, the necessity of choosing among societal ways of life, questions of social change, dealing with societal pluralism, the ideal of being responsible for one's own standards, and the search for true standards lead people to think about ethics.

Ethics focuses on basic and general standards that apply to many people and to large parts of their lives. Ethics tries to figure out both how an individual can live a good life and how people should treat one another in a good society. There are disagreements about whether what makes an individual's life go well would also agree with the rules for treating other people well. Ethics and moral philosophy are frequently considered to be the same thing, although there is also a narrower conception of moral philosophy. Ethics differs from social and political philosophy in that ethics focuses on the rules for how individuals should treat one another, while social and political philosophy consider which form of government and what economic and institutional systems are best.

Ethics includes both reasoning about basic and general principles and reasoning from those principles to what someone should do in a specific situation. Ethical theory attempts both to state basic and general principles for acting and judging and to find a basis for having one set of principles rather than another. Applied ethics tries to figure out for specific controversial issues what features are morally relevant and what general ethical principles apply to them.

Ethics is the branch of philosophy that rationally studies how to live and how to treat and judge other people. The study of ethics requires that we develop objective reasons for the views that guide our acting and judging. Rational reasons for an ethical position indicate or show that that position is true or better than any of the alternative positions. Ethical positions are supposed to be supported by facts, such as facts about human nature, about the individual agent and his society, and about what is intrinsically good or moral.

In studying ethics, we try to make concepts and positions as clear as possible in order to understand exactly what is meant by them. In seeking the best supported position on an ethical issue, we have to consider all of the reasonable alternatives and provide strong reasons why one position is better than any of its competitors. Even introductory works in ethics discuss the reasons for and against alternative positions, rather than teaching established ethical truths.

Selected Readings

Becker, Lawrence (ed.). *Encyclopedia of Ethics* (2 vols.). Hamden, CT: Garland, 1991.

Martinich, A.P. *Philosophical Writing*. Englewood Cliffs, NJ: Prentice-Hall, 1989.

Woodhouse, Mark. *A Preface to Philosophy* (2nd ed.) Belmont, CA: Wadsworth, 1980.

2

The Good Life

Throughout history, people have had very different ideas about the best way to live. We all probably know individual people whose values are radically different from one another's. Each does not want to live the sort of life that the others prize most highly. We may find ourselves tending to agree with each of them at different times. We feel inclined at different times toward different values and life-styles. Sometimes, pleasurable activities may seem to be most important. At other times you may feel driven to succeed at something without regard for pleasure, or feel that human suffering must be reduced even at the cost of personal sacrifice. Which route should you follow? What is worth doing, and what is not worth the effort? Philosophical theories have attempted to state what makes a life good and why such a way of living is better than any other.

SELFISHNESS

Perhaps the most common idea about living well is "to look out for yourself." Selfishness is concern only for oneself. A thoroughly selfish person does not care much about anyone else, about the good of society, about the progress of knowledge, or about following God's plan. Selfish people usually think that they have to look out for themselves because no one else is likely to do it. They may even think that society would be better off if everyone were selfish, although a completely selfish person is not very concerned about the good of society in general. There are different forms of selfishness that correspond to different ideas about what people's selfish interests are.

Hedonism

Hedonism is the view that the only good in life is pleasure. A person should try to get as much pleasure and avoid as much pain as possible. Different things may bring pleasure and pain. Eating, drinking, having sex, and sleeping are pleasurable. Sickness, physical injury, being too cold or hot or wet, being forced to do boring work, and being deprived of pleasurable things are painful. Some hedonists focus their energies on these things, but this is a pretty limited range of pleasurable and painful items. More sophisticated hedonists obtain pleasure from other things as well, recognize that we may have to suffer some pain in order to get a greater amount of pleasure, and are concerned with ensuring themselves a favorable balance of pleasure and pain.

SOPHISTICATED HEDONISM

Sophisticated hedonists are concerned about more than the simple pleasures and pains. They enjoy the company of other people, humor, music, movies, and other arts, enjoy perceiving and knowing about the world, so long as it is interesting, and may enjoy practically anything so long as it brings them pleasure. To increase their range of pleasures, sophisticated hedonists may develop a wider knowledge of what sorts of things are pleasurable and develop their own tastes, so that more things can bring them pleasure. Sophisticated hedonists also realize that it is usually not possible in real life to experience large amounts of pleasure continuously. It is usually necessary to put up with some unpleasant things that accompany or are a means to pleasurable things. The point is to get the greatest balance of pleasure over pain. A situation that brings the greatest overall amount of pleasure may still include some unpleasant things that cannot be avoided. It is also necessary to balance the attractions of short-term pleasure with those of long-term pleasure.

Thoughtful hedonists want to ensure themselves a favorable balance of pleasure and pain. They try to increase their control over the world so that they can bring about pleasurable events and avoid painful ones. Thoughtful hedonists want to develop their powers to influence events, even if the process of development is not itself very pleasant, because such powers can produce enough benefits in the future to make the development process worthwhile. For example, it is worth the effort to prepare for a high-paying job if the money that you later make will bring you enough pleasure and allow you to avoid enough pain. However, these sorts of estimates of overall amounts of pleasure and pain can sometimes be hard to make with any accuracy.

EGOISTIC HEDONISM

Hedonism advises people to pursue pleasurable experiences and anything else that will contribute to the overall balance of pleasure over pain.

Selfish hedonists are sometimes called "egoistic hedonists" because only their own pleasures and pains count. A person pursues her own pleasure, not the pleasure of anyone else. Sometimes the pleasure or welfare of someone else may contribute to her own pleasure. In such cases a hedonist will care about another's well-being, but this is only because another's welfare contributes to her own pleasure. What a consistent hedonist will not have is commitment to something, other than her own pleasure, for its own sake. A selfish hedonist will not care about the good of others or about art, science, the environment, or God except insofar as these bring her pleasure. She will never sacrifice any portion of her own pleasure for these projects. Other versions of hedonism may be altruistic or even concerned for the pleasure of all people (see chapter 4 on utilitarianism), but these forms of hedonism are not selfish.

Other people are usually suspicious of someone who is obviously concerned only with his own pleasure. They think that the selfish person will try to take advantage of them whenever the opportunity arises. This may not be true, because a thoughtful hedonist may judge that not taking advantage of someone will produce more benefits in the long run. Getting the person to be "on your side" may ultimately produce more benefits than taking advantage would. However, since many people do think that selfish hedonists will try to take advantage of them, many people dislike and may harm a selfish hedonist who is open about his view of the good life. Hence, a thoughtful selfish hedonist should deceive others about his values. He should pretend to care about the welfare of others, while secretly pursuing only his own pleasure. In this way he can get other people to like him and to help him to attain his goals.

PSYCHOLOGICAL HEDONISM

The theory of psychological hedonism is one way in which hedonists have defended the claim that a person should try only to get the most pleasure and to avoid the most pain in life. This theory claims that it is a psychological fact about people that they pursue only what they think will bring them pleasure and that they avoid what they think will bring them pain. Pleasure is the only "positive reinforcement," so that the things that become associated with pleasure are the things that a person automatically pursues. Things that become associated with pain are automatically avoided. However, the automatic pursuit of pleasurable things and avoidance of painful things are largely unconscious processes, because people do not realize that this is what they are doing. People generally do not realize that they are selfish hedonists and that they are presenting a false picture to other people in order to win their support. Most people are unconsciously manipulating everyone else with the talk about noble motives, moral duties, and concern for the public good.

According to psychological hedonism, no one ever sacrifices her own benefits for the benefits of anyone else. This is why the truth of psychological hedonism would support hedonism as the best way to live. If you cannot be obligated to do something that you are incapable of doing, and you are incapable of sacrificing your own benefits for the benefits of someone else, you cannot be obligated to make that sacrifice. Hedonists conclude that if people are going to pursue pleasure without realizing it anyway, it is better to embrace hedonism and to pay more attention to what actually brings you pleasure. Hedonists claim that by being aware of everyone's hedonism, you can increase the favorable balance of your own pleasures and pains.

Arguments Against Egoistic Hedonism

There are several arguments against the view that selfish hedonism is the best way to live. One argument is that egoistic hedonism is self-defeating, because constantly pursuing pleasure is not a good way to obtain it. Most of a person's pleasures occur in taking pleasure in some activity or taking pleasure in the well-being of other people and the success of various causes. To take pleasure in these things requires that one care about them, not simply about the pleasure they may bring. For example, to take pleasure in a game or sport requires that you care about playing it well and about the goal of the game or sport. If you focus only on trying to obtain pleasure in life, rather than on fulfilling other objectives, you will end up obtaining less pleasure.

Another argument is that egoistic hedonism prevents a person from having satisfying personal relationships. If you already care about some other people, you may get pleasure from their company or from knowing that their lives are going well. However, it is very hard to develop a new intimate and caring relationship with someone if you are pursuing only your own pleasure. It is particularly difficult to develop new relationships because a selfish hedonist usually must deceive others about his values. Furthermore, the thought that everyone else is a selfish hedonist, who is at least unconsciously trying to manipulate you, makes it very hard to care about them. It would be especially depressing to think that your mother, your father, your family, and your best friend had no commitment to your welfare, but were just deceiving you into thinking that they did. Someone with this attitude is not likely to have a very pleasant life.

A third objection to egoistic hedonism is that it is immoral. It is immoral because it is totally selfish. The interests of other people are never more than a means to one's own pleasure. A selfish hedonist will treat other people in the most terrible ways if doing so contributes to his pleasure.

Self-Development

Self-development is "becoming all you can be." The good life for a person is to develop her abilities and talents to their fullest extent. A person should achieve as much as possible in whatever fields he or she can. You should strive for accomplishment in athletics or music or science or politics or business or any other field. People who are very talented and develop their talents successfully may produce great results. However, recognition from other people or great accomplishments are not the goal. The goal is to do the best with what you have—that is, to develop yourself.

Self-development is an attractive idea. Self-development, like the pursuit of pleasure, need not be selfish if it is restricted by other goods. Most philosophers who advocate self-development, such as Aristotle (384–322 B.C.), do not endorse the purely selfish form of it. The purely selfish notion of self-development is that developing your own abilities is the only thing that counts for you. Developing other people's abilities or making their lives better is not the selfish person's concern. He will not let anything get in the way of his self-development. He develops his talents and strives to accomplish without any concern for other people. Some "creative geniuses" have this single-minded devotion to developing themselves at any cost, including any cost to other people.

OBJECTIONS

The main objections to selfish self-development are that it is immoral, that it prevents a person from having satisfying personal relationships, and that it ignores the importance of pleasure and pain. The first two objections are common to any form of selfishness. Selfish self-development, like egoistic hedonism, is immoral because it treats other people simply as means to one's own selfish goal. The welfare of other people is not considered to be intrinsically important. Satisfying personal relationships are scarce, because a person whose only concern is to develop her own abilities is unlikely to develop satisfying personal relations. Other people will mistrust and probably dislike the selfish self-developer if she is open about it. If she hides her values and tries to manipulate others to help her attain her goals, she will never have secure and intimate relationships with people.

The Goodness of Selfishness

Many economic thinkers claim that an economic system is better when people work for their own selfish gain, rather than for the good of the community at large. More wealth will be produced in the society because people will work harder for their own gain than for the gain of the community at large. A free-market system will also produce a better mix of products than a planned community will. People will produce what they can sell to other people, and each person's judgment of what he wants and needs individually is better than the general community's judgment of what individuals want and need. These features of an economic system are sometimes used to support the claim that there is a "virtue to selfishness." More people will be better off if everyone behaves selfishly than if they try to act for the good of everyone else.

It is important to note that the benefits of such an economic system do not show that being selfish is the best way to live. A person's willingness to work hard depends upon what she wants. Many people are willing to work just as hard or harder for the benefit of their spouse, relatives, and children as for their own selfish benefit. Some people are willing to work just as hard for a religious, moral, environmental, or artistic cause. Furthermore, the smooth working of an economic system depends upon a certain amount of social order. People have to obey the rules of buying and selling. Hence, the economic benefits of a free-market system occur only when people support certain rules for dealing with others.

SELF-INTEREST

Self-interest is the view that the good life consists of fulfilling one's interests. A person should act so as promote her own interests. Since a person's interests may include concern for other people or devotion to a cause, self-interest is not the same as selfishness. According to one frequent interpretation of self-interest, a person's self-interest consists of satisfying her desires or getting what she wants. This will make her happy. According to a second interpretation, a person's self-interest includes both the maximum satisfaction of informed wants and self-development.

Satisfying Wants

One interpretation is that self-interest consists of the maximum satisfaction of your desires and wants. Satisfying desires and wants makes you happy, and your self-interest is to be happy. To have the greatest amount of happiness through satisfying desires and wants is to live the best life possible.

This theory of self-interest says that you should act in order to maximize the satisfaction of your desires and wants, but it does not tell you what to desire and want. What you want can be something for yourself, something for other people, something for the world or environment, or something for God. A self-interested person may have many different concrete attitudes depending upon what sort of wants she has. One self-interested person may have mostly wants for things (such as pleasure, money or power) for herself, so that her self-interest is to be selfish. Another self-interested person may have mostly wants for the welfare of other people, so that her self-interest is to be altruistic or "self-sacrificing." A person may sacrifice some selfish interests for the welfare of others, yet still be acting in her self-interest.

Self-interest is sometimes equated with selfishness. This is because it is assumed that the person's wants and desires are for things only for himself.

Innate or "natural" desires are always selfish, according to this view, so that pursuing your "natural" desires is to be selfish. It is this selfish version of self-interest that Gautama Buddha (560–480 B.C.) attacked. He claimed that selfish desire was the source of all our dissatisfaction with life and that the good life required abandoning all selfish desire.

Self-interest need not be selfishness because a person need not want things only for herself. Perhaps all people do have some selfish desires, but practically all people want or desire things for other people as well, at least for their mother or friends or family. A self-interested person may want a natural park to be preserved or the environment to be cleaned up, even though this will bring no direct advantage to her. These are not selfish desires, but the satisfaction of these desires will please her. Acting to satisfy such nonselfish desires can contribute to the maximum amount of satisfaction of her desires.

MAXIMIZING SATISFACTION

To be as happy as possible, a person should act so as to bring about the greatest amount of satisfaction of his desires and wants. Any person wants or desires many different things. Some of these wants and desires are stronger or more intense than others. The more strongly you want something, the more satisfying it is to get it. Hence, this view advises people to try to satisfy their strongest desires. Since any person has many different wants and desires, including wanting some things not to happen, the combination of wants that you try to satisfy is also important. You may have two wants that cannot both be satisfied. They may contradict each other, such as wanting to diet but also wanting to eat a huge banana split, or the circumstances may just prevent you from satisfying both. The circumstances may require that in order to get something that you strongly want, such as the taste of a chocolate sundae, you will have put up with something that you want to avoid, such as the calories that the sundae will add to your weight. To obtain the most satisfaction, you should act to satisfy as many wants and desires of the highest strength as can be satisfied together. The greatest overall satisfaction is the result of how many positive wants are satisfied, how many negative wants to avoid things are not satisfied, and how intense each want is. You have to figure out what course of action will bring the greatest overall satisfaction in each set of circumstances. This is the course of action that maximizes satisfaction and makes you most happy.

Sophisticated followers of self-interest have to consider many of the same factors that sophisticated hedonists do. They have to consider for what period of time they should seek the greatest satisfaction of desires and wants and how to ensure high levels of satisfaction. It makes a difference whether you are seeking the greatest satisfaction of wants during the next day, the next year, or your entire lifetime. If you cared only about the next day, you could satisfy many desires during that day at the cost of many unsatisfying things later on. For example, you could borrow and spend lots of money to satisfy your wants today, but you would have to sacrifice to pay it back later. Most followers of self-interest try to maximize satisfaction over their entire lifetimes. To ensure high levels of satisfaction later on, followers of self-interest try to increase their control over the world. They develop their own abilities and powers to affect the world, because these will help them to satisfy their wants.

PSYCHOLOGICAL SUPPORT

The "maximum satisfaction of wants" theory of the good life is frequently defended by appealing to facts of human psychology. The argument is similar to the psychological argument for hedonism. It is a psychological fact about humans, the argument claims, that their actions are produced by their strongest current desires or wants. A person always does what she at the present time most wants to do. Whatever a person does must be motivated by her wants in order to be a voluntary action, and her strongest current wants or some combination of these motivate her actions. Since a person's actions are always attempts to satisfy her desires anyway, it is better to realize this fact. It is better to embrace acting from self-interest as the right or good way to live. This allows you to do a better job of figuring out which combinations of desires and wants and which courses of action will bring the most satisfaction in the long run.

Objections

The main objections to the "maximum satisfaction of wants" theory of the good life are that it does not tell you what to want, it does not distinguish between good wants and bad wants, and it does not promote full self-development. To satisfy wants and desires, you must already have wants and desires. People always already do have wants and desires, but they are also able to develop new wants and to strengthen or weaken old ones. Parents, educators, and friends try to cultivate the right desires and wants in children and other people, and people try to develop the right desires and wants in themselves. This theory of the good life, however, focuses on satisfying the wants that people already have. It does not tell you much about which wants to encourage in other people and in yourself. Should you try to change your current wants at all? Should you try to develop an appreciation of art or an appreciation of torture? This theory would tell you only to develop wants that contribute to the maximum satisfaction of wants. It would tell you to cultivate wants that can be satisfied easily and to weaken wants that cannot be satisfied without sacrificing too many other satisfactions. For example, if your desire to torture is likely to result in your suffering legal punishment, the desire to torture should be weakened or eliminated. Critics of the theory think that it should provide more specific guidance than this.

The "maximum satisfaction of wants" theory considers wants primarily in terms of how much satisfaction they might bring. Wants differ in their intensity, in their prospects or chances of being satisfied, and in their compatibility with other wants of the person. However, this theory does not distinguish wants and desires for good things from wants and desires for bad things. Many people consider this to be a serious flaw. Some wants may be for things that would be harmful or painful to a person if the wants were satisfied. You may strongly desire some food that in fact will make you ill. Satisfying such wants cannot be in the person's real self-interest, because it will not make him happy. A person may also not have wants for some things that he really needs or that would benefit him if he had them. In this case also, self-interest seems to be more than the maximum satisfaction of a person's *actual* wants. Finally, this theory gives no priority to moral wants over selfish wants. It does not require that a person want to be moral at all, and if he does want to be moral, it does not require that moral wants have priority over other wants when there is a conflict. According to this theory, a person can be totally selfish and treat other people horribly, yet live a good life.

To be sure that they will have a high level of satisfaction of their wants, sophisticated followers of the "maximum satisfaction of wants" theory will try to develop those abilities that help them to satisfy their wants. However, the theory does not advise them to develop other abilities that are not directly connected with their actual wants. Hence, they may not develop all their abilities and talents. Some of their abilities and talents may be wasted.

Maximum Satisfaction of Informed Wants and Self-Development

This interpretation of self-interest tries to remove the features that produced the objections to the "maximum satisfaction of wants" theory. Wants for things that would be harmful or painful to a person are to be excluded from her self-interest. If a person realizes that the outcome of satisfying a particular want would be harmful or painful to her, she would not try to satisfy that want. Her self-interest will include only the satisfaction of informed wants. Informed wants are those that are informed about what a person needs and what the result would be of satisfying a want. Wants that are informed by this knowledge will not be for things that are harmful or painful. Informed wants will include wants for things that the person needs and for things that would benefit her.

This interpretation also includes self-development as part of a person's self-interest. It is in a person's interest to develop his abilities and talents, whether he currently wants to do so or not. His life will be better if he develops himself. Since developing his abilities and talents would benefit him, his informed wants should include wanting to develop his abilities and talents. Hence, this view of the good life advises a person to try to develop some new wants in himself. He should cultivate wants to develop specific abilities and talents, such as wanting to develop his scientific understanding of things. He should also encourage wants and interests that are connected with these abilities and talents. The development of his scientific understanding of the world would be helped by a curiosity about scientific discoveries and an interest in scientific achievements. His life will become richer through these changes, because he will expand the range of things that can satisfy his wants.

Morality and Self-Interest

Many philosophers have claimed that it is in a person's self-interest to be moral. They claim that informed self-interest does not conflict with leading a moral life, but rather supports it. There are different accounts of how treating other people morally is in a person's self-interest. The most famous account was given by Plato (428–347 B.C.) in *The Republic*. Plato claimed that the happiest life belonged to the person whose soul had a good inner harmony. This good inner harmony is justice in the soul. Justice in the soul, in which each part of the soul is performing its proper function well, is far more pleasant and more productive than inner conflict and disunity. Good inner harmony is also far more pleasant and productive than control of the soul by appetites and passions. Thus, it is in your informed self-interest to have this good inner harmony. Just actions toward other people contribute to and follow from justice in the soul. They build up a good inner harmony in the person. Unjust actions toward other people destroy the soul's inner harmony and ultimately make a person unhappy. Therefore, in order to be happy, a person must cultivate a just and harmonious soul, and so must treat others justly.

There have been many other accounts of how being moral is in someone's self-interest. If someone has been raised to live a moral life, she may have very strong wants to act morally. To act immorally might produce a guilty conscience, which would make her unhappy. For such a person to satisfy her informed wants to the greatest degree, she will have to act morally. Other accounts emphasize the necessity of order in a society for any person to be able to satisfy her wants. Few people would be able to live a happy and successful life if no one in society accepted moral restrictions on their actions. A "war of all against all" would exist if there were no moral and legal restrictions. You could not satisfy many of your wants if everyone was trying to rob, cheat, kill, or take advantage of you for their selfish gain. According to social contract theories, it is in everyone's self-interest to have moral social rules that restrict selfish behavior. It is in your self-interest to have and to support such moral rules and laws. It is only through supporting morality that you can have any good chance of satisfying your wants. Therefore, it is in your self-interest to live a moral life.

MORALITY

Many philosophers have claimed that leading the good life is to be moral. The best way to live is to treat other people and oneself according to morality. We all have some understanding of what it is to live a moral life. Some actions are easily identified as moral actions, and other actions are clearly immoral. However, there have been some differences in moral standards in different historical periods and in different cultures. Some of those who think that self-interest supports morality think that moral standards are relative to cultures and historical periods (see chapter 3). However, most defenders of the view that the moral life is the best life think that there are objectively true moral standards. Different moral theories, such as those discussed in chapters 4 through 6, attempt to state exactly what it is to be moral. Although they differ about some details, all theories of morality share some basic features. They all claim that your actions must take the interests of other people into account, not simply your own selfish interests. Morality always includes requirements about how people are to be treated by other people. It always imposes some restrictions on acting from selfish interests. For example, morality prohibits harming other people just because you enjoy doing so.

Morality also includes requirements of how a person is to treat herself. It sets some goals for what you should and should not do with your life. Wasting abilities or resources that could contribute to the welfare of others is generally forbidden by morality. Morality also requires you to be concerned about the behavior of other people, not just your own behavior. You are supposed to disapprove of immoral actions, to encourage other people to act morally, and to support those who are the victims of seriously immoral treatment. Members of a moral community are supposed to regard and to treat one another in these ways.

Why Be Moral?

Why is living morally the best way to live? There are two main types of answer to this question. Some philosophers claim that living morally is in a person's self-interest. Living morally brings the person the most satisfaction of his informed wants and provides for the proper treatment of other people as well. There is no conflict between morality and enlightened self-interest, according to this first position. The second answer is that living morally is the intrinsically right or good way to live, whether or not it allows you to satisfy your wants. You ought to be moral even if it makes you unhappy or imposes severe burdens on you. Being moral is always more important than selfish interests or concern for anything else, such as art, science, or the environment. Being moral always has priority over any other interest whenever the two conflict. The second position is frequently expressed in terms of morality commanding you without conditions (without the condition that your wants be satisfied). You should do your moral duty, and this "should" is an unconditional requirement (a "categorical imperative," in Kant's terms; see chapter 5).

Justifications of Morality

If being moral sometimes conflicts with your self-interest, why should you be moral? Why should you follow morality rather than do what you want or what will make you happy? Four major types of justification of morality have been proposed. (A fifth type of justification is that morality does not conflict with self-interest).

DIVINE COMMAND

Many people think that God is the source of morality. God requires you to be moral whether or not being moral makes you happy in this life. You ought to be moral regardless of the costs, because being moral is following God's commands or acting in accord with God's wishes. You ought to obey God's commands because God is all-powerful, all-knowing, all-good, and inspires awe. Some divine-command theories stop at this point. However, some divine-command theories claim that you ought to obey God's commands because God will, in an afterlife, reward those who obey and punish those who disobey. The notion of a reward or punishment in an afterlife makes obeying God's commands a matter of enlightened self-interest. When you include the afterlife, not just your worldly life, it is in your long-term self-interest to be moral. Other divine-command theories claim that you ought to obey God's commands because this is the only way that humans can fulfill their nature. Finite beings yearn for a relationship with God and can be deeply satisfied in this world only through following God's wishes (see "Why Be Religious", p. 25).

INTUITION OF OBJECTIVE GOODNESS

Some philosophers have claimed that moral goodness is an objectively existing characteristic that somehow "attaches" to actions and states of affairs in this world. People can detect which actions and results of actions are objectively good or objectively evil with a special mental sense, which is called "moral intuition." Moral intuition tells you which actions are morally good, and their moral goodness requires that they be done. Moral intuition also tells you which actions are morally bad, and their moral badness requires that they not be done. Doing morally good actions and avoiding morally evil actions are required of a person by objective moral goodness and badness. Some people may be better at determining whether an action is morally good, morally neutral, or morally bad, but everyone is obligated in the same way by objective moral characteristics. Objective moral characteristics require that you live a moral life.

NATURAL LAW

This is another theory of objective moral characteristics and of how people know about them. According to natural law theory, there are laws that govern the behavior of all things. These "natural laws" concern the proper functioning of all things, including people. An animal body may function as it should or have diseases or deficiencies. Your heart may be doing its job well or may have defects. Similarly, there is a naturally good way or ways for a human life to go on, and there are deficient and deviant ways for a human life to go on. Using their reason and powers of observation, people can discover what the naturally good ways of living are. Being moral is living in agreement with the natural laws for human behavior, the naturally good ways of living. A person should live according to the morality of natural laws, even when he might receive some benefit from disobeying the laws. For example, a person should not keep other people in slavery—slavery violates their natural rights—even if he can make a large profit from it. Moral natural laws require a person to live a moral life. Some philosophers, such as Saint Thomas Aquinas (1225–74), have combined natural law theory with religion by considering God to be the source of these natural laws.

TRUE SELF OR DEEP SELF

A true self is an inner nature that is different from your everyday understanding of yourself. A true self is what you most truly are. Many moral and religious theories are based on the idea that people have a fundamental nature, such as to be rational, to be loving, or to be free, which needs to be developed. To develop your inner nature or true self is your ultimate self-interest. Your ultimate self-interest is to live in agreement with your "deep" self. According to different versions of the true-self theory, your ultimate self-interest may be to be fully rational, to love others fully, or to choose freely your values and perspectives. However, your ultimate self-interest is not the same as the maximum satisfaction of your normal informed wants. This is why being moral can sometimes conflict with what you normally consider to be your self-interest. Being moral is part of living in agreement with your true self. In different theories, being moral follows from being rational or being loving or being free. You should be moral even when it harms your everyday interests, because being moral is necessary for becoming your true self.

FREEDOM AND CREATIVITY

In recent years some thinkers have claimed that the best way to live is to be as free as possible. Freedom is most valuable, but the term "freedom" has many different meanings. Gaining more power to affect the world and removing obstacles to getting what you want have always been considered by most people to be good things. However, this type of "freedom to do" is not the main ingredient of the view that being free is the good life, although it is frequently included. The main ingredient is freedom to choose a way of life.

Freedom to Choose

Children acquire beliefs about the world, attitudes toward other people, and values from their families and culture. People find themselves with values, life-styles, and world views that they have passively absorbed without thinking much about them. The freedom that is supposed to make up the good life is the freedom to choose your values, attitudes toward other people, and world view. You think about these important features of yourself and decide for yourself which features to have. The good life is one in which you get your values, beliefs, attitudes, emotions, and other standards under your own control. Your situation and your own psychological makeup may limit your degree of control over yourself, but your goal should be to develop as much as possible your freedom to choose.

Why is being more free to choose better? Some traditional moral theorists, such as Immanuel Kant (1724–1804), have claimed that freedom to choose leads people to be moral (see chapter 5). They think that there is an essential connection between being free and being moral, so that increasing freedom to choose will lead to the good life of morality. Some existentialists, such as Jean-Paul Sartre (1905–80) and Simone de Beauvoir (1908–86), have claimed that normal humans are intrinsically free and that it is fear of anxiety that leads people not to make full use of their freedom (see chapter 7). They seem to think that being as free as possible is living in agreement with our true self and that failing to do so is something like cowardice or dishonesty. A third account of why being more free is better is that it is connected with being creative, and being free and creative is the best way of life.

Creativity

The type of creativity that is supposed to make your life good is the producing of new and significant ideas and perspectives on things. Just thinking or proposing something new is not sufficient. Many trivial, stupid, or worthless ideas and approaches have never before been thought by anyone, but the producing of them does not count as creativity. The results of creativity have to be significant, interesting, or valuable according to some standards. Creativity can occur in any area of human activity. You are probably most familiar with creativity in art, music, and literature, but creativity also occurs in business, politics, medicine, personal relationships, natural science, and other areas of knowledge. In each of these areas, new ideas, perspectives, or methods can add on to what has already been established or can transform what has already been established. Both the discovery of a new type of virus and a new theory of the nature of viruses are cases of creativity, although the new theory is usually considered to be more creative because it affects a larger area. Creative developments can also be more or less continuous with previous ideas, perspectives, and methods. Some advances seem to involve a sharp break with the past, while other advances seem to "carry forward" or be more continuous with past ideas, perspectives, and methods. Since all creativity involves going beyond standard and conventional ways of thinking, freedom to choose is helpful for it. A person who is more free is not automatically stuck with previous ideas, and so is more likely to be creative.

Why is a creative life the best way to live? Some thinkers consider creativity to be a basic part of human nature, so that acting creatively is fulfilling your nature or true self. A related idea is that creativity is good because it makes full use of a person's abilities and talents. Being creative is a type of self-development. Other thinkers emphasize the value of the results of creativity. A creative life is good because it produces valuable advances in scientific knowledge, artistic activity, political organization, or other areas.

RELIGION

Many people think that being religious is the best way to live. The good life is a life in relation with God or gods. Those who think that being religious is the best way to live claim that there is a God and that people should follow God's wishes.

The Existence of God

The main traditions of Judaism, Christianity, and Islam claim that there is only one God in whom all the powers and features of the divine are united. God is self-existent, eternal, the creator of the universe, all-powerful, all-knowing, all-good, holy, and personal. People can have a relationship with a God of this nature only if God exists. Hence, religious people claim that there are good reasons to think that a God of this nature exists. Because God's characteristics are different from those of ordinary physical objects, God cannot be perceived or detected in ordinary ways. God normally cannot be seen, touched, or found on radar. We have to find out about an all-powerful, all-knowing, and holy God in some other way. Religious believers think that there are several other ways to know that God exists.

Many religious believers think that God's existence can be proven from God's effect on the universe. One argument is that only a beneficent and all-powerful God could be the source of the complex, improbable order of the universe that is necessary for human life to be possible on earth. Another argument is that only a necessary and self-existent God could be the "first cause" of everything in the universe. A third argument is that God must exist because existence is one of the qualities of the most perfect being. A fourth argument is that only God could be the source of miracles, mysterious happenings that supposedly do not conform to the laws of nature.

Religious and mystical experiences are a different way of knowing that God exists. Those who have such experiences claim that they were directly aware of God's presence through a special intuition or perception. In religious experience they feel a communion with God, and in mystical experiences they feel that God reveals something of Himself (or Herself) to them despite their human limits. Those who have such experiences and those who do not consider other people's religious and mystical experiences to be hallucinations have reason to believe that God exists. However, some religious believers think that the existence of God must be accepted without the ordinary types of evidence. They think that belief in God is solely a matter of faith.

Why Be Religious?

If an all-powerful, all-knowing, and holy God exists, any reasonable person would want to know about God and would want to take God into account in organizing her life. However, a religious life requires more than just taking God into account. A religious life is devoted to God, because God is all-good, holy, and personal. Religious considerations have to be more important than anything else, including selfish interests, freedom and creativity, interpersonal relationships, and even morality. As Sören Kierkegaard (1813–55) noted, God's commands have to take precedence even over moral prohibitions. For example, in the Bible, Abraham is right to attempt to sacrifice his son, Isaac, because God commands it.

A religious life is thought to be the best way to live for several different reasons. Some thinkers claim that a person's long-term self-interest is to do whatever God wants, because God is all-knowing, all-powerful, and the ruler of the universe. No prudent person would rebel against such a God. Other thinkers emphasize that people need God in order to have an ultimate meaning in their lives. God has designed an order into the universe. God has decreed objective values, so that there are objectively right and wrong ways to live. God cares about human history and about each of our individual lives. Without a relationship with God, even the most happy and successful life lacks something. God completes human life by providing the ultimate meaning that people by themselves lack. A relationship with God shows people their place in the universe and tells them how to act in this world. God provides the direction for human development and is the source of morality.

That people need a relationship with God is sometimes described in terms of people's true selves. Human nature is such that people can be fulfilled only through a relationship with God. This religious relationship is in their ultimate self-interest, although it may not always promote the satisfaction of their worldly wants. Different religions, and different approaches within one religion, have very different views about the satisfaction of worldly wants and happiness in this life. Some claim that the relationship with God (or gods) will make a person happier in this life. Others claim that we may not be particularly happy, but we will know that we are living in the right way. Others claim that this life is not particularly important in comparison with a life after death, so that unhappiness in this life can be endured as a pathway to a better afterlife.

CLOSE PERSONAL RELATIONS

Most people think that close personal relations with other people are an essential part of the good life. Having friends, loving and being loved, and identifying with family and community are not all that there is to living well, but they are an important part of it. These close and emotionally charged relations partly form and remake a person's psychological makeup. They strongly influence what a person wants, what interests him, what his emotional reactions are, and what specific things will make him happy. Because they change a person, including what a person wants, positive personal relationships are not the same thing as the satisfaction of wants. The lives of people who do not particularly want positive personal relationships would still be improved by these relationships. Many people do want to have positive personal relationships, but when they do have them, they do not simply have their wants satisfied. They are altered by the relationships.

Love

Love is the strongest positive attachment between two people. The term "love" can be applied both to a mutual relationship—the love between two people—and to the feelings of one person for another—Jason loves Jennifer, whether she loves him or not. There are different types of love relationships. There is the love between parent and child, in which the parent may love the child differently from how the child loves the parent. There is the love between members of a family, in which it is usually assumed that a sister loves a brother in the same way that a brother loves a sister. There is the love between friends, and there is romantic love.

Romantic love is a major concern of most people. This is shown by popular culture, in which there is an extraordinary number of songs, stories, movies, and television programs about people's attempts to find a romantic love relationship. Romantic love normally includes a desire for sexual union, but there is much more to it than sex. Some philosophers have tried to state what our society's conception of an ideal romantic love relationship is and why love is so valuable. Some of the main features of an ideal love relationship are equality, intimacy, mutuality, and admiration. The equality of romantic love is that each lover considers the other to be his or her equal, regardless of differences in wealth, power, attractiveness, social standing, or education. The intimacy of romantic love is the detailed understanding that the lovers have of each other's conceptions and evaluations of the world. Lovers strive to develop and to help the other lover to develop this intimate understanding of all their most personal features. The mutuality of romantic love is the partial merging of two minds by each lover partially adopting the outlook and evaluations of the other lover. The two "I's" try to become a "we." The admiration of romantic love is the high regard and respect that, ideally, each lover has for the other. By being loved by such an admirable person, each lover gains a type of confirmation of his or her own worth. In loving and being loved, a person feels that there is a meaning to his or her life.

Friendship

Friendship can be considered to be love between friends. Friendship differs from romantic love in that there is not usually any urge toward sexual union. Perhaps for this reason friendship is much more common between members of the same sex, although it is possible between members of different sexes. Friendship usually differs from romantic love in the degrees of equality, intimacy, mutuality, and admiration that are involved. Friendship usually allows more inequality. Friendship is often less wholistic (the friend is loved for specific features rather than as a whole), and it can tolerate more separation and distance than romantic love. Friends do partially adopt each other's views, which is one reason why they care so much about what their friends think about things (see chapter 13). In this way friends partly transform each other, but to a lesser degree than lovers. There is usually more independence from your friend than from your lover.

Selfishness is concern only for yourself. A thoroughly selfish person does not care much about anyone else or about the good of anything else. Two selfish conceptions of the good life are hedonism and self-development at any cost. Hedonists try to get as much pleasure and avoid as much pain for themselves as possible. Sophisticated hedonists try to develop their knowledge and tastes, so that more things bring them pleasure, and try to increase their control over the world. Other people are usually suspicious of someone who is obviously concerned only with his own pleasure, so that an egoistic hedonist should deceive others about his values. Hedonists frequently use the theory of psychological hedonism to defend their view of the good life. The three main arguments against egoistic hedonism are that it is self-defeating, it prevents satisfying personal relationships, and it is immoral.

The good life of self-development is to develop your abilities and talents to their fullest extent. Self-development need not be selfish if it is restricted by other "goods." The purely selfish notion of self-development is that developing your own abilities is the only thing that counts for you. The main objections to selfish self-development are that it is immoral, it prevents satisfying personal relationships, and it ignores the importance of pleasure and pain. The benefits of an economic system in which people work for their own gain rather than for the good of the community at large do not show that being selfish is the best way to live.

Self-interest is the view that the good life consists of fulfilling your interests. One interpretation is that self-interest consists of the maximum satisfaction of your desires and wants. Satisfying desires and wants makes you happy, and your self-interest is to be happy. Self-interest need not be selfishness because a person need not want only things for herself. The greatest overall satisfaction is the result of how many positive wants are satisfied, how many negative wants to avoid things are not satisfied, and how intense each want is. Sophisticated followers of this view try to maximize satisfaction over an entire lifetime and to increase their control over the world. This theory is frequently defended by appealing to the supposed fact that humans always act according to their strongest current wants. The main objections to the "maximum satisfaction of wants" theory are that it does not tell you what to want, it does not distinguish between good wants and bad wants, and it does not promote full self-development.

Another interpretation of self-interest is that it is the maximum satisfaction of informed wants plus the development of a person's abilities and talents. Informed wants are those that are informed about what a person needs and what the result would be of satisfying a want. Many philosophers have claimed that in this expanded sense of self-interest a person's self-interest includes being moral. Plato claimed that the happiest life belonged to the person whose soul has a good inner harmony, which requires treating others justly. Social contract theories claim that it is in everyone's self-interest to have moral social rules that restrict selfish behavior. It is only through supporting morality that you can have any good chance of satisfying your wants.

Many philosophers have claimed that the good life is to be moral. Morality always includes requirements about how people are to be treated by other people. It always imposes some restrictions on acting from selfish interests. Why should you follow morality rather than just do what you want or what will make you happy? Four major types of justification of morality have been proposed. The divine command position claims that God is the source of morality and that God requires you to be moral, regardless of the costs. The intuition of objective goodness position claims that moral goodness is an objectively existing characteristic that people can detect with a special mental sense. Objective moral characteristics require that you live a moral life. The natural-law position claims that there are naturally good ways for a human life to go on and that moral natural laws require a person to live a moral life. The true-self position claims that your ultimate self-interest is to live in agreement with your true self and that being moral is necessary for becoming your true self.

Some people think that being as free and creative as possible is the best way to live. A person's goal should be to become more free to choose his values, attitudes, and world view. The freedom to decide for yourself about important features of yourself will also promote creative thinking in other areas.

Many people think that being religious is the best way to live. Religious people claim that there are good reasons to think that an all-knowing, all-powerful, holy, and personal God exists. God can be known either through proofs based on God's effect on the universe, through religious experience, or through faith. A religious life is devoted to God, so that religious considerations are more important than anything else. Different reasons for living religiously are that it is in your long-term self-interest to do whatever God wants, that you need God in order to have an ultimate meaning for your life, and that human nature is such that you can be fulfilled only through a relationship with God.

Most people think that close personal relations—such as having friends, loving, and being loved—are an essential part of the good life. These close and emotionally charged relations partly form and remake a person's psychological makeup. There are different types of love relationships. Romantic love is a major concern of most people. Romantic love normally includes a desire for sexual union, but an ideal love relationship also has the features of equality, intimacy, mutuality, and admiration. Friendship differs from romantic love in the degrees of these four features and in the absence of an urge toward sexual union.

Selected Readings

Butler, Joseph. *Five Sermons*. Indianapolis: Hackett, 1983.

MacIntyre, Alasdair. *A Short History of Ethics*. New York: Macmillan, 1966.

Mill, John S. *Utilitarianism*. Indianapolis: Hackett, 1979.

Plato, *The Republic* (several good translations).

Rand, Ayn. *The Virtue of Selfishness*. New York: New American Library, 1964.

Rowe, William. *Philosophy of Religion*. Belmont, CA: Wadsworth, 1978.

Sartre, Jean-Paul. *Existentialism*. B. Frechtman (tr.). New York: Philosophical Library, 1947.

Solomon, Robert. *Love: Emotion, Myth, and Metaphor*. New York: Doubleday, 1981.

3

Relativism and Subjectivism

In response to moral judgments, people sometimes say "Who are you to judge someone else's behavior? What gives you the right to impose your standards on him?" This type of reaction questions the legitimacy of moral judgments. The whole idea of blaming or criticizing someone's behavior on moral grounds is thought to be mistaken, unfair, or wrong in some way. There are many different reasons why people may be suspicious of moral judgments, including moral judgments of praise. This chapter examines the major reasons why some people doubt that moral judgments of other people can be legitimate, and considers the major defenses of moral judgment that have been proposed.

MORAL ABSOLUTISM

Throughout Western history, most people have thought that there are absolute moral standards. They believed that there was only one true morality and that it consisted of standards that applied to all people at all times in all conditions. If the practice of slavery was morally wrong for Americans in 1861, it was also morally wrong for the ancient Greeks and for Africans in 1861.

Absolute moral standards are both universal and objective. They are universal in that they apply to all people at all times in all conditions. Universal standards are different from relative standards that vary, relative to other factors. Relative moral standards are ones that exist only for some type of people, or only for some historical periods, or only for some environmental or cultural conditions. Absolute moral standards are objective in that they do not depend upon people's beliefs, emotions, or customs. Something is objective when it has a type of existence that is independent of people's beliefs. Something is subjective when its only existence is in people's thoughts of it or beliefs. Objective moral standards have some type of existence that is independent of people's belief in them. Objective moral standards are what make people's moral beliefs true or false. As both universal and objective, absolute moral standards are neither relative nor subjective.

Many people have believed not only that there are absolute moral standards, but also that the standards that they use are absolute. Members of a culture frequently assume that their societal standards are the intrinsically right ones. They assume that the ways of behaving that are considered to be morally wrong in their society are absolutely wrong, and that the ways of behaving that are considered to be morally good in their society are absolutely good. However, philosophers have always questioned whether the customs and attitudes of a society reflect the true moral standards. According to absolutism, the attitudes and customs of a society are fully moral only if they agree with the absolute moral standards. Societal views about what is right and wrong may agree with the absolute moral standards, but this agreement cannot be taken for granted. We cannot simply assume that the moral standards that we have learned from our society are the absolute moral standards.

MORAL RELATIVISM

Moral relativism is the position that moral standards are always relative to something else. Moral relativism denies that there are any absolute moral standards, because no moral standards are universal. Relativism claims that different moral standards exist for different people, different societies, or different historical periods. The same type of action, such as removing food and shelter from elderly parents when they can no longer contribute to the household, is supposed to be immoral in our society but moral in some other societies. Moral relativism does not deny that there are moral requirements on people's behavior, but it does claim that there are different requirements on different people.

Moral relativism is sometimes confused with the application of absolute moral standards to different conditions. Any action takes place in specific conditions, and these circumstances sometimes affect the morality of the action. The same absolute moral standard may consider cutting open someone's chest to be morally good when it is part of a surgery to save the person's life, but morally bad when it is done to harm the person. Although there are different theories of absolute moral standards, all theories agree that the absolute moral standards do not change when they are applied to different circumstances. The same absolute standards govern all circumstances, although these standards may say that a type of action is morally acceptable in one set of circumstances but morally forbidden in other circumstances. In contrast with absolutism, moral relativism claims that there are different standards that govern people in different cultures or historical periods.

Moral Diversity

Different societies have different moral codes. Throughout history there have been very different beliefs about the right ways to treat people. Slavery has been considered to be morally acceptable in many societies. Many groups consider outsiders to be "fair prey" for robbing, swindling, beating, and other things that members are not allowed to do to one another. The morally acceptable ways of treating people in the society vary greatly from one society to another. There are very different views about how women, children, sick people, the elderly, the poor, and others should be treated. This diversity of moral standards is the main support for moral relativism. Relativists claim that the diversity shows that different moral standards exist for different societies.

Moral relativism is a claim about how people should treat one another. It is important to understand that moral relativism is not just the claim that there are and have been many different moral codes in different societies. Both absolutists and relativists agree that different societies have used different standards. The historical and sociological fact of moral diversity is not itself moral relativism, because it might be that most of these societies are just wrong. If one society believes that the earth is flat and another society believes that the earth is round, there is diversity of beliefs, but one belief is true and the other belief is false. Absolutists argue that there is an important difference between what a society believes to be moral—its moral code—and what is truly moral—the absolute moral standards. Relativists claim that there is no difference in reality. Relativists claim that there are no other moral standards that are independent of societal moral codes. Societal moral codes are the only objective standards. The moral code of a society cannot be false or only partially true, because it does not refer to absolute standards that could make it false or only partially true. Relativists claim that moral diversity shows that there are different moral requirements for members of different societies, because there are no independent, absolute standards that could correct the societal moral codes.

Relativist Arguments Against Moral Absolutism

Moral relativists accept the existence of moral requirements, but deny that there is a set of absolute moral requirements that applies to all people at all times in all societies. The fact that there are and have been different moral codes is the main support for the rejection of absolute standards.

This fact of moral diversity is used in three relativist arguments against absolute standards.

AVAILABILITY OF MORAL STANDARDS

Moral requirements have to be known by people in order to influence their behavior. If people do not know that they are morally required to do something, the moral requirement could not serve its purpose of getting people to behave morally. Hence, moral requirements and moral standards must be known or be available to be known. They cannot be hidden or impossible to know, because then they could not lead people to act morally.

Relativists claim that the only moral standards that are available to be known in a society are the standards of the moral code of that society. People in the society understand these moral standards, and do not look beyond them to absolute standards that might make the societal code right or wrong. People generally do not have any idea how they would find such absolute standards. Even if people did have the idea of absolute standards, relativists claim that they would always be limited by their cultural tradition. Relativists claim that people are unable to be objective about an independent reality, and so could not appreciate absolute standards even if they existed. Therefore, since moral standards have to be available and absolute standards are not available, there are no absolute moral standards.

FAIRNESS

Relativists also argue that absolute moral standards would be unfair. Since people know only the moral code of their society, the existence of some other standards that would make their behavior intrinsically right or wrong would not be fair to them. If there were absolute moral standards, people's actions could be morally wrong even though the people thought that they were acting morally. If someone follows the moral code of her own society, she thinks that she is doing the right thing. According to absolute standards, her action might be morally wrong; if so, her action would deserve moral blame and punishment. Relativists claim that someone who is trying to do what is moral cannot deserve moral blame and punishment. Therefore, there cannot be absolute moral standards.

MORAL CODES ARE NOT APPROACHING THE SAME STANDARDS

Another relativist argument against absolute standards is that societal moral codes do not seem to be different approximations of the same absolute standards. If there were absolute standards and these standards were available to be known, every societal moral code should show the influence of the absolute standards. Although societal moral codes are different from one another, they should each reflect the absolute moral standards. Each societal moral code should be that society's attempt to conform to the absolute standards as understood within the society. Relativists claim that they cannot find any influence of a set of absolute standards on all societal moral codes. They claim that there is no evidence that each is an attempt to conform to the same absolute standards. Relativists frequently also claim that there is no evidence that societal moral codes throughout history have been all moving toward the same position.

Absolutist Responses

Defenders of the existence of absolute moral standards usually accept the idea that moral standards have to be available. They respond to the availability argument by claiming that people within any society can find out more about the absolute standards. People in any society or culture discover in the same way what absolute morality requires of them. According to different absolutist theories, people know about moral standards by reason, by moral intuition, by conscience, or by divine revelation. Hence, the fact that people in different societies are taught somewhat different moral codes does not prevent them from discovering, at least to some extent, the absolute standards.

The absolutist response that absolute moral standards are available to members of different societies provides one answer to the fairness argument. It is fair for absolute moral standards to govern the morality of people's actions, because members of different societies can discover what morality requires of them. A person can find out whether following some part of his societal moral code is absolutely right or wrong. A second response to the fairness argument involves distinguishing absolute wrongness from deserving moral blame and punishment. A person who is trying to do the right thing by following his social moral code may be doing something wrong, according to absolute standards. However, he does not deserve moral blame or punishment if he is mistaken, through no fault of his own, about the correct moral action. Faultless ignorance is an excuse against moral blame and punishment. A third response to the fairness argument is that it is self-refuting. It presupposes that fairness is an absolute standard that must apply to all moral standards.

Defenders of absolute moral standards claim that different societal moral codes do show the influence of absolute standards. Some absolutists claim that all moral codes share some general features, such as prohibiting incest, requiring people to tell the truth, and parental responsibility for young children. The differences in moral codes, according to these absolutists, are largely a matter of the different conditions that exist in different societies. For example, societies that permit families to leave elderly parents to die are very poor ones in which supporting unproductive elderly people would threaten the survival of the whole family or group. The moral codes of such societies do not ignore absolute moral standards against killing people. Rather, these moral codes reflect other absolute moral standards, such as the necessity of ensuring the survival of the family or group. These absolute moral standards take precedence in the impoverished conditions over not allowing someone to die. Other absolutists accept the differences between moral codes, but still consider them to be different approximations of the absolute standards. These absolutists usually think that societal moral codes will become more similar to one another over time, as each code more closely approximates the absolute standards.

TYPES OF MORAL RELATIVISM

There are several different versions of moral relativism. They all reject absolute moral standards, but they differ from one another in their positive claims. Different versions make different positive claims about how a moral relativist should treat and judge people outside his own society and how he should treat and judge people within his own society.

Respect for Other Moral Codes

The most frequent version of moral relativism claims that people should live according to the moral code of their own society, and they should respect the moral codes of other societies. According to this view, a person should obey the moral code of her own society—society A—and judge members of her own society by that code. Furthermore, she should obey the moral code of society A in any actions that affect members of another society—society B. The same moral restrictions on selfish behavior and moral requirements of helpful behavior that govern her actions toward members of her own society should govern her actions toward members of other societies. For example, if the moral code of society A forbids her to rob weak people in society A, she should also not rob weak people in society B, even if the moral code of society B allows robbing the weak.

According to this version of moral relativism, people should obey the moral code of their own society. Since members of society B should obey the moral code of society B, a member of society A should not use the standards of society A to reward, punish, praise, or blame a member of society B. A member of society A should not enforce the moral requirements of society A on the members of other societies. If the moral code of society B allows people to take possessions from the weak, a member of society A should not interfere with, blame, or punish such an action by a member of society B. If it is morally praiseworthy in society B to force people to engage in religious practices, a member of society A should praise a member of society B for doing this, since it is the morally right thing for a member of society B. In general, people should accept the relative character of moral requirements. What is morally right for a member of society A may be different from what is morally right for a member of society B, and members of both societies should recognize this. Members of all societies should respect the moral codes of all other societies.

Problems with Respect

One major problem with the respect version of moral relativism is that it can be logically impossible to obey it. The moral code of one's own society may require a person to treat members of another society in a way that does not respect their moral code. For example, the moral code of society B may require members of society B to try to convert all people to the "one true religion." It would be logically impossible for a member of society B to obey her own societal moral code, and at the same time to respect the moral code of society C, which does not practice the "one true religion." This is why the example of Nazi Germany is frequently used against relativism. Many people feel that it is impossible to follow their own moral code and to respect the societal code of Nazi Germany.

There are also problems in respecting the moral codes of two different societies when these codes conflict with each other. If the moral code of society B requires its members to promote the equality of women with men, and the moral code of society C requires its members to subordinate women to men, there are situations in which it is difficult for a member of society A to respect both moral codes fully. A member of society A would have to praise and encourage a member of society B for trying to liberate women in society C, yet also praise and encourage members of society C for trying to prevent this.

A second problem with this version of moral relativism is that there can be disagreement within a society about what is morally right and wrong. Some members of a society may want to change some of the customary ways of acting, treating other people, and judging them. Those who favor the changes will consider the changes to be moral progress, while those who oppose the changes will consider them to be morally bad. Such disagreements about what is morally right and wrong are a serious problem for the relativist, both with respect to his own societal moral code and other societal moral codes. Disagreements in his own society make it unclear how he is to act. There is no definite societal moral code for him to follow, at least on the points of disagreement. Disagreements in another society make it unclear which side of the disagreement he should respect. There is no definite moral code in the other society for him to respect.

A third problem is that the boundaries of a society are frequently not completely definite. A societal moral code is supposed to govern the actions of all the members of the society, but which people are members? Are all social classes and all religious, ethnic, racial, sexual, and age groups in a geographical area part of the same society? Any society usually has some subgroups whose customs and values differ somewhat from the mainstream society. Should subgroups be evaluated according to the moral code of the larger society? Should all subgroups be treated as separate societies whose moral codes must be respected? How should people who belong to more than one subgroup be treated? If there is not one societal moral code that governs particular people's actions, the relativist will not be able to respect that societal moral code.

Respect for Tolerant Moral Codes

Another version of moral relativism respects only tolerant moral codes. This version claims that people should live according to the moral code of their own society insofar as it is tolerant of the moral codes of other societies, and that they should respect the moral codes of other societies insofar as they are tolerant of the moral codes of other societies. This revised version is designed to improve moral relativism so that it does not require contradictory actions (see the first problem in "Problems with Respect"). If your own societal moral code requires you to treat people in another society in a way that interferes with their tolerant moral code, you should not follow this feature of your societal moral code. A person should follow the moral code of her society for most actions, but not for actions that would interfere with the nonintolerant features of the moral code of another society. However, she could follow her own moral code in actions that were designed to change the intolerant features of another society's moral code.

The same considerations apply to respecting the moral codes of two or more societies. A relativist is not required to respect the intolerant features of other societal moral codes. Hence, he is not required to respect both societal moral codes in cases in which they come into conflict with each other.

Problems for the Revised Version

One major problem with this revised version is that it makes tolerance into an absolute standard. Tolerance of the tolerant moral codes of other societies seems to be required of everyone, regardless of what their own societal moral code claims. The revised version does not tell people simply to accept the moral code of their own society and to respect the moral codes of other societies. Rather, it tells people to evaluate all societal moral codes in terms of their respect for the tolerant features of other societal moral codes. By distinguishing what is universally morally right from the claims of a person's societal moral code, the revised version uses an absolute standard. Tolerance is used as an absolute standard by which all societal moral codes are evaluated.

The revised version also retains two of the problems of the original version. There can be disagreements within a society about what is morally right and wrong, and the boundaries of a society are frequently not completely definite. These problems make indefinite the societal moral codes that the relativist is supposed to respect.

Tolerance for Everyone

Another revised version of moral relativism claims that people should tolerate the moral standards of all other people. A person should live according to his own moral code, which may be widely shared by people in his society. However, he should not judge by his moral code the actions of other people, either in his own society or in other societies. People can be judged, according to the tolerance view, only by their own moral standards. A tolerant relativist should evaluate people, even people in his own society, only by the moral standards that they accept. A tolerant relativist should reward or punish people only on the basis of their moral standards, not on the basis of societal moral standards. Such a tolerant attitude toward everyone will avoid some of the problems of respecting other societal moral codes, because the relativist does not have to deal with the moral code of a whole society.

Problems with Tolerance

One major problem with the tolerance view is that it would be practically impossible to be tolerant of many people who had different moral codes whose actions affected you. Tolerance is easier when people around you have the same basic moral code, so that only minor differences in behavior have to be tolerated. Tolerance is also easier when people who have very different moral codes do not have any important effects on your life; for example, if they live in distant lands. Tolerance becomes more difficult in proportion to how different other people's moral codes are and how much effect they have on you. Not trying to change the standards of people whose actions, following those standards, have serious negative effects on you would make a person's life unhappy and unsuccessful. For example, a completely tolerant person would have to tolerate muggers, robbers, rapists, and murderers if they thought that their actions were morally acceptable.

It is also unlikely that a society could survive if most of its members were tolerant relativists. Children could not be taught to follow the societal moral code, because this would interfere with their own standards. Adults could not be forced to follow the societal moral and legal code for the same reason.

Another major problem with the tolerance version of ethical relativism is that it seems to make tolerance into an absolute standard. Everyone is supposed to be tolerant of other people's moral standards. A person's own moral standards may require her to convert others to the "one true religion" or to free women from subordination to men. According to tolerant relativism, she should not follow her original standards, because her actions would interfere with the moral standards of others. In such cases tolerance is being used as an absolute standard to correct the original standards.

MORAL SUBJECTIVISM

Moral subjectivism is the position that moral standards are always a matter of personal opinion, individual emotions, or societal customs. Subjectivists claim that morality is only what people think or feel should be done, but that people project their own subjective evaluations on to things. Nothing is objectively morally good or morally bad. Subjectivists deny that moral goodness and badness are objective features of the universe that are independent of what people believe. They claim that moral judgments are really like judgments of taste. Various foods do not intrinsically taste good or taste bad. The good or bad taste depends upon the taster, although the taster may project his own subjective reaction on to the food. Subjectivists claim that people similarly project on to worldly things their own subjective reactions. Moral standards are not an objective part of the universe, so that worldly things do not by themselves have moral features. While it may be an objective fact that an action causes unnecessary pain to some other person, it is not an objective fact that such an action is morally wrong. The moral evaluation is a matter of people's subjective reactions.

In denying the objectivity of moral goodness and badness, moral subjectivism also denies that people are obligated or intrinsically required to follow moral rules and to pursue moral goals. No moral standards have any intrinsic authority over people, so that no one is unavoidably obligated by either a societal moral code or absolute moral standards. Morality is a human invention that is based on various features of individuals, societies, and circumstances. Since morality does not intrinsically govern everyone's actions, the good life for an individual need not be a moral life (see chapter 2). Subjectivists have different positive views about the best way to live, but they all deny that there are objective moral requirements.

Moral relativism and moral subjectivism both deny that objective and universal moral standards exist. Since the denial of absolute moral standards is such an important point, the terms "moral relativism" and "moral subjectivism" are sometimes used loosely to mean the same thing. However, there is a difference between the two positions. Standard versions of moral relativism claim that there are objective moral requirements on people. Relativists think that a person is obligated to treat other people in moral ways, whether or not he believes in the moral standards. Moral subjectivism claims that there are no objective moral standards and no intrinsic moral requirements. People may mistakenly think that they are governed by objective moral standards, but in reality there are only their own beliefs, other people's beliefs, and societal customs. People mistakenly think that there are objective moral obligations, because other people may require them to act in moral ways. Being required by other people—

according to their subjective standards—is mistaken for being intrinsically required to act morally.

There are universal, societal, and individual versions of subjectivism. The universal version claims that all people share some subjective evaluations, such as feeling sympathy for an innocent person's suffering. No one has an obligation to feel sympathy or to have any other type of subjective response, but it is a fact about humans that they all have many of the same subjective reactions. The societal version claims that all people in a society share some subjective responses because they are socialized to have these responses. Their training, education, and interactions with other people produce these subjective responses in all members of a society. The individual version claims that different people may have very different subjective evaluations.

Subjectivist Arguments Against Moral Objectivity

Subjectivists argue that there are neither absolute nor relative moral standards that unavoidably obligate people. Subjectivists have made the following arguments against the objectivity of morality.

DIVERSITY

Subjectivists use an argument against objective moral standards that is just like one of the relativist arguments against absolute moral standards. Subjectivists claim that the diversity of societal moral codes and the fact that these codes do not seem to be different approximations of one set of objective moral standards shows that there are no objective moral standards. If moral goodness and badness were objective features of the universe, all societies should recognize them to some extent. Subjectivists claim that different societal moral codes are too different from one another to be different views of one set of objective standards of moral goodness and badness.

Subjectivists modify this argument, and use it against objective but relative moral standards. Relativists usually claim that societal moral codes are objective for members of the society. Members of a society are morally obligated to follow the societal moral code, because it is objective for them. The idea of objective but relative moral standards can be understood by considering the theory that God gives moral standards to people. An absolutist would claim that God gives the same moral standards to all people at all times in all conditions. An objective relativist would claim that God gives somewhat different moral standards to different societies or to different historical periods. For example, Christianity usually considers the moral requirements on people before Christ to be different from the moral requirements on people after Christ. Both sets of moral standards are supposed to be objective, but they are also relative to exposure to Christ's message.

Subjectivists use the fact that even within societies there are disagreements about moral standards to argue against objective but relative moral standards. Subgroups and individual people have their own moral codes. Subjectivists argue that individual moral codes may be so different from one another that they could not be different views of one set of objective standards of moral goodness and badness.

ALTERNATIVE EXPLANATION

Subjectivists argue that objective moral standards are unnecessary fictions. There is no good reason to think that objective moral standards exist, because everything about morality can be explained without them. Objective moral standards are not needed in any way to explain why societies have had the different moral codes that they have had or why societal moral codes change. Societal moral codes, and changes in these codes over time, can be completely explained by natural factors. Human needs, instincts, powers to act, environmental conditions, the level of technology, the influence of neighboring groups, cultural traditions, human creativity, and other natural factors can, combined, give a complete account of societal moral codes. History, anthropology, and sociology can explain why humans develop their specific societal moral codes without bringing in any objective moral standards.

STRANGENESS

Subjectivists claim that objective moral standards would be very strange parts of the universe if they did exist. Objective moral standards would have to be very different from ordinary natural things—such as rocks, plants, and animals—and from the scientific laws that describe the behavior of natural things. Objective moral standards would have to be "supernatural" or nonnatural existents that somehow had authority over how humans should act. Objective moral standards would have to be special, nonworldly existents that intrinsically applied or attached to worldly events. For example, standards of moral badness would not themselves be located in space or time, but they would intrinsically apply to worldly events, such as to an action that causes unnecessary pain to another person. Because objective moral standards would be such strange things, our ways of knowing about them would have to be different from our ways of knowing about the natural world. Subjectivists doubt that these other ways of knowing exist. They claim that there are no objective ways of testing diverse claims about objective moral standards, so that there is no reason to think that there could be knowledge about them.

Defenses of Moral Objectivity

Defenders of the objectivity of morality respond to the diversity argument by claiming that different moral codes do show the influence of objective moral standards (see the discussion on pages 34–35). They respond to the alternative explanation argument by claiming that something more than these natural factors is needed to explain morality in society. People's awareness of objective moral standards, although limited and imperfect, does influence their moral standards and help to bring about moral progress.

Defenders of objectivity respond to the strangeness argument in several different ways. All defenders believe that moral standards are something other than properties of natural objects or scientific laws. They all point out that this supposed strangeness also applies to mathematical entities, logical laws, standards of reasoning, and standards of knowledge. Hence, they all agree that there is nothing wrong with such nonnatural existents, since nonnatural standards are necessary for any reasoning or scientific knowledge. However, defenders of objectivity have different theories of the way objective moral standards exist. They have different accounts of the metaphysical status of moral standards, which correspond to different reasons for living morally. Some think that moral standards are part of God's nature. Others think that God creates moral standards to govern human behavior. Others think that moral standards exist in some supernatural way, like Plato's Forms, but are independent of God. Others think that moral standards are fundamentally connected to humans' true natures, so that humans can reach their full potential only by following the moral standards. Each theory of moral objectivity is more than a response to the strangeness argument. It is a positive account of how moral standards exist and why people should live according to those standards (see "Justifications of Morality" pp. 21–22).

Emotivism

Emotivism is one type of subjectivism that focuses on the meaning of moral language. Emotivism claims that moral judgments in language are expressions of emotional reactions to worldly events and attempts to influence other people's behavior. To say "causing unnecessary pain to other people is morally wrong" is not to state a fact, according to emotivists. That sentence does not say something that is either true or false. Rather, it expresses a negative emotional attitude toward causing unnecessary pain and commands or invites other people to make the same negative evaluation. According to emotivists, that sentence says something like "Down with causing unnecessary pain to other people." Positive moral judgments, such as "It is morally good to feed starving people," also express emotional evaluations and command or invite others to make the same positive evaluation. That judgment means something like "Hurrah for feeding starving people."

Social Morality

Although subjectivists deny that any moral standards are objective, most subjectivists do not reject morality as a social practice. Most subjectivists think that some shared standards for how people should treat one another are necessary to have a functioning society. Many also think that each individual's self-interest is better served by having social rules that restrict selfish behavior (see "Morality and Self-Interest," page 19). Universalist subjectivists, such as David Hume (1711–76), claim that all people have some of the same emotional reactions, such as approving of actions that help other people when one's own selfish interests are not involved. These universal but subjective reactions can be the basis for shared moral views. Societal subjectivists similarly think that members of a society can agree on moral standards, because they all have the same basic subjective reactions to things. Even individual subjectivists frequently think that people can agree on social rules that restrict selfish behavior.

Absolute moral standards are both universal and objective. They are universal in that they determine moral goodness and badness for all people at all times in all conditions. They are objective in that they have some type of existence that is independent of the beliefs and customs of a society. The attitudes and customs of a society are truly moral if they agree with the absolute standards. Moral relativism is the position that there are no absolute standards and that different moral standards exist for different people, different societies, or different historical periods. Relativists claim that there are different moral requirements on different people.

Relativist arguments against absolute moral standards are mainly based on the fact that different societies have had different moral codes. One relativist argument is that absolute moral standards would have to be available to members of a society, but only societal moral codes are available. Another argument is that it would be unfair for absolute standards to condemn someone who was doing what was right according to her societal moral code. A third argument is that societal moral codes do not seem to be different approximations of the same absolute standards. In response to the first argument, absolutists claim that absolute standards are available to members of any society. In response to the second argument, absolutists claim that someone who is faultlessly ignorant of the absolute standards does not deserve moral blame. In response to the third argument, absolutists claim that societal moral codes do show the influence of absolute standards.

The most frequent version of moral relativism claims that people should live according to the moral code of their own society, and they should respect the moral codes of other societies. There are three problems with this version. First, it is impossible to obey it if the moral code of one society requires a person to treat members of another society in a way that interferes with their moral code. Second, disagreement within a society about what is morally right and wrong make indefinite which side a relativist should respect. Third, the boundaries of a society are frequently not completely definite.

Another version of moral relativism claims that people should live according to the moral code of their own society insofar as it is tolerant of the moral codes of other societies, and that they should respect the moral codes of other societies insofar as they are tolerant of the moral codes of other societies. The major problem with this version is that it makes tolerance into an absolute standard.

A third version of moral relativism claims that people should tolerate the individual moral standards of all other people. The major problems of this version are that it also makes tolerance into an absolute value and that it might be impossible to obey it.

Moral subjectivism is the position that moral standards are always a matter of personal opinion, individual emotions, or societal customs. People project their own subjective evaluations on to things. Nothing is objectively morally good or morally bad, and no moral standards have any intrinsic authority over people. People are not obligated or intrinsically required to follow moral rules and to pursue moral goals.

Subjectivists use three basic arguments against objective moral standards. The diversity argument is that different societal moral codes or different individual moral codes do not seem to be different approximations of one set of objective moral standards. The alternative explanation argument is that objective moral standards are not needed to explain anything about morality in societies. The strangeness argument is that objective moral standards would be very strange parts of the universe if they did exist. Defenders of objectivity respond that moral codes do show the influence of objective standards, that input from objective standards is necessary to explain morality, and that many types of supposedly strange standards do exist.

Most subjectivists do not reject morality as a social practice. If all people, or all people in a society, have the same basic subjective reactions to things, they can easily agree on social rules for treating people.

Selected Readings

Harman, Gilbert. *The Nature of Morality.* New York: Oxford University Press, 1977.

Hume, David. *A Treatise of Human Nature.* Oxford: Oxford University Press, 1888.

Krausz, M., and J. Meiland (eds.). *Relativism: Cognitive and Moral.* Notre Dame, IN: Notre Dame University Press, 1982.

Ladd, John (ed.). *Ethical Relativism.* Belmont, CA: Wadsworth, 1973.

Mackie, John. *Ethics: Inventing Right and Wrong.* New York: Penguin, 1977.

4

Utilitarianism

he most common response to the question "Why is a certain act wrong?" is to point out the consequences of the act. Why is it wrong to kick someone? Because it causes pain. Utilitarianism is a family of views that develops this common sort of response into sophisticated moral theories. From the late nineteenth century until the late 1960s, utilitarian views dominated moral discussion. But recently many have argued that, no matter how utilitarianism is revised, it has fatal flaws.

CONSEQUENTIALISM

Utilitarian moral theories are part of a larger family of moral theories called "consequentialist." Consequentialism is the view that whether an act is right or wrong is determined, directly or indirectly, by the act's consequences and not by its intrinsic features. Consider the act of throwing a rock into a pond. Even this trivial act has consequences. There is one less rock on the shore of the pond. There are ripples on the surface of the pool for a short period of time. While the concept of consequences of an act is straightforward, the concept of intrinsic features is more complex. The following are intrinsic features of throwing a rock into a pond: it is an act of throwing; it is a physical (not a mental) act; it involves a rock.

This example might lead one to think that the intrinsic features of an act are unimportant. But consider the act of telling a lie. Telling a lie might have many consequences. Often people rely on what one says and make plans supposing that one did not lie. If you tell a lie, then people who have relied on what you said may be hurt. This would be a consequence of your lie. But whether people are hurt or not, a lie is a lie. In other words, all lies have the intrinsic feature of being lies. According to consequentialism, lying is wrong only because of its consequences—it hurts others. But sometimes lies do not hurt anyone. In these cases, consequentialists say that lying is not wrong. Those who object to consequentialism argue that there are cases in which lying hurts no one and yet is still wrong. They think that acts that have the intrinsic feature "being a lie" have a moral defect—whether or not the lie hurts anyone.

Why does the phrase "directly or indirectly" appear in the definition of consequentialism? Because there are many different versions of consequentialism, and different versions hold that the rightness of acts is related in different ways to their consequences. For example, according to some versions of consequentialism, an act is right when the act produces the most happiness. On this theory, the act's immediate or direct consequences determine whether it is right or wrong. According to other versions of consequentialism, an act is right if it is allowed by the system of rules that produces the most happiness. On this theory, the act's indirect consequences determine whether it is right or wrong.

Every version of consequentialism embodies a position on three issues: What sort of consequences are morally important? Who is morally important? What is the correct amount of the morally important consequences?

What Sort of Consequences Are Morally Important?

Acts have all sorts of consequences. Which of these consequences are morally important and which are morally irrelevant? The preceding definition of consequentialism does not answer this question. The (silly) view that an act is right if it produces more hats than any other act is a (silly) version of consequentialism. In chapter 2 we discussed four sorts of consequences that are frequently singled out by consequentialists as morally important. First, some consequentialists are hedonists. They think that the only morally important consequence is pleasure. They might argue that an act is right when it produces the most pleasure. Second, some consequentialists argue that the consequences that are important are self and/or other development. They might argue that an act is right when it assists the development of others. Third, some consequentialists think that want satisfaction is what is important. They might hold that an act is right when it produces the most want satisfaction. Finally, some consequentialists hold that informed want satisfaction is important.

Philosophers have also argued that consequences not discussed in chapter 2 are the morally important consequences. For example, one might hold that whether an act is right or wrong is determined by its effect on the amount of rights violation. An act is right if it minimizes the number of rights violated. Or one might hold that whether an act is right or wrong is determined by its effect on promise-keeping. An act is right if it maximizes the number of promises kept.

It is important to see that these theories are different from moral theories that hold that the intrinsic features "being a rights violation" or "being a breaking of a promise" are morally important. Compare two simple (and therefore implausible) theories to illustrate this difference. One might hold that an act is wrong if it violates a right. Another might hold that an act is wrong if it fails to produce the least possible number of rights violations. The first theory is not consequentialist because it holds that an act is wrong if it has a certain intrinsic feature (being a violation of a right). The second theory is consequentialist because it holds that an act is wrong if it has certain consequences (failing to produce the least possible number of rights violations). This is a difference which makes a difference. Suppose that your violating one of Tom's rights would change the world so that many fewer rights violations would occur. The first theory implies that it would be wrong to violate Tom's right, while the second theory does not have this implication.

When consequentialists argue that only certain sorts of consequences are morally important, they do not mean that other consequences are completely unimportant. Rather, they mean that other consequences are morally important only because of their effect on the morally important consequences. For example, hedonistic consequentialists think that pleasure is the only morally important consequence. They argue that it is important for people to have sufficient food only because people with sufficient food feel more pleasure than those with insufficient food.

Many philosophers have argued that the only morally important consequence is happiness. They understand happiness to be the balance of pleasure over pain. One is happier, according to this view, the more pleasure and the less pain one has in one's life. In the rest of this chapter we will use the term "happiness" to refer ambiguously to whatever consequences are morally important. So "happiness" might refer to pleasure, self and/or other development, want satisfaction, rights violation, or anything else that someone proposes as a morally important consequence. (Some philosophers have used the term "utility" in the way that we will use the term "happiness," and this is what led to the name "utilitarianism.")

Who Is Morally Important?

Not only do acts have all sorts of consequences; they have varying consequences on different people. Leyanda's sending a love letter to Al might make Al happy and Kohki unhappy. The definition of consequentialism does not impose any restrictions on whose happiness is relevant. So the following is a (silly) consequentialist view: An act is right if it produces the most happiness for people in New Jersey. Egoistic ethical hedonism is a version of consequentialism. According to this view, an act by any person is right if it produces the most pleasure for that person. This theory says that you ought to produce as much of your own pleasure as possible, and I ought to produce as much of my pleasure as possible. So egoistic consequentialists think that only they are morally important. Egoistic *ethical* hedonism must not be confused with egoistic hedonism—a view discussed in chapter 2. Egoistic hedonism is a view about what sort of life is the best sort of life—the view that the best sort of life is the one that contains the most pleasure for me. Egoistic *ethical* hedonism is a view about what acts are right.

Egoistic ethical hedonism seems to have problems similar to the problems with egoistic hedonism that were discussed in Chapter 2. For this reason most consequentialists are not egoists; rather, they are universalists. Universalistic consequentialists think that everyone is equal in moral importance. So the following is a universalistic view: An act is right if it produces the most happiness for everyone in the world. According to this view, you and I act rightly when our acts produce the most happiness for everyone in the world. Each of us ought to consider our own happiness as well as that of everyone else. And we ought to consider everyone's happiness equally. We ought not give any greater weight to our own or anyone else's happiness. For the rest of this chapter we will focus on versions of universalistic consequentialism.

Consequentialists disagree over whether we ought to count the happiness of nonhuman animals when we consider whether acts are right or wrong. One's view on this controversy is greatly affected by one's view of what consequences are morally important. If pleasure and pain are the important consequences, then, because nonhuman animals feel pleasure, it seems natural to count them. If, on the other hand, self-development is the important consequence, then it seems natural not to count nonhuman animals. They do not seem to develop in the way that humans do. We will return to this issue in chapter 14.

What Is the Correct Amount of the Morally Important Consequences?

Consequentialists hold that the right act is the act whose consequences lead to the correct amount of happiness. But what is the correct amount of happiness? One obvious answer is: as much as possible. Consequentialists who give this answer are maximizing consequentialists. But there are nonmaximizing versions of consequentialism. Unlike maximizing consequentialism, this view allows for the possibility that an act will produce too much happiness or distribute happiness in the wrong way. Different versions of nonmaximizing consequentialism have different views about what the correct amount of happiness is. For example, some think that an act is right if it contributes to everyone's having an equal amount of happiness. According to this view, we ought to do an act that would contribute to distributing happiness equally even if this would decrease the total happiness in the world. Other versions of nonmaximizing consequentialism hold that happiness ought to be distributed according to merit or according to need.

Maximizing Consequential-ism

The phrase "produces as much happiness as possible" is ambiguous. To be more precise in our understanding of maximization, let us represent happiness with numbers. Positive numbers indicate happiness, negative numbers indicate unhappiness, and zero indicates indifference. Suppose that there are five actions you can do in a certain situation and that only three people are affected by your actions. The following chart represents the effects of the five actions open to you:

		PERSON		
Act	P1	P2	P3	Total
1	9	-2	2	9
2	2	2	2	6
3	-1	0	-3	-4
4	-4	-2	1	-5
5	1	1	4	6

P1, P2, and P3 are the people affected by your action. To maximize happiness, one follows a step by step procedure. Of the acts open to you which produce some happiness, choose the one that produces the most happiness. If all five acts described in the chart were possible, Act 1 produces the most happiness, so you ought to do this act. If all the acts open to you decrease the amount of happiness, do the act that produces the smallest decrease. If you had only Acts 3 and 4 to choose from, you ought to do Act 3. If two acts have the exact same effect on the amount of happiness, then these acts are equally right. If you had only Acts 2 and 5 to choose from, then it would not matter which you chose to do.

Expected Happiness

This maximization procedure is possible only if you know the consequences of every act open to you. But often people do not know this. Rather, they know only that the consequences of their action will be affected by other events and the probabilities that these other events will occur. Suppose you are trying to decide whether to take an umbrella to work today. You are the only person whose happiness will be affected by this action. There are two possible actions: take the umbrella, leave the umbrella. You do not know the consequences of these actions because the consequences depend on whether it rains or not, and you do not know whether it will rain or not. But, having heard the forecast, you know that there is a 20 percent chance of rain (and an 80 percent chance of no rain). A chart to represent your decision might look like this:

| | STATE | |
Act	Rain	No rain
Take	10	-5
Leave	-20	30

If you take your umbrella and it rains, you are happy because the umbrella keeps you dry. But if you take your umbrella and it does not rain, you are unhappy because you have to carry the umbrella around all day. If you leave your umbrella at home and it rains, you are very unhappy because you get wet. If you leave your umbrella and it does not rain, then you are very happy because it is sunny and you are not carrying the umbrella around.

Ought you take the umbrella? You ought to consider the probability that it will rain. You can consider this probability by calculating the *expected happiness* of each action. The expected happiness of an action is the sum of product of the happiness produced by every possible outcome of the action and the probability that the action will produce that outcome. Given that the chance of rain is 20 percent, the expected happiness of taking your umbrella is:

$$(10)(.2) + (-5)(.8) = 2 + -4 = -2$$

The expected happiness of leaving your umbrella at home is:

$$(-20)(.2) + (30)(.8) = -4 + 24 = 20$$

Because the expected happiness of your leaving the umbrella (20) is greater than the expected happiness of taking it (-2), you ought to leave the umbrella at home. All these numbers are used merely for illustrative purposes. Consequentialists do not think that we can actually generate numbers such as these. They think that we must reply on less precise comparisons of actions. But these examples illustrate the sort of factors that consequentialists think we ought to consider, as well as how we ought to consider them.

We are now in a position to be more precise about the phrase "produces as much happiness as possible." One produces as much happiness as possible when one maximizes universal expected happiness. Hereafter, we will abbreviate "maximize universal expected" to "maximize."

ACT UTILITARIANISM

Act utilitarianism is a version of maximizing universalistic consequentialism. The view has two forms. Classical act utilitarianism is the view that an act is right if it maximizes happiness, and that otherwise the act is wrong. Average act utilitarianism is the view that an act is right if it maximizes average happiness, and that otherwise it is wrong. Average happiness is the total happiness in the world divided by the number of people in the world. Classical act utilitarianism and average act utilitarianism are both versions of act utilitarianism because both share the view that whether an act is right or wrong is determined directly by that particular act's consequences. According to both views, every time I act I ought to consider the effects of my doing this particular act in this particular situation. Both forms of act utilitarianism have many different versions. For example, there is a different version for each of the possible meanings of "happiness" discussed above in the section on what sort of consequences are morally important.

Many have objected to classical act utilitarianism on the grounds that it has implausible implications concerning population control. One way to increase happiness is to have children. As long as each new child's life has a bit more happiness than unhappiness, then having that child increases the total amount of happiness in the world. But an increasing population may strain resources and cause unhappiness. In other words, an increasing population may increase total happiness (and therefore maximize happiness), while at the same time causing average happiness to fall. It may lead to a society with a great many not very happy (but not unhappy) people, instead of one with fewer, happier people. Certain countries in Africa and Asia may currently face this problem. Classical act utilitarianism seems to imply that these countries ought not to adopt population-control programs when it seems clear to many that these countries desperately need these programs. Average act utilitarianism obviously avoids the population problem. It implies that one ought to have children only if this would increase the average happiness in society.

OBJECTIONS TO ACT UTILITARIANISM

Cannot Do Calculations

Sometimes determining the consequences of an act is easy. I can easily know that kicking someone will cause pain. But sometimes determining the consequences of an act can be very difficult. Suppose a legislator is trying to decide which tax plan she ought to support. On the one hand, act utilitarianism gives her straightforward guidance—vote for the one that maximizes happiness. But determining the effects of the plans may require a great deal of study. She would have to consider effects on inflation, unemployment, investment, and so forth. In many cases act utilitarianism requires knowing a great deal of information and making a great many calculations.

Some have objected that we do not have the time to do all these calculations every time we act. Sometimes we must act immediately without stopping to consider every possible option. If a car pulls out in front of you while you are driving, you must immediately decide what to do. In addition, some point out that it is extraordinarily difficult to know *all* the consequences of our actions. Even a seemingly trivial act may have dramatic consequences. Suppose that Hitler's parents met while both were taking a walk in a park. Then the decision to take that walk transformed the world. Finally, some argue that we cannot compare one person's happiness to that of another person. There is no happiness meter that we can use to determine whether Todd likes ice cream more than Michelle does.

In response, act utilitarians acknowledge that all these facts are true. It is hard to make interpersonal happiness comparisons, to know all the consequences of our actions, and to do the relevant happiness calculations. But they argue that we can and do make accurate judgments about happiness. When deciding what gift to give someone, we attempt to figure out which gift would make the person happiest, and we often pick the right gift. We cannot be absolutely certain that we know all the consequences of our acts, but often we can be very sure that a certain act will have a certain effect. If I am considering whether to take a walk in the park, I can be very sure that this will make me happy and that the probability that this will cause another Hitler is minuscule. Therefore, this possibility's effect on expected happiness will be tiny. As for the time to calculate, act utilitarians argue that calculating happiness is an act like any other and sometimes it may not maximize happiness to stop and consider an action at great length. This might well be the case if a car pulls out in front of me. In general, act utilitarians respond to this objection by asserting that they never said acting morally would be easy. It can be very difficult to figure out what act is right, and act utilitarianism merely reflects this fact.

Allows All Consequences to Count

A black woman and a white man meet and fall in love. They live in South Africa. They are considering whether to marry or not. According to act utilitarians, when making this decision, they ought to take into account that they will offend a great many people and so cause a great deal of unhappiness. Of course, it may be that their own happiness will outweigh the unhappiness of others. But then again it may not. Some object to act utilitarianism on the grounds that even if the happiness of these two people will outweigh the unhappiness of others, the unhappiness of these prejudiced people ought not be counted at all. These sorts of consequences, the objectors argue, are completely irrelevant and ought never to enter into anyone's decisions.

Act utilitarians argue that these objectors are being unrealistic. Prejudiced people really exist and they make their presence felt in all sorts of ways. Perhaps they will fire the couple from their jobs. Perhaps they will kill them. Act utilitarians think that the couple ought to consider possibilities like these when considering whether to marry. They argue that prejudice is immoral because it produces a great deal of unhappiness. Therefore, we ought to work to eliminate prejudice. But until it is eliminated we ought to consider its effects.

Distribution

Suppose that there are two possible distributions of happiness in society. In one distribution 80 percent of the population live very well and are very happy. The reason they are so well off is that the other 20 percent of the population are their slaves. These slaves are very unhappy. In the other distribution no one is a slave. Everyone is about equally well off and happy. In this second distribution everyone is happier than the slaves in the first distribution, but not as happy as the slave owners. The total and average happiness in these two distributions is exactly the same. According to act utilitarianism, we ought to be indifferent between these two distributions. According to this theory, the distribution of happiness is morally irrelevant. All that counts is the total or the average happiness.

Many people think that this is a serious problem with act utilitarianism. They argue that the second distribution is clearly morally superior to the first, even though the total and average happiness are the same. They often go on to claim that the second distribution would be a morally better one even if the total and average happiness were somewhat less than they were in the first distribution. This point has been most forcefully made by John Rawls. In *A Theory of Justice*, Rawls argued that act utilitarianism fails to take the separateness of persons seriously. According to Rawls, this view treats a group of people as if they were one big person. Many people try to maximize their own happiness. Rawls thinks that act utilitarians have noted this and moved from the fact that many individuals try to maximize their happiness to the claim that society ought to maximize total happiness. This fails to see that groups are composed of separate individuals. Therefore, according to Rawls, who within a group is happy is more important than the maximization of happiness.

Too Demanding

You are trying to decide whether to buy a VCR or a stereo system. Both cost about $400. Most people think that either option is perfectly moral. But some have argued that act utilitarianism implies that buying either the VCR or the stereo is wrong. Note that you could send that $400 to organizations that are feeding starving people in Africa. Of course, if you did that you would lose the happiness that the VCR or the stereo would have given you. But $400 could quite literally save 1,000 lives in Africa. So the action that maximizes happiness is sending the money to Africa. But this is not only true of this $400. It is also true of the $7 spent on a movie, the $15 spent on a CD, and thousands of other expenses. Act utilitarianism seems to demand that most of the people in the West send large portions of their money to those overseas. (We will discuss this issue further in chapter 11.) This leads many to argue that act utilitarianism demands too much of us. Surely one may go to a movie every now and then. Some act utilitarians respond by arguing that one may not. They accept this consequence of act utilitarianism.

Intrinsic Features

Possibly the most direct challenge to act utilitarianism, and to all forms of consequentialism, is the claim that intrinsic features of acts are morally important—that consequences are not the only things of moral importance. People have argued that many different kinds of acts are wrong independent of their consequences. Let us consider an example.

A white woman is raped in a Southern town during the 1940s. She knows that her attacker was a black man but she cannot identify him. The sheriff cannot find any evidence that would allow her to determine who attacked the woman. The white people in the town are threatening to go on a rampage through the black part of town, destroying homes and severely beating many black people. From past experience the sheriff knows that they will carry out this threat and that the only way she can prevent this rampage is to arrest, convict, and hang a black man. The unhappiness that the rampage will cause is greater than the unhappiness that would be caused by killing one black man.

The sheriff is an act utilitarian. It seems she would arrest and hang a black man to avoid the rampage. She would choose the man carefully. It is better if the man is someone no one cares about, because then there will be less unhappiness caused by the man's death. She will not choose one of the productive members of the black community. Such a person is doing something useful and thus making people happy. So the sheriff finds a black drifter who was not even in town the night of the rape. She trumps up charges and easily wins conviction from an all-white jury. The black drifter is hanged and the rampage is avoided.

Many think that not only did the sheriff not do the right thing, she did something horribly wrong. They argue that act utilitarianism implies that this act is right because it overlooks the fact that this act has a morally important intrinsic feature—it was the arrest and hanging of an innocent person. It was unjust. Many argue that injustice is a morally important intrinsic feature of acts. It is this intrinsic feature that explains why the sheriff ought not to have hung the drifter even if it was the only way she could prevent a rampage that would cause a greater loss of happiness.

Act utilitarians have a common response to the claims that their view does not consider distribution, is too demanding and fails to consider intrinsic features. They argue that in making all these objections, people have relied on odd, abstract situations. They assert that one could never really be in a position to choose between the two possible distributions of happiness discussed above, that it is not really true that one could cause more happiness by sending one's movie money to Africa, and that the Southern-sheriff example did not and will not really happen. They argue that we are being confused by bizarre and unfamiliar examples. Those who made these arguments respond that their cases are not bizarre at all. They think these cases really could and do occur.

RULE UTILITARIANISM

Rule utilitarianism comes in two forms. Classical rule utilitarianism is the view that an act is right if the system of rules that would, if followed by everyone, maximize happiness includes a rule that states that the act is right. Average rule utilitarianism is the view that an act is right if the system of rules that would, if followed by everyone, maximize average happiness includes a rule that states that the act is right. Recall that according to act utilitarianism the rightness or wrongness of an act is determined directly by its own consequences. According to rule utilitarianism, on the other hand, the rightness or wrongness of an act is not directly determined by that act's consequences; rather, it is determined indirectly by determining whether the act would be right according to the system of rules that would, if everyone followed them, maximize happiness.

Rule utilitarianism allows for the possibility that some right acts will not maximize happiness. Suppose you are visiting the Grand Canyon. You would like to take home a rock as a souvenir. If were an act utilitarianism, you would compare the consequences of your taking a rock with the consequences of your not taking a rock. Because there are so many rocks in the Grand Canyon, no one would notice one less. So the only person affected by your act is you, and you will be happier if you take a rock. So act utilitarianism implies that you ought to take a rock. But according to rule utilitarianism you ought to compare the system of rules that allowed people to take rocks from the Grand Canyon with the system of rules that did not allow them to take rocks. Because millions and millions of people visit the Grand Canyon, if lots of them took home a rock, the Canyon would be severely damaged. This would make millions and millions of future visitors unhappy. So a rule prohibiting the taking of rocks would maximize happiness. Rule utilitarianism implies that you ought not to take the rock.

Too Demanding   Notice that the phrase "otherwise the act is wrong," which was part of the definition of act utilitarianism, is not part of the definition of rule utilitarianism. Most people think that some acts are morally required, some are morally forbidden, and some are permitted. We think stopping at Stop signs is morally required, killing others is morally forbidden, and going to a movie is morally permitted. As we saw above when considering the view that act utilitarianism is too demanding, it seems that act utilitarianism implies that all acts are either forbidden or required—required if they maximize happiness, and forbidden if they do not. That is the effect of the phrase "otherwise the act is wrong" in the definitions of classical- and average-act utilitarianism. This feature of act utilitarianism leads many to object that the view is too demanding—it did not imply that going to the movies is permitted. But according to rule utilitarianism an act can be required, forbidden, or permitted.

The category an act falls into is determined by the system of rules that would, if followed by everyone, maximize happiness. If this system includes a rule that states that the act is required, then the act is required. If it includes a rule that states that the act is forbidden, then the act is forbidden. If it includes a rule that states that the act is permitted, then the act is permitted. Some think that rule utilitarianism's allowing for permitted acts makes the view an improvement over act utilitarianism because it avoids the problem of being too demanding. Others think that rule utilitarianism, like act utilitarianism, is too demanding. They claim that a rule that those who make more than $20,000 per year send $10,000 per year to those who make less than $100 per year would maximize happiness.

OBJECTIONS TO RULE UTILITARIANISM

Rule Worship   Act utilitarians object that rule utilitarianism is nothing but irrational rule worship. Why, they ask, follow a rule in those cases in which following the rule will decrease happiness? Act utilitarians argue that past experience will allow us to establish general guidelines for determining whether our acts maximize happiness. Past experience tells us that an act of washing our hands before dinner will probably maximize happiness by reducing the incidence of disease. But, according to act utilitarians, past experience gives us only guidelines. In a particular, unusual situation the guideline might not apply. One might be starving and there might be no place to wash one's hands. In these cases act utilitarians think that following the guideline would be wrong. Rule utilitarians respond that, as the Grand Canyon example illustrates, sometimes the effect of a set of particular acts that maximize happiness is a decrease in happiness. Therefore, we ought to consider the effect of sets of acts—not of particular acts.

Collapses into Act Utilitarianism

Some argue that rule utilitarianism collapses into act utilitarianism. Whether it does or not depends on what system of rules would, if followed by everyone, maximize happiness. Some think that the system of rules that would do this includes only one rule: Do those acts that maximize happiness, and do not do those that do not. They think that the best way to maximize happiness is for everyone to try to maximize happiness with every act. But this is just act utilitarianism. Rule utilitarians argue that this rule system with a single rule would not maximize happiness. They point to cases like that of the Grand Canyon to support their view.

Intrinsic Features

Rule utilitarians have argued that their view avoids the problems raised by the claim that intrinsic features are relevant. Recall the example of the Southern sheriff. Let us assume that the sheriff is a rule, not an act, utilitarian. Rather than ask herself which act would directly maximize utility, she asks herself what rule would, if followed by everyone, maximize happiness. She then notes that a rule permitting sheriffs to hang innocent people would not maximize happiness. If people knew that sheriffs sometimes knowingly hanged innocent people, they would be afraid that they might be hanged. Therefore, they would be unhappy. It seems that a rule prohibiting all hangings of innocent people would maximize happiness.

Those who object to all forms of utilitarianism think that rule utilitarianism is no better than act utilitarianism when it comes to intrinsic features. They argue that the rules that maximize happiness often permit or even require intrinsically unjust acts. For example, in the sheriff case, while it may very well be true that a rule permitting sheriffs to hang innocent people *whenever they want* would not maximize happiness, it may also be true that a rule that sheriffs ought to hang innocent people *to prevent a violent racial riot* does maximize happiness. They point out that the rule-utilitarian argument in the last paragraph does not distinguish these two rules. If the second rule maximizes happiness, then rule utilitarianism, like act utilitarianism, implies that the sheriff ought to hang the innocent drifter. Those who object to all forms of utilitarianism go on to argue that utilitarianism has not even correctly framed the sheriff's problem. The sheriff ought to try to figure out which act is intrinsically just—not which act would, directly or indirectly, maximize happiness. They argue that not only does utilitarianism have the wrong implication, but it arrives at it in the wrong way.

IS UTILITARIANISM SELF-EFFACING?

Recently some have suggested that utilitarianism is self-effacing. A view is self-effacing when the view implies that people should not believe the view. Egoistic ethical hedonism seems to be self-effacing. Recall that egoistic ethical hedonism is the view that everyone ought to act so as to maximize her own pleasure. Suppose you attempt to maximize your own pleasure by checking constantly to see if you are doing what brings you the most pleasure. If you do this, you will not get very much pleasure. Instead of enjoying a movie, you will be wondering constantly whether staying at the movie is maximizing your pleasure. You would constantly be asking yourself: Is there another movie that I would like more? This would keep you from enjoying the movie you are watching. To maximize your own pleasure, you have to forget about maximizing your own pleasure and become wrapped up in the movie. So egoistic ethical hedonism is self-effacing.

Similarly, some argue that society maximizes happiness if people do not try to maximize happiness. Suppose you were always trying to maximize happiness. You meet someone whom you like. You realize that it is possible that you will fall in love with this person. But you are constantly asking yourself whether your actions maximize happiness. You might take the person you like out to dinner. But then it would maximize happiness to send the money to feed hungry people. If you are always thinking about maximizing happiness, you will never fall in love. This is not only true of you, but of most people. So in a society where everyone is constantly trying to maximize happiness, few people will fall in love. But falling in love is an excellent way to produce happiness. People who never fall in love are usually unhappy. So if everyone is constantly trying to maximize happiness, they will miss one of the best ways to produce happiness. Therefore, people will maximize happiness by not trying to maximize happiness. The problem is that to fall in love, you have to care about (and so want to maximize the individual happiness of) someone more than you care about others. But, because utilitarianism is universalistic, it requires us to maximize everyone's happiness. (Some have argued that all universalistic moral theories, including Kantianism, have a similar problem with love. See chapter 5.)

Some do not think utilitarianism is self-effacing. They argue that the reasoning in the previous paragraph is flawed. They claim that since falling in love is one of the best ways to produce happiness, utilitarians will seek to fall in love. Those who think utilitarianism is self-effacing argue that as long as people seek to maximize happiness, they will fail to fall in love. As long as they are trying to maximize everyone's happiness and not show favoritism by treating someone as special, they will never fall in love.

Is Being Self-Effacing a Problem?

Those who think that utilitarianism is self-effacing disagree over whether this is a problem with, or a virtue of, the view. There are utilitarians who think that utilitarianism is self-effacing. They see this as a virtue of their theory. They argue that the self-effacing character of utilitarianism allows it to respond to some of the objections to the theory. Suppose rule utilitarianism is true and self-effacing. Then we ought not to try to maximize happiness. Instead, we ought to try to follow those rules that would, if followed by everyone, maximize happiness. Because being in love produces so much happiness, one rule would tell us to try to fall in love. Because entertainment makes people happy and a country of people who never went to the movies would be less happy, one rule would be that going to the movies every now and then is permitted. On this view we ought to forget about maximizing happiness and follow rules like these. Therefore, we ought not try to calculate the precise effects on happiness of each of our acts. So one of problems noted previously—the problem of calculating the effect on happiness of each of our actions—is avoided.

Some argue that being self-effacing is a problem with any view. Therefore, they claim that if utilitarianism is self-effacing, we have good reason to reject it. A self-effacing moral view seems to be inconsistent in some sense. After all, it is very odd for a view to imply that people ought not believe the view. Those who object to utilitarianism also argue that it is psychologically impossible for human beings to live according to a self-effacing moral theory. Suppose that Juanita is a utilitarian who thinks that utilitarianism is self-effacing. After careful consideration she is convinced that utilitarianism is the correct moral theory. But because she also believes, after equally careful consideration, that utilitarianism is self-effacing, she must resolve to try to stop believing utilitarianism. Some argue that Juanita cannot succeed in changing her beliefs in this way. She might try not to believe a theory she believes is true. But, some argue, if she really believes it is true, then she will not be able to fool herself into believing that it is not true.

VIRTUES OF UTILITARIANISM

In this chapter we have focused on the many problems that seem to plague utilitarianism. Many think that these problems are so serious that we must turn to other moral theories—perhaps to some version of Kantianism (see chapter 5). But we should also note the many virtues of utilitarianism. First, utilitarianism is a very clear and straightforward theory. While it may be very difficult in practice to do the relevant happiness calculations, utilitarianism gives us clear guidance. It tells us in a very clear way what we ought to be trying to do—even if doing it is difficult. In chapters 5 and 6 we will see that other moral theories have trouble being as clear as utilitarianism. Second, utilitarianism gives us a principled way to resolve all moral conflicts. Suppose that one is not a consequentialist. One thinks that the intrinsic features of acts are morally important. One must decide between telling a lie or breaking a promise. One thinks it is intrinsically wrong to do either of these sorts of actions. But in this case one has no choice but to tell a lie or to break a promise. How can one resolve this conflict? It is not clear. But utilitarianism tells us how to resolve these conflicts—do the act that maximizes happiness. These reasons account for the continuing plausibility of utilitarianism in the face of many objections.

Utilitarianism is one version of consequentialism—the view that whether an act is right or wrong is determined, directly or indirectly, by the act's consequences and not by its intrinsic features. Different versions of consequentialism pick out different consequences as morally important. The definition of consequentialism does not impose any restrictions on whose happiness is relevant, but most consequentialists are universalists. Universalistic consequentialists think that everyone is equal in moral importance. Universalistic consequentialism requires us not to give any greater weight to our own or anyone else's happiness.

What is the correct amount of the morally important consequences? Maximizing consequentialists answer: The correct amount is as much as possible. But this is ambiguous. Most consequentialists understand this phrase to mean "maximize universal expected happiness." To maximize happiness, one is guided by the following procedure. Of the acts open to you that produce some happiness, one chooses the one that produces the most happiness. If all the acts open to you decrease the amount of happiness, one chooses the act that produces the smallest decrease. If two acts have the exact same effect on the amount of happiness, then one is indifferent between these two acts.

There are two basic versions of utilitarianism— act utilitarianism and rule utilitarianism. There are, in turn, two basic versions of act utilitarianism and two basic versions of rule utilitarianism. Classical act utilitarianism is the view that an act is right if it maximizes happiness, and that otherwise the act is wrong. Average act utilitarianism is the view that an act is right if it maximizes average happiness, and that otherwise it is wrong. Classical rule utilitarianism is the view that an act is right if the system of rules that would, if followed by everyone, maximize happiness includes a rule that states that the act is right. Average rule utilitarianism is the view that an act is right if the system of rules that would, if followed by everyone, maximize average happiness includes a rule that states that the act is right. Many have objected to classical utilitarianism on the grounds that it has implausible implications concerning population control. An increasing population may maximize happiness, while at the same time causing average happiness to fall. It may lead to a society with a great many not very happy (but not unhappy) people, instead of one with fewer, happier people.

Many people have objected to act utilitarianism. They have raised sev-

eral objections. They argue that we cannot do the happiness calculations that utilitarianism requires of us. They claim that we ought not to let the happiness of prejudiced people enter into our happiness calculations. They hold that the distribution, not merely the maximization, of happiness is morally important. They argue that utilitarianism is too demanding. Finally they argue, using examples like the case of the Southern sheriff, that intrinsic features of acts, such as whether an act is just or not, are morally important.

Rule utilitarianism is an attempt to respond to these objections. It allows for the possibility that some right acts will not maximize happiness. Rule utilitarianism allows for permitted acts and so might avoid the problem of being too demanding. Rule utilitarians also claim that their view avoids the problems with intrinsic features that plagued act utilitarianism. However, others argue that there are examples of clearly unjust rules that would maximize happiness.

Some argue that utilitarianism is self-effacing. A view is self-effacing when the view implies that people should not believe the view. Those utilitarians who think that their view is self-effacing see this as a strength of the view. They think that its self-effacing nature allows it to avoid the problems that nonself-effacing utilitarianism seems to have when it comes to the morality of loving others. Other utilitarians do not think their view is self-effacing. Some think that utilitarianism's being self-effacing is a problem with the view. They are argue that it is psychologically impossible for human beings to live according to a self-effacing moral theory.

Selected Readings

Hare, R. M. *Moral Thinking: Its Levels, Method, and Point.* New York: Oxford University Press, 1981.

Mill, John Stuart. *Utilitarianism* (several editions are available).

Quinton, A. *Utilitarian Ethics.* London: Duckworth Press, 1989.

Rawls, J. A *Theory of Justice.* Cambridge, MA: Harvard University Press, 1971.

Scheffler, S. *The Rejection of Consequentialism.* New York: Oxford University Press, 1982.

Smart, J. C. C. and B. Williams. *Utilitarianism: For and Against.* New York: Cambridge University Press, 1973.

5

Kant and Kantianism

Most people think that everyone is morally required to treat other people in moral ways. Whether or not you should treat other people morally is not a matter of how you happen to feel or of personal opinion. Some people have very nasty feelings toward people in general, and many people are not extremely kind or sympathetic. Their particular sentiments do not affect their moral obligations, because moral obligations are objective. The German philosopher Immanuel Kant (1724–1804) developed one of the strongest and most influential theories of how moral obligations are objective.

MORALITY AND RATIONALITY

Kant claimed that morality is based entirely upon rationality. Reason gives us moral requirements that all of our actions must meet. All rational beings are familiar with these moral requirements. They are our moral duty that everyone should obey. Acting according to moral duty does not always make you happy or serve your ordinary self-interest. In an imperfect society, acting according to moral duty may not even make other people happy or promote other people's ordinary self-interests. Nevertheless, you are required by your essential nature (rationality) to follow the Categorical Imperative (see page 66), which is the underlying principle of morality.

Moral Requirements

Kant claimed that everyone is familiar with moral requirements on their actions. Everyone realizes that there are some things that they morally ought to do, and some immoral actions that they should not do. For example, you are aware that you should not steal things from someone, even if you strongly desire the things and are sure that you will not be caught. These moral requirements that are expressed as "ought" or "should" are different from nonmoral "oughts" or "shoulds." A person is intrinsically required to do what is morally right, regardless of her desires, her emotions, or societal customs. Morality commands or requires people to do the right thing, regardless of other considerations. Nonmoral "oughts" or "shoulds" are dependent on other conditions. In many cases nonmoral "shoulds" tell people what is the best means for attaining some objective that they want. For example, if you want to prepare a good dinner, you ought to acquire fresh ingredients. Kant calls this type of statement a "hypothetical imperative." The "ought," or imperative, tells you to do something—to acquire fresh ingredients—as a means to accomplishing a goal—to prepare a good dinner. If you did not have this goal, the "ought" would not apply to you. If you did not especially want to prepare a good dinner, you would have no obligation to acquire fresh ingredients. The imperative commands you only hypothetically—that is, only if you have that goal. In contrast, moral imperatives command people, regardless of what goals they have or what they want. According to Kant, moral imperatives command people without any conditions. Moral imperatives command people categorically, not hypothetically.

Moral requirements, according to Kant, are not based on happiness. Morality does not command you to do whatever will make you most happy. Morality may require you to do things that will not make you happy at all, such as requiring that you not kill yourself, even though you will continue to be depressed and miserable. Morality does not always command you to do whatever will make other people most happy either. Kant's account of morality directly contradicts utilitarianism on this issue (see chapter 4). Although he recognizes that there is a duty to promote the welfare of others, Kant claims that moral requirements are not always directed toward producing the greatest amount of happiness for people in general. Doing your moral duty may produce happiness in other people, but it sometimes does not. In an imperfect world, the morally right action does not always promote other people's goals or please them. For example, sometimes you might produce the most happiness for other people by telling a lie, but morality requires that you not lie. Morality is not based on the goal of making people happy.

Another feature of moral requirements, according to Kant, is that the same basic moral requirements are made on all rational beings. We experience the basic moral requirements that are made on our behavior to apply to other people as well. Other people ought also to do what we ought to do. Morality is objective and absolute. The same basic moral standards must apply to all people at all times in all conditions. An action that is fundamentally morally wrong for Germans in 1786 is also morally wrong for Ethiopians in 1786 or Americans in 1995.

Moral Requirements and Objectivity

The experience of moral requirements on our behavior is basic to Kant's moral philosophy. If we do experience moral requirements that command us without conditions and have to be the same for all people, morality cannot be based on desires and emotions or on societal customs. Morality must be objective rather than subjective (see "subjectivism" in chapter 3). Absolute moral requirements that command categorically cannot depend upon the existence of desires and emotions in us or on societal customs outside us. If the requirements did depend upon the existence of specific desires and emotions in us or specific societal customs outside us, the requirements would not command without conditions. The requirements would apply to us only if certain desires and emotions or certain social customs existed. Furthermore, desires and emotions may vary from person to person or from society to society, and customs may vary from society to society. If moral requirements depended upon having kind feelings toward others and some person happened not to have those kind feelings, morality would not apply to him. If morality were based on desires or emotions and some society trained its members to have other desires or emotions, such as to want to take advantage of all outsiders, morality would not apply to that society. If morality were based on societal customs, and a society's customs included human sacrifice or robbing and beating outsiders, moral restrictions against these actions would not apply to that society. Since the same basic moral requirements must apply to everyone, according to Kant, morality cannot be based on desires and emotions or on social customs.

Kant claimed that moral requirements are objective. There is a true morality that governs all rational beings. The standards of this true morality are contained in rationality (see "Reason and the Categorical Imperative," page 68). The nature of rationality, which is objective, is the source of the moral requirements on the behavior of all rational beings. This is why all rational beings are aware of the same basic moral requirements on their behavior. All people, as rational beings, have some understanding of the basic requirements of morality. This basic understanding can be helped or hindered by a person's individual upbringing and education and by the customs and practices of her society. These can promote or interfere with the full development of a person's innate rationality. Nevertheless, all people have access to the true moral standards through their rationality. Even the worst conditions cannot remove a person's basic understanding of what is morally right and wrong.

Moral Worth

Kant had a very strict doctrine about the moral worth or moral goodness of actions. He claimed that an action has moral worth only if it is done because it is morally right. A person's actions are morally good only when she intends to obey moral requirements. She must be motivated by the idea of moral duty. This intention to obey moral requirements is what makes a will morally good, and a "good will" is the only thing that is good without conditions.

Kant denied that actions that are done only in order to satisfy desires are morally good actions. He denied that actions that are only expressions of emotions or feelings—even kind feelings toward others, such as sympathy or generosity—are morally good actions. Although these actions may be in agreement with what morality requires, they do not have moral worth unless they are done from moral duty. To be morally good, an action must be done because it is the moral thing to do, not because you feel like doing it. From an external perspective, how you treat other people or yourself may be the same, whether you are acting from the motive to be moral or acting out of desire or feeling. For example, a shopkeeper's outward behavior is the same whether he gives a child a fair deal out of a sense of moral duty or out of a sense of what will be good for business in the long run. It is better for society if all outward behavior is in agreement with moral behavior. Outward behavior that agrees with moral behavior is good, but not morally good. Actions are morally good and have moral worth only if the internal intention is to do your moral duty. If the shopkeeper's intention is only to serve his long-term self-interest by doing what will be good for his business, there is no particular moral goodness to his action.

Kant thought that this doctrine about moral goodness agrees with our ordinary moral thinking. He thought that everyone would agree that the moral goodness of an action depends entirely upon the intention to do what morality requires. However, other moral theorists, such as Aristotle (see chapter 6) and the utilitarians (see chapter 4), disagree with this claim.

Motivation of Moral Action

To experience moral requirements is one thing; to obey them is another. It is difficult for people to act morally because we all have desires and emotions that incline us toward nonmoral behavior. We all have desires to have and to do things, and some of these things are immoral. The satisfaction of desires is usually pleasurable. The satisfaction of the best combination of desires would bring us a type of happiness (see "Self-Interest" in chapter 2). It is easy for people to do what they think will bring them pleasure and happiness. However, morality does not have the basic purpose of making people happy. It can be difficult for a person to motivate herself to act as morality requires.

People are able to motivate themselves to behave morally because they are rational beings. Rational or reasoning beings do not automatically do what they feel like doing. They do not automatically follow their inclinations, which is Kant's term for both desires and emotions. Reason allows people to think about what they are inclined to do. Reason produces a type of detachment from desires and emotions in which you can think about whether to do what you feel like doing. In thinking about what you feel like doing, you can consider whether the proposed action is moral or immoral. If a proposed action does not violate moral requirements, you can follow your desires or emotions. In many cases moral requirements permit you to do what you feel like doing. If a proposed action does violate moral requirements, you can choose not to do it. The detachment from inclinations that rationality provides makes a person able to act contrary to his desires and emotions. You are free not to follow your inclinations and to do something else instead. Reason makes a person able to obey moral requirements and to do an action simply because it is your duty. Of course, you are also able to disobey moral requirements and to do an action that you know to be immoral.

Kant claimed that moral requirements make sense only for rational beings who have inclinations. A rational being who had no desires or emotions would automatically follow her rationality. Since she would have no inclinations to do anything else, such a "holy will" would not have to be required to follow rational moral principles. However, all humans have both inclinations and reason. Reason gives humans the freedom of will to obey moral requirements despite their desires and emotions. Nonrational animals are governed entirely by their desires and emotions. They have no choice but to follow their inclinations. Since nonrational beings are unable to obey moral requirements, moral requirements do not apply to them. This is why we do not consider cats, dogs, and other animals to be morally responsible for what they do. See chapter 14.

THE CATEGORICAL IMPERATIVE

Kant claimed that all moral requirements are instances of one general moral requirement, which he called the Categorical Imperative. An imperative is a command or requirement, such as "You must do this." A categorical or unconditioned imperative would be a requirement that did not depend upon any conditions. Kant claimed that there is one command or requirement that is made of all rational beings without any conditions. It does not depend upon what a person wants, upon her emotions, upon what will make her happy, or upon societal customs. Rational beings are commanded to be moral without any of these conditions. All people are subject to the one general moral requirement or Categorical Imperative.

The Categorical Imperative can be stated in several ways. Kant claimed that each of these formulas is ultimately equivalent to the others. Each emphasizes one feature of the Categorical Imperative, but they are all expressing the same thing. The two most important statements of the Categorical Imperative are the Formula of Universal Law and the Formula of the End in Itself.

UNIVERSAL LAW

Act only according to that maxim whereby you can, at the same time, will that it should become a universal law.

END IN ITSELF

Act in such a way that you treat humanity, whether in your own person or in the person of another, always at the same time as an end in itself and never simply as a means.

The Formula of Universal Law states the moral requirement to do only those actions whose guiding idea (maxim) can be willed to become a universal law. The basic thought here is that whether an action is moral or not depends upon whether it is consistent that all people in similar circumstances act in a similar way and whether rationality would favor all people acting in that way. Rational consistency is the basis of morality. In everyday life the appeal to rational consistency is expressed in questions such as "What if everybody did that?" To determine whether an action is moral, you have to consider whether you could consistently will that everyone do what you are thinking of doing. If what you are thinking of doing in these circumstances is not moral, you could not consistently want everyone who is in such circumstances to do it. In performing immoral actions a person wants to treat himself differently from other people. He wants to be able to act in a way that other people are not allowed to act. The Formula of Universal Law commands a person to do only actions that he could consistently will that everyone else do in similar circumstances.

To apply the Formula of Universal Law to your action, there are two tests that you should carry out. First, ask yourself if it is logically possible that everyone who is in similar circumstances could do what you are thinking of doing. Most immoral actions will fail this test. For example, if you are considering telling someone a lie to gain some advantage for yourself, you have to ask yourself whether it is logically possible for everyone to lie in such circumstances. Since lying will help you only if people believe what you tell them, and people believe what someone tells them only because people generally tell the truth, if everyone regularly lied whenever they could gain some advantage by it, no one would believe the lies. It is not logically possible for everyone to gain some advantage by lying, so that this proposed action does not pass the first test. The second test is necessary only if an action passes the first test. The second test is to ask yourself whether you could rationally want everyone who is in such circumstances to do what you are thinking of doing. Is it consistent with the nature of willing and the human condition to will that everyone behave that way? For example, if you are considering being lazy and not developing your abilities, you have to ask yourself not only whether there could be a society in which no one developed her talents, but also whether it is rational to want this society to exist. Since all reasonable people want a society in which some people have developed their abilities—such as doctors who can cure you chemists who can detect and neutralize dangerous chemicals—it would be irrational for you to want a society in which no one developed her talents. Wanting all people not to develop their talents would contradict these other wants that all reasonable people have.

The Formula of the End in Itself states the moral requirement of treating people, including yourself, as intrinsically valuable. People are intrinsically valuable because they are reasoning beings who can think about whether to do what they feel like doing. Any rational being, whether human or not, deserves respect for his freedom to set his own goals and to motivate himself to act morally. Morality requires that you respect rational actors who have these powers and that you never treat them only as useful to accomplish your goals. You should never treat someone only as a means to your goals. You can treat a piece of lumber or any other thing that is not a rational agent solely in terms of its usefulness for what you want. Kant claimed that such things have value only because rational beings value them, so that nonrational things do not deserve to be treated in any special way. However, rational beings have intrinsic value, so that morality requires that you treat them as ends in themselves.

The requirement to treat rational beings as ends in themselves does not mean that you cannot treat someone at all as a means to your goals. You have to interact with people in everyday life in many ways that treat them as useful to your goals. You treat the grocer as a means to satisfying your desire for food and the auto mechanic as a means for accomplishing your goal of fixing your car. These are not immoral so long as you do not treat people only as a means. You cannot enslave them or bypass their powers to make their own decisions. So long as the auto mechanic agrees to fix your car, you are not treating her only as a means. The Formula of the End in Itself says that you should treat people only in a way to which they could in principle reasonably consent.

REASON AND THE CATEGORICAL IMPERATIVE

Kant claimed that the Categorical Imperative comes from people's rational nature. The command to be moral does not come from an external source. An external God or other authority does not impose moral requirements on you. You impose moral requirements on yourself, because your fundamental rationality requires that you consider whether your proposed actions are moral. In obeying moral requirements, you are acting autonomously because you are the source of the requirements. You can refuse to act morally, but then you are going against your basic rationality.

The exact way in which the Categorical Imperative is supposed to follow from rationality itself is stated by Kant in a rather indirect way. The basic idea is that rationality requires that you treat similar things in similar ways. It is irrational to treat two things differently unless there is a significant difference between them. Kant then applies this idea to a person's consideration of what to do. Rationality requires you to treat the action that you are considering as you would treat the action of any person in these circumstances. From the standpoint of rationality, it makes no difference that it is your action. You should do it only if you could will that everyone in these circumstances do it. This leads to the Formula of Universal Law. The Formula of the End in Itself comes from reason's valuing of rational motivation. Rationality should lead you to value agents who operate in terms of rationality. Rational beings should consider other rational beings to be intrinsically valuable, because they are able to consider all inclinations to act in terms of rational consistency and able to motivate themselves to do what rationality requires.

Metaphysical Background

In his metaphysical writings, such as *The Critique of Pure Reason*, Kant argued that our familiar world of physical objects is not the ultimately real world. Our minds impose structures on everything that can appear to us in perception and in thought. Our minds perceive and think of things through structures of space, time, substance, causation, number, and some other basic categories. These structures shape the appearing or "phenomenal" world. The independently real or "noumenal" world is not spatial and temporal and is not governed by causation.

According to Kant's metaphysics, people's minds are part of the noumenal world. The mind that imposes structures on the appearing or phenomenal world is itself ultimately real or noumenal. This metaphysical theory affects Kant's moral theory in three important ways. First, it helps to explain the intrinsic value that rational agents are supposed to have. Rational agents are part of the ultimately real world, whereas all ordinary physical things are only part of the appearing world. Second, it supports the priority of reason over inclinations. Reason is a main feature of everyone's true self, but inclinations are always dependent upon the appearing world. Desires and emotions are about objects and events in the appearing world. Third, natural causation is, according to Kant, only a structure that the mind employs. Causation according to natural laws is not part of the noumenal world. Hence, the mind's thinking and deciding are not subject to natural causation, since the mind is itself noumenal. Rational agents are free to choose for themselves whether to follow their inclinations or to follow their rationality. This freedom cannot be observed in the phenomenal world, but we are each aware of our own freedom to choose. Freedom cannot be explained by scientific thought, but in practical action we have to consider ourselves free to choose moral or immoral alternatives.

OBJECTIONS TO KANT'S MORAL THEORY

There have been many different types of objections to Kant's moral theory. Some of the most frequent objections concern Kant's account of ordinary moral views, the application of the Categorical Imperative, and the objectivity of morality.

Account of Ordinary Moral Views

One type of objection is that Kant's moral theory does not accurately express our ordinary moral views. The theory is supposed to provide an explicit statement of the basic principles and underlying ideas of everyday morality. Although it can clarify and emphasize some features of morality that we may not have noticed before, Kant's moral theory is not supposed to be different from our ordinary moral views. Some critics claim that Kant's account of moral worth conflicts with our everyday morality. They claim that an action need not be done out of a sense of moral duty in order to be morally good. Actions that are done solely from benevolence, kindness, sympathy, caring, or love are motivated by emotions, but they can have moral worth. For example, it is morally good to aid the poor out of kindness and to prevent a mugging out of anger, even if the agent does not think about her moral duty. We all recognize that having the right emotions and acting from them is an important part of our ordinary moral life (see chapter 6). Kant's notion that moral worth depends entirely on dutifully obeying moral requirements is a distortion of real moral behavior, according to these critics.

A related objection is that Kant's theory does not easily make room for special relationships, such as love, family relations, and friendship. Most people think that they have special moral obligations for their children, family members, and friends. You should provide special care and attention for these people that you need not and cannot provide for all rational beings (see chapter 13). Kant's theory does not oppose special relationships, but they are hard to include under the Categorical Imperative. The Formula of the End in Itself seems not to allow treating some people better than others, because all rational beings are supposed to be treated as intrinsically valuable. However, the Formula of Universal Law might allow all people to give special care and attention to those specially related to them, because this could be willed to be a universal law.

Applying the Categorical Imperative

There are many objections to Kant's notion that the Categorical Imperative is the one fundamental principle of morality. One objection is that it is not clear exactly what applying the Categorical Imperative is supposed to show. Is applying the Categorical Imperative supposed to be a procedure for deciding whether you are morally required to do some action, morally required not to do some action, or morally permitted either to do it or not to do it? If a maxim can be willed to be a universal law, is the action morally required or morally permitted but not necessarily required? For example, the maxim "In normal circumstances, always tie your left shoelace before your right shoelace" could consistently be willed to be a universal law. However, this action seems to be morally permitted but not morally required. If a maxim cannot be willed to be a universal law, is the action morally forbidden or not morally required but perhaps permitted? Kant seems to think that such actions are morally forbidden. However, the action of withdrawing all your money from the bank at ten o'clock seems to be morally permitted, even though it would be impossible for everyone to do this. Kant usually states that applying the Categorical Imperative tells you what you are morally required to do. However, almost all his examples of applying the Categorical Imperative are cases in which some action is said to be morally forbidden—you are required not to do it—because its maxim cannot be willed to be a universal law or it does not treat other people as ends in themselves.

Another objection is that the Categorical Imperative is so general or formal that applying it will not provide specific moral answers. A person who tries to find out what morality requires in any situation by applying the Categorical Imperative will frequently not get a specific answer. You will not get a specific answer because there are many possible ways of describing some action that you are considering. In Kant's language, there are many different maxims that you might form for the same external behavior. You might include more or less of the specific circumstances in which your proposed action would be done. For example, the same behavior might be described as "speaking a sentence," "telling a lie," "telling a lie to a professional killer," or "telling a lie to a professional killer when it is necessary to save someone's life." You might include more or less of the predictable consequences of your proposed action. For example, the same behavior might be described as "telling a lie," "saving the life of someone who would otherwise be killed," or "perpetuating mass murder by saving the life of a leader like Hitler." How much of the specific circumstances and the predictable consequences of some external behavior should be included in the maxim that you would have to will to be a universal law? You would come to different moral conclusions if the action were described as "speaking a sentence," "telling a lie," "saving the life of someone who would otherwise be killed," or "perpetuating mass murder by saving the life of a leader like Hitler."

Objectivity of Moral Requirements

Many objections have been raised against Kant's arguments for the objectivity of moral requirements. One objection is that rationality need not imply the Categorical Imperative. Although being reasonable about your action includes taking into account all relevant factors, including the actions of other agents, it is not obvious that a rational person need consider whether his proposed action could be performed by all agents. Why does a rational person have to think about all agents, rather than just about those who might have some effect on the person himself?

Another objection is that Kant's moral theory requires that reason always has priority over bodily feelings, desires, and emotions. Even if the Categorical Imperative comes from people's rational nature, why are people required to follow their rational nature rather than their feelings, desires, or emotions? Since all of these are part of a person's mind, why should rationality always be what is most important? Many people claim that their emotions are at least as important to them as their rationality.

Kant defended the priority of rationality over inclinations through his metaphysical theory. He claimed that inclinations are dependent on the phenomenal world and that rationality is part of one's true self and the basis of freedom. Kant's metaphysical defense of the objectivity of moral requirements has been attacked in many ways. Most philosophers and scientists consider the spatial, temporal, and causal world to be independently real. They consider the human mind to be a special part of the natural world. The development of evolutionary biology has provided an account of the natural origins of human beings. Studies of the human brain and of the effects of brain damage have shown that the human mind and reasoning processes depend upon a properly working brain. These scientific developments undermine the idea that reason is otherworldly and almost divine. Studies in psychology, anthropology, and sociology also challenge the noumenal status of reason's commands. They claim that moral requirements are learned from and imposed by people's family, society, and culture, rather than coming from their rational nature.

KANTIANISM

Kant's moral theory continues to be very influential. Moral theories are called "Kantian" because they resemble Kant's moral theory. Kant's moral theory has many complex features. Kant wrote several books about moral issues, and his writings are sometimes difficult to interpret. Scholars continue to argue about the details of Kant's moral philosophy. Many contemporary moral philosophers accept some features of Kant's theory, but reject or revise other features. These Kantian moral theories do not all accept and reject the same features of Kant's theory, and they also revise some features in different ways. Hence, Kantian moral theories do not all share the same basic principles.

The features of Kant's moral philosophy that have been developed in the most influential Kantian moral theories are: reason as the basis of morality, moral principles as universalizable, rational agents as ends in themselves, and the rejection of consequentialism.

REASON AS THE BASIS OF MORALITY

Many Kantian moral theories base morality on reason. Reason has its own goals, such as rational consistency or respecting rational nature, rather than being merely "the slave of the passions." In having its own goals, reason is supposed to provide one or several basic rules for action from which the rest of morality is developed. Morality can require us to do things in opposition to our feelings, desires, and emotions, because its requirements come from reason. This Kantian notion that reason is the basis of morality is frequently contrasted with attempts to base morality on happiness and the satisfaction of desires or on virtue and dispositions to act in agreement with human nature and societal practices.

MORAL PRINCIPLES AS UNIVERSALIZABLE

Many Kantian moral theories use a basic principle that is like the Formula of Universal Law. They claim that moral principles have to be universalizable. Moral principles have to be the same for all people. If one person is to be morally required to do an action in certain circumstances, all people who are in similar circumstances must be morally required to do similar actions. Societal rules for acting that cannot pass the universalization test are not moral.

RATIONAL AGENTS AS ENDS IN THEMSELVES

Many Kantian moral theories consider rational agents to be ultimately valuable. The autonomy of rational agents to decide on their own goals for themselves should be respected. The autonomy of rational agents should be promoted by social and economic structures. This respect for rational agents is the basis for human rights, such as the rights to life, to liberty, to the means necessary for self-development, and to fair treatment. The rights of individual people should not be sacrificed, even if this would increase the overall amount of happiness or fulfill other societal goals. The rights of individual people should not be sacrificed, because this would treat something else as more valuable than rational agency or ignore the individuality of rational agents.

THE REJECTION OF CONSEQUENTIALISM

Kantian moral theories reject consequentialism (see chapter 4). They reject the idea that whether an act is right or wrong is determined, directly or indirectly, by the act's consequences. Kantian theories claim that the intrinsic features of an act in its context are what make it morally right or wrong. This is one major difference between Kantian and utilitarian moral theories.

Kant claimed that morality is based entirely upon rationality. Reason gives us moral requirements that all our actions must meet. Moral requirements are categorical imperatives; they command without any conditions. Hypothetical imperatives tell you to do some action if you want to accomplish some goal. Moral requirements are not based on happiness. Morality may require you to do things that will not make you or other people happy. The same basic moral requirements are made on all rational beings, so that morality is absolute. Morality is objective, because moral requirements do not depend upon our desires, our emotions, or societal customs. Moral standards come from reason, so that all reasonable beings are aware of the same basic moral requirements on their behavior.

Kant claimed that an action has moral worth only if it is done because it is morally right. A person's actions are morally good only when she is motivated by the idea of moral duty. From an external perspective, outward behavior may be the same whether you are acting from the motive to be moral or acting out of desire or feeling. People are able to motivate themselves to behave morally because they are rational beings. Reason produces a type of detachment from desires and emotions in which you can think about whether to do what you feel like doing. Rational agents are free not to follow their inclinations and to obey moral requirements. Moral requirements make sense only for rational agents who have inclinations.

Kant claimed that all moral requirements are instances of one general moral requirement, which he called the Categorical Imperative. The two most important statements of the Categorical Imperative are the Formula of Universal Law—act only according to that maxim whereby you can, at the same time, will that it should become a universal law—and the Formula of the End in Itself—act in such a way that you treat humanity, whether in your own person or in the person of another, always at the same time as an end in itself and never simply as a means. The basic idea of the Formula of Universal Law is that whether an action is moral or not depends upon whether it is consistent that all people in similar circumstances act in a similar way and whether rationality would favor all people acting in that way. To apply this formula, you ask yourself whether you could rationally want everyone who is in such circumstances to do what you are thinking of doing. The Formula of the End in Itself states the moral requirement of treating rational agents, including yourself, as intrinsically valuable. You should never treat someone only as a means to your goals.

Kant claimed that the Categorical Imperative comes from people's rational nature. The basic idea is that rationality requires that you treat similar things in similar ways. Rationality requires you to treat the action that you are considering as you would treat the action of any person in these circumstances. Kant's metaphysics supports freedom and the primacy of reason by arguing that rational agency exists in the noumenal world that lies behind the spatial, temporal, and causal world.

Some of the most frequent objections to Kant's moral theory concern its account of ordinary moral views, the application of the Categorical Imperative, and the objectivity of morality. Critics claim that Kant's theory does not accurately express ordinary moral views about the moral worth of actions and about special moral obligations for family members and loved ones. Other objections are that it is not clear what applying the Categorical Imperative is supposed to show and that applying it will not provide specific moral answers because there are many possible ways of describing an action. Some critics claim that rationality need not imply the Categorical Imperative or that people need not always follow their rational nature rather than their feelings, desires, or emotions. Scientific and social scientific accounts have also undermined the noumenal status of reason.

Moral theories are called "Kantian" because they resemble Kant's moral theory. Kantian moral theories do not all accept and reject the same features of Kant's theory, so that they do not all share the same basic principles. The most influential Kantian moral theories have developed the following features: reason as the basis of morality, moral principles as universalizable, rational agents as ends in themselves, and the rejection of consequentialism.

Selected Readings

Acton, Harold. *Kant's Moral Philosophy*. St. Martin's Press, 1970.

Kant, Immanuel. *Grounding for the Metaphysics of Morals* (also translated as *Groundwork of ...* and *Foundations of ...*) (several good translations).

Kant, Immanuel. *The Metaphysics of Morals*. M. Gregor (tr.). New York: Cambridge University Press, 1991.

O'Neil, Onora. *Acting on Principle*. New York: Columbia University Press, 1975.

Paton, H.J. *The Categorical Imperative*. London: Hutchinson, 1947.

Wolff, Robert. Kant: *A Collection of Critical Essays*. Garden City, NY: Doubleday, 1967.

6

Virtue Ethics

The views discussed in chapters 4 and 5, utilitarianism and Kantianism, focus their attention on figuring out what acts are right and wrong. Some have argued that these theories have little to say about what makes a person good or evil and that this is a serious problem. They have proposed a different family of moral theories, virtue ethics, which focus primarily on figuring out what makes a person good or evil.

VIRTUES AND DISPOSITIONS

We morally evaluate both acts and persons. Acts can be, among other things, morally right, morally wrong, morally permitted, or morally obligatory. Kantianism and utilitarianism, the two moral theories that have dominated modern philosophical discourse, are action-based ethics. They are primarily concerned with the moral evaluation of acts. Recall that according to classical act utilitarianism, an *act* is right if it maximizes happiness. According to Kant, an *act* is right if it passes the test of the Categorical Imperative. But we often focus our moral evaluation not on acts but on people. You might tell a friend who was considering dating someone, "Don't go out with him, he is arrogant." You might say of a job candidate, "We ought to hire her, she is industrious." A person can be honest, dishonest, impartial, biased, generous, miserly, courageous, cowardly, sensitive, insensitive, loyal, disloyal, tolerant, intolerant, wise, foolish, humble, arrogant, merciful, merciless, temperate, intemperate, just, unjust, charitable, uncharitable, industrious, lazy, prudent, imprudent, or simply good or bad. The terms that we use to evaluate persons are called virtues and vices. Virtues are good qualities of people, and vices are bad qualities of people.

Philosophers disagree about the precise nature of virtue and vice. Most agree that a virtue is a desirable disposition, and a vice is an undesirable disposition. Something has a disposition when it is disposed to do such-and-such. And something is disposed to do such-and-such when it usually does such-and-such in certain circumstances. For example, water is disposed to freeze when the temperature is below zero degrees Celsius. Water is disposed to freeze even though it does not always freeze when it is below zero. The water might be moving too fast to freeze or it might contain chemicals that keep it from freezing. Glass is disposed to break when struck by heavy objects, and paper is disposed to burn when placed in a fire. People, like objects, have dispositions. For example, Kluane might be disposed to slightly underestimate how well he performed a task. Kluane is modest. Mary might be disposed to spend a great deal of time watching TV when she has important things to do. Mary is lazy. If you look at the list of virtues and vices above, you will find that they are all dispositions. But not every disposition is a virtue or a vice. To be a virtue, a disposition must be desirable; to be a vice, a disposition must be undesirable. Laziness is undesirable, and modesty is desirable. Some dispositions are neither desirable nor undesirable. For example, a person might have a disposition to walk slowly or put her hands in her pockets. Such dispositions are neither virtues nor vices because they are neither desirable nor undesirable.

While most agree that virtues are desirable dispositions, there is debate over the precise sense in which virtues are desirable. Some think that the virtues are morally desirable. Others argue that there are non-moral virtues, intelligence, for example, that are not morally desirable. For a disposition to be a virtue or a vice, it must be stable. Suppose that, as a result of his father's dying, Tyrone is disposed to snap at people for a month. We would not say that the death of his father made Tyrone short-tempered. We would say that Tyrone is not really short-tempered but acted that way for a while after his father died. But if this disposition lasted for the rest of his life, then we would claim that his father's death made Tyrone short-tempered. Precisely how long a disposition must last to be stable is a matter of debate. Those who study the virtues have also debated whether the dispositions that are virtues must be in some way significant or special. Some think, for example, that a disposition not to wet one's pants, even if stable and desirable, is too common and banal to be a virtue. Others think that the disposition not to wet one's pants is a virtue. They think it is, like the disposition to write legibly, a virtue that most adult humans possess.

TWO FORMS OF VIRTUE ETHICS

One can distinguish two different sorts of virtue ethics: weak virtue ethics and strong virtue ethics.

Weak Virtue Ethics

Weak virtue ethics are ethical theories that hold that, while action-based approaches are correct and useful, they are incomplete because they fail to give the virtues the analysis they deserve. Those who defend weak virtue ethics do not claim that there is anything wrong with action-based ethical theories, but they argue that those who consider ethics must expand what they do to include thinking about virtues. Utilitarians and Kantians can be, and most are, weak virtue ethicists. This explains why much of virtue ethics is weak virtue ethics. Examples of this sort of virtue ethics include analyzing particular virtues, studying relationships between virtues, and considering how one becomes virtuous. What, exactly, is humility? What is the relationship between sympathy, empathy, generosity, and compassion? How does one become just? One can seek to answer questions like these and think that these questions are important without attacking action-based ethics. This is what weak virtue ethics does.

Strong Virtue Ethics

Strong virtue ethics are ethical theories that hold that action-based ethics are not only incomplete but seriously flawed because they have ignored the virtues. To understand strong virtue ethics, we must first lay out the structure of action-based ethics. Action-based ethics begin with a theory of right action. According to classical act utilitarianism, an act is right when it maximizes happiness. Then action-based ethics give an account of the virtues. Virtues are the dispositions that lead people to do the right acts. So, according to classical act utilitarians, a person is virtuous when she has the set of dispositions that cause her to do the acts that maximize happiness. A strong virtue ethic claims that action-based ethics begin in the wrong way. Rather than beginning with a theory of right action, a strong virtue ethic begins with a theory of virtue, of what it is to be a virtuous person. For example, one might hold that a virtuous person is one who has achieved the natural goals of a human being. (We will discuss this theory later in this chapter.) Then a strong virtue ethic gives an account of right action. Right actions are the actions that would be done by a virtuous person. The defender of strong virtue ethics claims that action-based ethics have considered the parts of morality in the wrong order. Rather than beginning with a theory of right action and then defining the virtuous person in terms of right action, we ought to begin with a theory of virtue and then define right action in terms of virtue. This, claim strong virtue ethicists, will give us a more accurate picture of morality. Because weak virtue ethics are accepted by most utilitarians and Kantians, the rest of this chapter will focus on strong virtue ethics. From now on "virtue ethics" will refer to strong virtue ethics.

OBJECTIONS TO UTILITARIANISM AND KANTIANISM

Virtue ethicists often begin by proposing objections to the most plausible action-based moral theories—utilitarianism and Kantianism.

Personal Relationships

Many virtue ethicists argue that action-based ethics cannot provide an adequate account of the moral obligations of personal relationships. Personal relationships are the relationships we have with those we care about. They include the relationships one has with friends, lovers, and family members. Consider an example made famous by Michael Stocker. (See the Selected Readings section at the end of this chapter.) Stocker focuses on friendship. What moral obligations does one have toward one's friends?

Suppose that you are sick and in the hospital. A person you think of as a friend, Van, comes to visit you regularly. You are touched by this and so you thank him. He responds that you should not really thank him; he is merely doing his duty. Puzzled, you ask Van why he thinks that he has a duty to come and visit you. He explains that he is a utilitarian. Further, Van says, coming to see you causes a slight loss in his happiness but a great increase in your happiness, so it maximizes happiness for him to visit you regularly. You would very likely think that Van is not a real friend. After all, if visiting the person in the next room maximized happiness, he would be visiting her, not you. The problem seems to apply to Kantianism as well because you would feel the same if Van told you that he was visiting you because he believed it was required by the Categorical Imperative.

Virtue ethicists think that Van has not met the moral obligations of friendship. Van's actions seem morally inferior to those of someone else, Alison, who visits you because she likes you. This seems to show that the morality of actions turns not only on what is done but also on the character, the virtues, of the person who does the act. One has an obligation to do things for one's friends *because* one has certain feelings for them. If one does the acts associated with friendship merely because they are required by an action-based ethic, then one is not fulfilling the moral obligations generated by friendship. In personal relationships, one has an obligation to be a certain sort of person, to have certain virtues, not merely to do certain actions. Virtue ethicists think that cases like these show that action-based ethics are flawed. What is wrong with Van has nothing to do with what he has done, but instead with the kind of person he is.

Action-based ethicists make several responses to this objection. First, they argue that virtue ethics are subject to the same problem. Suppose that Van had said that he came to visit because he had become convinced that a virtue ethic is correct and that a virtuous person would visit his friends in the hospital. In an effort to be a virtuous person, he decided to visit you regularly. One's reaction to this case seems to be the same as it is if Van is a utilitarian.

Second, some deny that personal relationships generate moral obligations to be a certain sort of person. They claim, for example, that morality requires us to do only certain things for our friends. It might be nice if they also have certain feelings for us, but they have no moral obligations to have these feelings. Virtue ethicists think that this sort of response ignores the importance of personal relationships in our lives. Given the importance of personal relationships, a moral theorist who holds that the essence of these relationships—the feelings involved—is beyond the pale of moral obligation offers an impoverished moral theory. They claim that people who, like Van, do things only because they are required by an action-based ethic reveal themselves to be deeply morally flawed people.

Third, some utilitarians respond to this problem by arguing that their view is self-effacing. Recall from chapter 4 that a view is self-effacing when the view implies that people should not believe the view. In chapter 4 we saw that some think that utilitarianism is self-effacing and that this is a strength of the view. If utilitarianism is self-effacing, it may imply that Van should not believe utilitarianism, even though the view is true. In that case, Van has failed to do something that utilitarianism says he ought to do—stop believing utilitarianism. That is why, according to some utilitarians, Van's actions are not as good as Alison's.

Fourth, some Kantians argue that virtue ethicists have overlooked the fact that one can have a duty to have certain feelings and not to have others. Kantians argue that among the acts we have a duty to do are acts that will lead us to have certain feelings and not have others. For example, we have a duty not to do acts that will lead us to have a desire to hurt people. If it were true that viewing certain films caused this desire, then we would have a duty not to see those films. We might also have a duty to do acts that will lead us to care about people. Alison might have done this. Suppose that after asking why she visits you (to which question she truthfully responded that she was your friend), you ask Alison why she is your friend. She responds that it is her Kantian duty to do things that will lead to her developing friendships. In the past she did that, and this is why she is your friend. Kantians argue that there is nothing wrong with such a person, but virtue ethicists often disagree.

Action-Based Ethics and Authority

Other virtue ethicists argue that the concepts of action evaluation, concepts such as right, wrong, permitted, and obligatory, make no sense without an authority. They claim that an act is right when it is permitted or obligatory, and that an act is wrong when it is forbidden. They then claim that it makes no sense to say that an act is permitted, forbidden, or obligatory unless it is permitted or forbidden by someone—some authority. So it makes sense to say that an act is legally wrong. This means that the act is forbidden by the government. It also makes sense to say that an act is morally wrong *if* one believes that God exists and that He is the authority who forbids immoral actions. But many virtue ethicists, like many philosophers, do not believe in God. They claim that since God does not exist, it makes no sense to say that an act is morally wrong—there is no moral government to do the forbidding.

Some action-based ethicists respond to this argument by arguing that God exists. Other action-based ethicists argue that action- based moral concepts are not based on authority. For example, utilitarians claim that the moral wrongness of an act has nothing to do with whether anyone forbids the act. Rather, the moral wrongness of an act is determined by whether the act maximizes happiness. Kantians claim that moral wrongness is determined not by any authority, but by the Categorical Imperative.

Endless Quarrels

A final objection to action-based ethics is the claim that action-based ethics have produced nothing but quarrels that have gone on for at least 200 years with no results. Virtue ethicists see the long history of action-based ethics as nothing more than a collection of dry arguments that are never resolved. Action-based ethicists respond that the length of the argument is to be expected. They point out that in other fields debate also continues for hundreds of years. Consider, for example, the debate over whether our emotional characteristics are the product of nature, our choices, or our early-childhood experiences. Debate will be long, action-based ethicists claim, when issues are difficult ones. They also deny that action-based ethical debate has produced no results. They point out that at one time slavery, women's right to vote, and patient consent to medical procedures were hotly debated moral issues. Now these debates have been resolved. Slavery is immoral, women ought to have the right to vote, and doctors ought to get consent from their patient before operating.

ARISTOTLE

Far and away the most influential example of a virtue ethic is the moral theory proposed by Aristotle (384–322 B.C.). His view is so influential that most virtue ethicists see themselves as calling for a return to an Aristotelian conception of moral theory. As we shall see, this does not mean that all contemporary virtue ethicists accept all of Aristotle's moral theory.

Aristotle's Theory of Virtue

Aristotle, like contemporary virtue ethicists, thinks that moral theory ought to begin with a theory of virtue. A theory of virtue is a theory that tells us what dispositions are virtues. It answers the question "What is a good person?" or, to put the same question in another way "What sort of person should I be?"

THE FUNCTION ARGUMENT

The center of Aristotle's theory of virtue is the function argument. This argument begins with an analogy to objects. What is a good person? We begin by considering the question "What is a good X?," where X is an object. What is a good car or a good sauce pan? Aristotle thinks that a good X is an X that performs the function of an X well. A good car is a car that performs a car's function well. The function of a car is to transport people from place to place. So a good car does this well. To do this well a good car is fast, reliable, and comfortable. A car that cannot go more than twenty miles an hour is not a good car. Neither is one that breaks down frequently or is uncomfortable to sit in. By analogy, Aristotle thinks that a good person is a person who performs the function of persons well.

This obviously raises a crucial question: What is the function of people? On this point Aristotle is not as clear as one might wish, but he seems to think that the function of something is what it does better than anything else. That is why the function of a car is transporting people and not cooking food. One can cook food with a car—the engine gets hot enough—but this is not a car's function, and one can see this because it is much easier to cook with a sauce pan. The one thing a car does better than anything else is transport people. Therefore, this is its function.

Applying this test to humans, Aristotle notes that living or feeling pleasure cannot be the function of humans because nonhuman animals do these things as well as humans. Killing nonhuman animals cannot be our function because other nonhuman animals do that much better than we do. According to Aristotle, the one thing humans do better than anything else is reason. Therefore, Aristotle thinks that the function of humans is to reason. Since a good X is an X that performs the function of X well and the function of humans is to reason, a good person is a person who reasons well. A virtuous person is a person who reasons well.

HUMAN FLOURISHING

Aristotle goes on to argue that humans flourish when they reason well. He thinks that a thing flourishes when it is fulfilling its function well, and since the function of humans is to reason, humans flourish when they reason well. When a thing is performing its function well, it is, in some sense, doing what it is meant to do and will therefore flourish. Aristotle assumes that everything, objects as well as nonhuman animals and humans has a function. Things flourish when they fulfill this function. So Aristotle thinks that virtuous humans are flourishing humans. A person who is reasoning well is both virtuous and flourishing.

Aristotle goes on to point out that to reason well and so to flourish, humans require many things. At the most basic level humans cannot reason well when they do not have enough to eat or a warm place to sleep. To reason well humans need a certain amount of leisure time, education, experience, and contact with other humans. Humans reason better when their lives contain Sunday mornings in a warm bed while someone else makes breakfast, hikes in the woods, falling in love, listening to music, or things like these. So all these things are important, according to Aristotle, because they help humans reason well and so to flourish. Aristotle points out that one can reason well in many different sorts of ways. So people can flourish in many different sorts of lives. Engineers, teachers, doctors, lawyers, and auto mechanics must all reason well. So a person could flourish in any of these roles. However, according to Aristotle, it may be very hard to reason well if one's life is filled with routine, dull labor. Such a life would leave no time to reason well, and humans who live this sort of life are not flourishing.

DOCTRINE OF THE MEAN

Aristotle thinks that flourishing requires a very complex set of dispositions, of virtues. But which dispositions are virtues and which are vices? The short answer is that the dispositions that lead to reasoning well are virtues, and the dispositions that lead to reasoning poorly are vices. But Aristotle believes that he can tell us more than this. He argues that for every virtue there will be two vices—a vice of excess and a vice of lack. This is Aristotle's doctrine of the mean. Every virtue is a mean, an intermediate, between two vices. One of his examples is courage. Courageous people avoid two vices—the vice of recklessness and the vice of cowardice. Reckless people are those who overcome fear too easily. In battle, they attack even when an attack will serve no purpose. They have a vice of excess. Cowardly people do not overcome fear easily enough. They do not attack even when attacking is essential to winning the battle. They have a vice of lack. Courageous people overcome fear in the right way and at the right time. Similarly, being self-confident is the mean between the excess of arrogance and the lack of subservience. Being industrious is the mean between the excess of being a workaholic and the lack of being lazy. Aristotle emphasizes that the mean is different for different people and in different situations.

Aristotle's Theory of Right Action

Aristotle's doctrine of the mean leads to his theory of right action. Aristotle thinks that people become virtuous by acting virtuously. Being a virtuous person, according to Aristotle, is not merely a matter of doing certain things, but of having a certain mental attitude about doing them. One who advances to meet the enemy because she is more afraid of her commander than of the enemy is not courageous, even though she is doing what a courageous person does. To be courageous one must advance because one overcomes fear of the enemy at the right time. Aristotle thinks that one becomes courageous by acting as a courageous person acts. This will lead to one's having the mental attitude of a courageous person. One who repeatedly advances because she is afraid of her commander will eventually learn to overcome her fear of the enemy and so become courageous. A person who lacks the virtue of self-confidence can, according to Aristotle, gain it by acting as self-confident people do. So if we wish to be virtuous (as we should, according to Aristotle, because virtuous people are flourishing), we ought to act as virtuous people do. This is Aristotle's theory of right action.

Problems with Aristotle's Theory of Virtue

Many of the objections to Aristotle's theory of virtue focus on the function argument.

HUMANS HAVE NO FUNCTION

Many object to a basic premise of Aristotle's view—that humans have a function. They think that only objects used by intelligent beings have functions. Functions are given to objects by intelligent beings when these beings create or modify objects for their use. One of the millions of stones lying on the ground has no function. It simply has effects on other things—adds to the mass of the earth and diverts a raindrop. The stone has these effects and more, but none of them is the function or purpose of the stone. It has no purpose or function until an intelligent being, such as a human being, takes the stone and uses it for something. If a human takes the stone and uses it to secure a tent stake, then and only then does the stone have a function.

God and Function One response to the claim that objects have no function until given one by an intelligent being is to claim that there is an intelligent being that has given stones and human beings a function. God is this being. During the Middle Ages many argued that the function argument as given by Aristotle could be replaced by a theistic theory of human function. As before, we must set aside this claim because it takes us into a complex question beyond the scope of this book—whether or not God exists.

Natural Function Another response to this objection to Aristotle's view is to claim that there are natural functions. People who make this argument point to complex interactions within the natural world. Sparrows control insect populations and distribute seeds. Seeds create new plants that nourish insect populations, hide and feed birds, and produce coal. An hour watching a nature program on TV will show many more of these interactions. It seems that nature is a large, complex entity and that each part of nature—bird, insect, plant—has a function in the ecosystem. Perhaps we should look for a human function by looking for our place in the earth's ecosystem.

Two objections have been made to this natural-function argument. First, some claim that the interrelations in nature are merely interrelations, not functions. Sparrows have not been given the function of controlling insect populations. They have simply evolved so that they have this effect. Some claim that it is no more a sparrow's function to control insect populations than it is a stone's function to divert a raindrop. These are merely effects that sparrows and stones have—not their functions. The second apparent problem with the natural-function argument is that it is not clear what the natural function of humans is. Is it to control the population of some animals? Which animals? What else could it be? Some think that Aristotle has not demonstrated that reasoning is the natural function of humans.

REASON IS NOT THE ONLY THING THAT HUMANS DO BETTER THAN ANYTHING ELSE

A final objection to Aristotle's function argument is the claim that reasoning is not the only thing that humans do better than anything else. It seems that humans drive cars, laugh, talk, make tools, and destroy ecosystems better than anything else. But surely these are not the function of humans. Most people who make this argument use it to reenforce the claim that humans have no function. That is why, they claim, the search for a human function leads to such odd answers.

CONTEMPORARY VIRTUE ETHICS

Many contemporary virtue ethicists think that Aristotle's theory of virtue, with its reliance on the function argument, must be modified. Some have argued that Aristotle's concept of human flourishing can be detached from his function argument and developed into a theory of virtue. This theory begins with the claim that a good person is not, as Aristotle thought, a person who is performing the function of a person well. Instead, a good person is a person who has the dispositions that lead to human flourishing. Clearly the next step in this sort of theory of virtue is answering the following question "What is human flourishing?"

We have already considered this question in this book. The question "What is human flourishing?" is simply an Aristotelian way of asking

"What is the good life?" This is the topic of chapter 2. There we considered several theories of the good life or human flourishing. We considered the views that a human flourishes when she acts selfishly, develops herself, or satisfies her wants. We will not review these possibilities here. But we will consider briefly some other theories of human flourishing, of the good life, that have been suggested by the virtue ethicists.

FLOURISHING AS REASONING WELL

As we saw above, Aristotle thought that humans flourish when they reason well. One might claim that while humans have no function, they flourish when they reason well. When Aristotle claims that a person who lives a life filled with dull, mindless labor is not flourishing, this seems to be plausible. One crucial ingredient of human flourishing does seem to be reasoning well. But many claim that it is not plausible to assert that reasoning well is all there is to human flourishing. There seem to be crucial parts of human flourishing that have nothing to do with reasoning well. Restful Sunday mornings may well be a component of human flourishing because they lead to better reasoning. But many argue that these things are also valuable on their own—not merely as a means to improve one's reasoning ability. Some argue that restful Sunday mornings are not part of human flourishing because they help us reason well. They are part of human flourishing independent of their effect on our ability to reason.

FLOURISHING AS A UNIFIED SELF

Some have suggested that humans flourish when they are developing and expressing a unified self. This view suffers from the problem that it is not very clear what a unified self is. But we can give examples of someone with a unified self and someone with a nonunified self. If someone is constantly and genuinely torn between doing very different things—say, going to Australia to live in the outback and going to medical school—then her self is not unified. One who is constantly tempted to harm others and yet knows that this is wrong and does not want to do it also has a nonunified self. Having a self that is torn in this way can be profoundly disturbing and genuinely ruin a life. Someone who has always wanted to become a social worker and have a family might well have a unified self. These two desires are compatible and might be the central elements that shape one's life. So one would avoid the torn feeling that a person who wanted to live in the outback and go to medical school might feel.

Even if we assume that the notion of a unified self can be spelled out with sufficient precision, this view still seems to face a serious problem. That one's self is unified is no guarantee that it will be unified around a moral life plan. One might want to kill people and torture cats. One could have a self unified around these two compatible desires just as one could have a self unified around the desires to be a social worker and have a family. But many claim that a person whose life is organized around killing people and torturing cats is not flourishing.

FLOURISHING AS THE SEARCH FOR HUMAN FLOURISHING

Some have suggested that a human is flourishing when she is involved in trying to figure out what human flourishing is. A human is flourishing when she spends her life trying different things in an attempt to discover what human flourishing is. This view seems to face the problem of the satisfied person. Some people, although perhaps not very many, find something that they consider very satisfying and have no desire to try anything else. Suppose that the person who wanted to be a social worker and have a family realized these goals and found that his life was profoundly satisfying. He has no desire to try anything else. It seems that he might be flourishing despite the fact that he is not trying to figure out what human flourishing is.

Some people look at all these accounts of human flourishing and claim that they are all flawed because they assume that there is only one sort of human flourishing. They claim that human flourishing is as different as humans are. This seems to be a serious problem for virtue ethicists. Recall the virtue ethic strategy. A theory of virtue is offered, and then right acts are defined as those acts a virtuous person would do. If virtue is defined as a disposition that leads to human flourishing, and if human flourishing is as different as humans are, then the virtues will be different for different people. And this will mean that different acts will be right for different people. Suppose that killing others is central to Patricia's flourishing. In that case, killing others might not be wrong for her.

MORAL RULES

There is nothing in the definition of a virtue ethic that prevents a virtue ethicist from providing a detailed set of rules that describes the actions done by a virtuous person. A virtue ethicist might begin with the rule "Act like a virtuous person," and then offer a very precise description of how a virtuous person acts. This would tell us what right action is and allow nonvirtuous people to do the right acts. However, most virtue ethicists have claimed that there are no moral rules or that moral rules are not very important. While denying the need or importance of moral rules is not required by a virtue ethic, it is clear that there is an understandable tendency to do this. If one is a virtue ethicist, one thinks that what is important in moral theory is the evaluation of persons, not the evaluation of actions. Since the evaluation of acts is less important than the evaluation of persons, there is less of a need to come up with rules for evaluating acts.

Virtue ethicists often cite three problems with moral rules. First, most virtue ethicists argue that we do not become virtuous people by following rules. Rather, they claim that we become virtuous by imitating virtuous people. They claim that most of moral education occurs when one is small. At this stage, children are too young to learn complex moral rules. But they naturally imitate their parents and others around them. This, say virtue ethicists, is how people become moral. Even later in life people do not learn moral rules and then put them into practice. Rather, they imitate moral exemplars—for example, real and fictional heroes. Action-based ethicists respond that children learn simple moral rules from their parents and people continue to learn more complex moral rules later in life.

Second, virtue ethicists often hold that rule-following is not really being virtuous. They claim that someone who is merely following a set of rules is acting like a virtuous person but is not really a virtuous person. They are just going through the motions. Following Aristotle, they claim that being a virtuous person is not only a matter of doing certain things, but of having a certain mental attitude about doing them. Recall that one who advances to meet the enemy because she is more afraid of her commander than of the enemy is not courageous. Virtue ethicists think that each virtue is a disposition to do certain actions because one has or does not have certain desires or emotions. A courageous person overcomes fear. A compassionate person cares about others. In response, action-based ethicists claim that their theories are perfectly compatible with the claim that being virtuous requires not only doing certain actions, but having or not having certain desires. Action-based ethics are merely ethics that begin with a theory of right action and then define a virtuous person as one disposed to do the right actions. But being disposed to do the right action might very well involve having or not having certain desires or emotions.

Third, most virtue ethicists claim that no rule can be complete enough to tell us what to do in every situation. They think that the situations people face are so different—different people, different cultures, different friendships, different promises, and so forth—that no rule can possibly cover them all. One set of rules could not possibly cover the actions of college students in the United States and the actions of village elders in Thailand. Action-based ethicists simply deny this claim. For example, utilitarians think that there is ultimately one, relatively simple rule that shows what one should do in any situation. Other action-based ethicists acknowledge that the moral rules are complex and that we do not know them all. But they assert that we know some of them, for example, "Do not keep slaves" and that we can discover others.

MORAL RELATIVISM

Virtue ethicists are, like action-based ethicists, divided over the issue of moral relativism. Recall from chapter 3 that moral relativism is the view that different moral standards exist for different people, different societies, or different historical periods. Some virtue ethicists, Aristotle, for example, think that the basic virtues will be the same everywhere. Aristotle thought that the function of all humans is to reason, and so a good person in every culture and every time period is a person who reasons well. But other virtue ethicists are relativists. For example, a virtue ethicist might adopt the human-flourishing approach discussed above and then claim that human flourishing is different for people in different cultures. Therefore, on this view, the virtues will be different in different cultures. The arguments for and against moral relativism in virtue ethics are parallel to the arguments for and against action-based moral relativism discussed in chapter 3.

OBJECTIONS TO VIRTUE ETHICS

Action-based ethicists have raised several objections to virtue ethics.

Trivializes Immoral Acts

Some object to virtue ethics on the grounds that they seem to trivialize immoral acts. According to virtue ethics, evaluating persons is more important than evaluating acts. So, some argue, a virtue ethic implies that an immoral act committed by a good person is not a serious problem. Suppose that an otherwise extremely virtuous person simply cannot stand her husband—who really is a very unpleasant person. She is forced to live with him day after day. One day she cracks and kills him. Suppose that a vicious person enjoys tripping people. He trips people on a regular basis. This never causes anything more than scrapes and bruises. Virtue ethics seem to imply that the killing is not as serious as the tripping. What really counts is the evaluation of persons, and the killing was an aberrant act by an otherwise virtuous person, while the tripping is the sign of a vicious person. This strikes many as very implausible. Some action-based ethicists, especially those who find utilitarianism plausible, point out that it is actions that hurt others. They argue that while actions are of course done by people, it is only when people *act* (or fail to act) that harm can be caused. These action-based theorists claim that a person who was vicious but so stupid or clumsy that she never succeeded in hurting anyone would not be very morally important. But if this person could carry out the acts she wants to do, then this would be morally important.

No Guidance

One of the most common objections to virtue ethics is the claim that it cannot provide guidance in concrete moral dilemmas. Suppose that you are a doctor with an elderly, terminally ill patient who is no longer mentally capable of making decisions for himself. You must decide whether to continue very expensive treatments that cannot save, but may slightly lengthen, his life. According to action-based ethicists, virtue ethics tell you nothing more helpful than "Act as a virtuous person would." This clearly is not very helpful. The virtuous person is one who has certain dispositions. Recall that something is disposed to do such-and-such when it *usually* does such-and-such in certain circumstances. Suppose you know that a virtuous person would usually end treatment in these circumstances. You still need to know if this case is a usual case. It might be one of the unusual cases in which a virtuous person would continue treatment. Virtue ethicists respond to this problem by claiming that they do not merely tell people "Act as a virtuous person would." They tell people to do that and then provide a theory of virtue. We considered some of these theories above. According to the virtue ethicists, it is the theory of virtue that will help people guide their actions. This brings us to another common objection to virtue ethics.

No Good Theory of Virtue

A basic objection to virtue ethics is the claim that virtue ethicists have offered no plausible theory of virtue. Action-based ethicists look at Aristotle's theory of virtue and the other theories considered above and claim that all are extremely vague and subject to serious objections. It seems fair to say that virtue ethicists have yet to offer a theory of virtue that is as powerful, plausible, and precise as the theories of right action proposed by action-based ethicists such as utilitarians and Kantians. The best response to this objection would be for a virtue ethicist to propose a powerful, plausible, and precise theory of virtue. Virtue ethics are, philosophically speaking, a very new line of thought. While Aristotle is a virtue theorist, the recent revival of virtue ethics occurred only in the mid-1970s. This is a philosophical yesterday. Virtue ethicists think that with time and further study they will be able to propose moral theories more powerful than utilitarianism and Kantianism.

The terms that we use to evaluate persons are called virtues and vices. A virtue is a desirable disposition, and a vice is an undesirable disposition. Virtue ethics are defined in contrast to action-based ethics—ethics that are concerned primarily with the moral evaluation of acts. Kantianism and utilitarianism, the two moral theories that have dominated modern philosophical discourse, are action-based ethics. Virtue ethics are primarily concerned with the evaluation of persons. There are two different sorts of virtue ethics:

weak virtue ethics, and strong virtue ethics. Weak virtue ethics hold that action-based approaches are incomplete because they fail to give the virtues the analysis they deserve. Strong virtue ethics hold that action-based ethics are not only incomplete but seriously flawed because they have ignored the virtues. A strong virtue ethic begins with a theory of what it is to be a virtuous person. Then it defines right actions as the actions that are done by a virtuous person. The defender of strong virtue ethics claims that action-based ethics have considered the parts of morality in the wrong order. Action-based ethics begin with a theory of right action and then define the virtues as the dispositions that lead people to do right acts.

Virtue ethicists make three objections against action-based ethics. The first concerns personal relationships. The example of friendship seems to show that the morality of actions turns not only on what is done, but also on the character, the virtues, of the person who does the act. The second objection is the claim that the concepts of action evaluation make no sense without an authority. The third objection is the claim that action-based ethics have produced nothing but long quarrels with no results.

The most influential example of virtue ethics is Aristotle's moral theory. The center of Aristotle's theory is the function argument. He thinks that a good X is an X that performs the function of an X well, and the function of something is what it does better than anything else. Aristotle thinks that the thing humans do better than anything else is reason. Therefore, Aristotle thinks that a good person is a person who reasons well. He also thinks that good people will flourish. According to Aristotle's doctrine of the mean, for every virtue there will be two vices—a vice of excess, and a vice of lack. Many think that the function argument is flawed because humans have no function, because a thing's function is not what it does better than anything else or because reasoning is not the only thing that humans do better than anything else.

Contemporary virtue ethics, abandoning Aristotle's function argument, often hold that a good person is a person who has the dispositions that lead to human flourishing. They then offer an account of human flourishing. Some propose that humans flourish when they reason well. Others propose that humans flourish when they are developing and expressing a unified self. This view suffers from the problems that it is not very clear and that even if one's self is unified this is no guarantee that it will be unified around a moral life plan. Still others have suggested that a human is flourishing when she is involved in trying to figure out what human flourishing is. This view seems to face the problem of the satisfied person. Some people look at all these accounts of human flourishing and claim that they are all flawed because they assume that there is one sort of human flourishing. Whatever their theory of virtue, most virtue ethicists think that action-based ethics have exaggerated the importance of moral rules.

There are three common objections to virtue ethics. Some object to virtue ethics on the grounds that they seem to trivialize immoral acts. According to virtue ethics, evaluating persons is more important than evaluating acts. So, some argue, a virtue ethic implies that an immoral act committed by a good person is not a serious problem. Others claim that virtue ethics cannot provide guidance in concrete moral dilemmas. According to action-based ethicists, virtue ethics tell you nothing more helpful than "Act as a virtuous person would." Virtue ethicists respond to this problem by claiming that they do not merely tell people to "Act as a virtuous person would." They tell people to do that and then provide a theory of virtue. But the third objection to virtue ethics is the claim that virtue ethicists have offered no plausible theory of virtue. Virtue ethicists think that with time and further study they will be able to offer such a theory.

Selected Readings

Aristotle. *The Nicomachean Ethics* (several good translations).

Foot, Phillippa. *Virtues and Vices*. Berkeley, CA: University of California Press, 1978.

French, Peter, et al. Midwest *Studies in Philosophy, Vol 13: Ethical Theory, Character, and Virtue*. Notre Dame, IN: University of Notre Dame Press, 1988.

Kruschwitz, Robert, and Robert Roberts. *The Virtues*. Belmont, CA: Wadsworth Publishing Company, 1987.

MacIntrye, Alasdair. *After Virtue*. Notre Dame, IN: University of Notre Dame Press, 1984.

Rorty, Amelie. *Essays on Aristotle's Ethics*. Berkeley, CA: University of California Press, 1980.

Stocker, Michael. "The Schizophrenia of Modern Ethical Theories," *The Journal of Philosophy*, vol. LXIII, no. 4 (August 12, 1976), pp. 453–66.

7

Existentialism

Many people worry about existential issues without knowing anything about the philosophy of existentialism. People worry about the meaning of life, about whether they are free to do anything or destined to continue as they have been, and about how to relate to other people, particularly in close personal relationships. Existentialism is a philosophy that emphasizes issues that make a major difference in everyday life, rather than more technical philosophical and moral issues. Existentialism emphasizes personal decisions about how to live. Many existential authors disagree with one another about the best responses to these issues, so there is not one specific set of existentialist doctrines.

THE MEANING OF LIFE

Everyone at some point asks herself what the point is of living as she does. Why should you put up with all of the difficulties and frustrations of your current life? Why bother to struggle against the obstacles that get in the way of accomplishing your goals? What do your efforts, achievements, and failures amount to in the big picture? What will living the good life get you in the end? Does anything ultimately make any difference?

Confronting the Questions

One response to the raising of such uncomfortable questions is to try to avoid the issues. A person may try not to think about the meaning of life because such thinking is too disturbing. He may want to immerse himself in everyday activities and return to living in the customary ways in which he has been living. Existentialism emphasizes the importance of raising and hinking through such questions about the meaning of life. Existentialism aims that once a person has experienced such questions, he has to think licitly about them.

Existential philosophers have given both negative arguments against to avoid these questions, and positive arguments for the benefits of inking about them. The negative arguments claim that trying to ignore or avoid such questions is a type of cowardice and self-deception. A person is running away from issues that she needs to confront, and she is deceiving herself in thinking that the issues can be successfully avoided. Issues about the meaning of life will continue to arise until a person takes a definite position on them. The positive arguments claim that a person becomes a distinct individual only when she confronts questions about the meaning of life, about how to think and act, and about how to treat other people. It is by taking a stand on these issues that a person defines herself as an individual who is distinct from the crowd. It is by thinking about these issues and deciding on her own positions that a person becomes something more than a set of socially defined roles. A person becomes fully free and authentic.

Different Existential Questions

Worrying about the meaning of life usually includes several concerns that can be distinguished from one another. Some types of concern focus more on the universe, and other types focus more on oneself.

ULTIMATE PURPOSE

Concerning the universe, one question that is usually contained in wondering about the meaning of life is whether there is a divine plan or rational world order that governs everything that happens. People wonder whether everything in the universe has an ultimate purpose and what that purpose might be. Does everything that happens fit into some large-scale, prearranged, and basically good order, or is it just a matter of fact? Does history show the influence of a divine plan or rational guiding principle? Do human and natural events show progress, or do they just happen without being directed toward a goal? Western religions have traditionally taught that God created the universe and watches over it. God ensures that things will not ultimately go badly. The religious belief in God's benevolent control over everything is one possible answer to the question about ultimate purpose. Doubts about God's benevolent control are a frequent source of worries about the meaning of life.

There are both religious existentialists, such as Sören Kierkegaard (1813–55), Martin Buber (1878–1965), and Gabriel Marcel (1889–1973); and atheistic existentialists, such as Friedrich Nietzsche (1844–1900), Albert Camus (1913–60) and Jean-Paul Sartre (1905–80). Religious existentialists believe in God, but they usually think that God's ways are not knowable by humans. God's nature and purposes cannot be understood by reasoned investigation. Hence, even religious existentialists deny that people can find a divine plan or guided progress in the workings of the universe and human history. Atheistic existentialists directly deny that there is a God or any superhuman force that guides the happenings of natural and human history. They consider the universe not to have any direction or purpose and to be unconcerned about human welfare. Humans find themselves thrown into this unfeeling and uncaring environment and have to create their own purposes.

OBJECTIVE GOODNESS

Another question that is frequently contained in wondering about the meaning of life is whether objective goodness and value exist. Does any thing or state of the world have intrinsic value, or is all value projected on to things by valuers? Do any standards of goodness exist independently of people, or is goodness dependent upon people's desires, emotions, and thoughts? In chapter 3 we considered similar issues about the objectivity or subjectivity of moral standards. In wondering about the meaning of life, the subjective-objective question is extended to all standards for living. Is there some objectively good or right way to live, or is it all a matter of social conventions and individual preferences?

All existentialists claim that some ways of living are better than others. They are not complete nihilists because they all believe that some values have a type of objectivity. No existentialist thinks that any action or any life-style is just as good as any other. Existentialists share some very general values, such as the value of individual freedom and responsibility for yourself (see "Freedom and Authenticity," page 98). However, they also disagree with one another about many, more specific values and about the metaphysical status of values.

THE GOOD LIFE FOR YOU

Worrying about the meaning of life usually includes a concern for the meaning of your own individual life. Applying the question of ultimate purpose to yourself, you wonder whether there is some larger reason why things happen in your life as they do. Are you supposed to play some role in a larger plan? Within your life itself, is there some intrinsic purpose that you should fulfill? Applying the question of objective value to yourself, you wonder whether there are things that you should and should not do. Are there intrinsically good goals that you are ignoring? Are you unknowingly following bad, evil, or self-destructive courses of action? Are you too dedicated to some goals or not dedicated enough to any? People sometimes wonder why they should care about anything. Particularly when you are feeling tired, bored, or lacking in energy, you may ask yourself why you should make the effort to try to accomplish some goal. Why bother?

As noted above, existentialists deny that humans can find any ultimate purpose. Hence, existentialists think that individuals should not try to fit their goals into some larger external order. Many existentialists also think that there is no detailed intrinsic purpose for individual lives, although religious existentialists consider relating to God to be a goal built in to human existence. All existentialists think that some values have a type of objectivity, but these values are very general ones that do not provide specific goals. Individual freedom and the energetic carrying-out of freely chosen goals are two values that all existentialists accept. However, many existentialists reject the idea that individuals are subject to objective and universal moral requirements. They think that moral requirements would interfere with individual freedom.

IMPACT ON THE UNIVERSE

Thinking about the meaning of life frequently includes wondering whether you or anyone else will have any noticeable effect on the universe. People frequently remark that even great kings and conquerors of the past are now dead and largely forgotten. A million years from now no one will know anything about you, your struggles, your accomplishments, and your failures. In terms of the incredibly large expanse of the universe, all events on earth seem insignificant. The significance of all your actions seems to disappear when you realize that they will have no impact on the universe at large.

Different existentialists respond differently to the fact that a person's actions will have no causal affect on the universe at large. Some religious existentialists claim that God cares about everyone, so that your actions do have a type of transcendent importance. They are important to God. Some atheistic existentialists think that people just have to bear up under the load of not having any ultimate importance. People have to learn to live with this absurdity. Others claim that people should emphasize the significance their lives have for themselves. Your thoughts and actions have a tremendous impact on your later self. You should focus on their importance for you, rather than consider them from the perspective of the universe at large. Your perspective should count more than this external perspective.

DEATH

All normal people know that every person will eventually die. However, people frequently do not include the ever-present possibility of their own death in their everyday planning. The explicit realization that you will die sometime and that you might die suddenly at any time strikes people very hard. Like the idea that your actions will have no impact on the universe at large, the realization that you will eventually die seems sometimes to drain everything of importance. What does anything matter since you are going to die anyhow? Whether you accomplish great things or are a total failure seems not to make any difference, since you will be gone anyhow. There will shortly come a time when you will no longer be here to enjoy or suffer the consequences of your former actions.

All existentialists reject the idea that the inevitability of death makes a current life meaningless. The fact that you are going to die sometime does not mean that your life is insignificant for you now. You should not let your inevitable death destroy your commitment to projects. However, existentialists differ on the meaning of death. Some religious existentialists hope for an afterlife. For them, death is not the total end, but a point of transition. Other existentialists think that death is basically absurd and just intrudes on life. Others, such as Martin Heidegger (1889–1976), claim that people should include the ever-present possibility of death in the choosing of their projects. You should consider the possibility that you might die at any time in deciding what life-style and long-term courses of action to pursue.

Heidegger thinks that death is the end of human existence, but he claims that human mortality is, in an important way, a good thing. Human mortality is necessary for valuing current activities. It is only by understanding that your life is limited that you can commit yourself to choices, projects, and values. If you thought that your time was unlimited, no decision would be of any importance to you, because you could always change your mind later without losing anything. Nothing would be risked by choosing one alternative over another. For example, if you were dissatified with your choice of a college, you could start over again at some other school. No action would be of any importance to you, because you could always go back and do things over again. If you thought that you were immortal, you would think that you had an infinite amount of time to do things, and this would lead to not valuing any particular moment of time. Since valuing choices and actions is essential for human existence, and mortality is necessary for valuing, mortality makes a positive contribution to human life. Sartre criticized Heidegger's argument by claiming that passing through time, not mortality, is all that is necessary for valuing current activities. Sartre claimed that the passing of time makes previously rejected choices unavailable to you, so that even an immortal person could not completely do things over again. For example, you could start over again at a new college, but at your second school you could not have your first college course.

Absurdity

Albert Camus expressed many of these concerns about the meaning of life in his famous work *The Myth of Sisyphus*. Camus started his inquiry from the experience of absurdity. The type of absurdity that Camus described was not lighthearted or humorous, but rather a frightening sense that things are not the way that humans need them to be. This feeling of absurdity arises from the confrontation of what people want and expect to find in the universe with what they actually find. According to Camus, people want and expect to find several things. They want and expect the world to be familiar and easy to understand, rather than strange and incomprehensible. They want and expect the world to show an underlying unity, so that everything fits together into a rational whole. They want and expect to find that human actions are obviously important and that objective standards of goodness exist that tell them what to do. The feeling of absurdity arises when you begin to realize that these things are missing. You do not find in the universe what you assumed was there. This is very disturbing and threatens your whole world view and accepted values. The experience of absurdity is the starting point for existential decision. According to Camus, you can either face absurdity and live with a constant recognition of it, or try to deny that the universe is lacking the meaning and value that you want and expect it to have.

Critics of Camus's notion of absurdity claim that he is mistaken either about the expectations that people have for the universe or about what they actually find. Some critics claim that it is not necessary for people to want and expect to find that the universe is easy to understand, has a simple rational order, and has objective standards of goodness. Other critics claim that such things can be found, so the experience of absurdity can be avoided or overcome.

FREEDOM AND AUTHENTICITY

Individual freedom is the basic concern of existentialism. The type of freedom with which existentialists are concerned is the freedom to choose your own values and way of life. Responsibility for yourself is included in this type of freedom. A person is responsible for her values, way of living, and world view to the degree that she has freely decided on them for herself. It is fair for other people to hold you responsible for your values, way of living, and world view, because you have chosen them freely and they make up your basic self. It is fair for other people to hold you responsible for your actions because they are expressions of your self.

Freedom from Convention

As we noted in chapter 1, people first learn how they are supposed to live and what they are supposed to do from their family and society. Their natural inclinations are shaped, modified, suppressed, and redirected according to the customs and morals of the society. The type of individual freedom that existentialism emphasizes is the power to determine your goals, standards, and values for yourself. An existentially free person does not unthinkingly accept goals, standards, and values from his upbringing and society. An existentially free person has somehow to choose to have the goals, standards, and values that he has. Hence, the exercise of existential freedom requires that you not be causally determined to follow natural inclinations, societal customs and standards, or some combination of these. You must be able to detach yourself to some extent from these factors in order to be able to decide for yourself what goals, standards, and values to have. Although they may differ about the exact nature of free will, all existentialists share the view that people are not forced or causally determined to continue to have the same goals, standards, and values.

Using Your Freedom

Existentialists think that not only do people have the power to choose goals, standards, and values for themselves, but also that people should use this power fully. The full development and use of your freedom are basic values for existentialists. They think that people should recognize their fundamental freedom and make full use of it. Most existentialists think that all people are intrinsically required to exercise their freedom at all times. The value of freedom is built in to human existence, so that the exercise of freedom in everything that you do is an intrinsic good. Humans have to use and develop their freedom in order to fulfill their natures, and this using of freedom should be involved in all acting, thinking, and deciding. However, some existentialists think that people are not always required to be free, but rather that they are only required to deal honestly with questions about the meaning of life when these are raised. If the questions are never raised or are raised only sometimes, a person does not have any duty or requirement to worry about them continuously, or continuously to question what she already values.

Existentialists claim that people always have freedom as a power, and many think that people are always exercising this power. A person's continuous use of his existential freedom to choose his goals, standards, and values would mean that he would always be at least partly in flux. He would always be in the process of defining himself, and the process would never be complete while he was alive. Existentialists disagree about whether a person is always defining everything about himself, or rather defining some features of himself from the standpoint of other features that are currently unquestioned. Do you have to redefine yourself completely at every moment? Should you be always deciding about all your goals, standards, and values, or should you be always deciding about some goals, standards, and values while keeping many others constant? The second position allows people to have a continuing but changeable character. A person would not be totally in flux, because he would have a continuing character based on earlier choices. Choices about your goals, standards, and values would produce a continuing self. This self would then decide about some other goals, standards, and values, but not about all the features that make up a self. Any goal, standard, or value could be considered at any time, but you would not consider all of them at the same time.

Choosing Values

All existentialists claim that a person's choice of goals, standards, and values is to some degree unjustified. You have to commit yourself to goals, standards, and values without having sufficient reasons that fully justify the specific things that you choose. If there were sufficient reasons that directed you definitely to specific goals, standards, and values, there would not be any choice to make. You could just figure out from the evidence exactly what projects you should have. There would be one right answer and many wrong answers to the question of what you should value. Existentialists claim that there is always a "leap" involved in choosing goals, standards, and values, because there is always a gap between them and the reasons for them. You have to commit yourself to things that are of vital importance to you without having a guarantee that you are choosing the best ones.

Existentialists disagree about two main features of the process of choosing goals, standards, and values. One feature is whether there are fixed options from which a person must choose her own position. Must a person choose between being good or evil, selfish or moral, for God or against God? Are there several main types of goals, standards, and values so that a person is forced to choose only between these types, or can a person creatively blend types and perhaps create some new types? Nietzsche and Sartre emphasized the individual creation of individually tailored values. They opposed the idea of fixed options. On the other hand, Kierkegaard claimed that there were basically three types of values and life styles. An aesthetic life is devoted to pleasure, being interested in things, and avoiding pain and boredom. An ethical life is devoted to living according to universal moral principles that are particularized in a community. A religious life is devoted to establishing and maintaining a relationship with God. Kierkegaard claimed that choices of values and life styles have to make one of these ways of life dominant over the others. One type of concern has to have priority over other types whenever there is a conflict. For example, if God commanded Abraham to sacrifice his son, and morality forbade human sacrifice, a religious Abraham would follow God's command, but an ethical Abraham would refuse.

The second feature about which existentialists disagree is the degree and type of influence that antecedent factors have on the free choice of goals, standards, and values. All existentialists agree that antecedent factors do not completely determine your choice and that choices are always partly unjustified by antecedently known reasons. However, some existentialists, such as Sartre, think that antecedent factors have little or no influence on your choice and that there cannot be any antecedent reasons for choosing one project rather than another. Sartre claims that the choice of a fundamental project creates reasons for actions, but that there can be no antecedent reasons for choosing a specific fundamental project. Other existentialists, such as Nietzsche, think that biological drives and social pressures strongly influence individuals' choices and that there are good reasons for individual people to choose certain sorts of goals, standards, and values, rather than other sorts. Certain types of values are well suited to the instincts, desires, abilities, and environment of particular people, while other types of values are not.

Anxiety

Existential freedom is difficult. It is not just a freedom from restrictions. It is a freedom that forces people to make decisions that define their lives, but without having fully sufficient reasons. Existential freedom includes a feeling of anxiety. Existentialists claim that anxiety is a mood of life uncertainty that necessarily accompanies existential freedom. They think that this mood of anxiety (or anguish or dread) is part of existential freedom because the person involved is staking his life on his choices without any guarantee that these are the right choices. A person is anxious because he must commit himself to goals, standards, and values that define him and motivate his behavior without having adequate guidance. In anxiety the person is aware of various possibilities for himself. There are alternative ways in which his life could go on. He does not know which are the best choices, but he has to choose and live out the consequences.

Many existentialists think that the experience of anxiety shows that people are free. It is very hard to make sense of free will from a detached, external perspective, but we each consider ourselves to be free in all our practical activities. Like Kant, existentialists claim that from your internal perspective of involvement and action in the world, your freedom makes good sense. The experience of anxiety reveals your freedom because it is your ability to choose various possibilities that produces anxiety. If you were causally determined to do everything, there would be no reason for anxiety.

Authenticity

Authenticity is being your own person or being responsible for what you are. You are authentic by considering the grounds for your world view and values and committing yourself to some position. You might wonder how it is possible not to be your own person. Existentialists claim that you are not your own person when you do not and have not exercised existential freedom. A person who allows herself to be defined completely by other people, societal customs, and biological givens is not her own, because she has not actively defined herself. Not being your own, inauthenticity, is tempting because of the anxiety that accompanies existential freedom. It is easier and more comfortable to live and think as everyone else does without having to face the anxiety-producing questions about what conceptions, goals, standards, and values to have. It is even easier to deceive yourself into thinking that you have no choice in the matter. You may deceive yourself into thinking that you are causally determined to do things or that you have an unchangeable character that inevitably directs you. These seem to excuse you from responsibility. It is not your fault because you have no control over these things. Sartre and Simone de Beauvoir (1908–86) call this "bad faith." Bad faith is self-deception that is designed to avoid freedom and responsibility for yourself.

RELATIONS WITH OTHER PEOPLE

Existentialists claim that relations with other people are always complicated because people are intrinsically free. Existential freedom is very individualistic. An individual person has to detach himself from automatically following the customs and morals of his society. He cannot unthinkingly interact with people in the standard ways. Social roles and customs ordinarily make people's interactions with one another go smoothly because each person has assigned parts to play. You treat other people in stereotyped ways, and they treat you similarly. An existentially free person can choose to adopt conventional roles, concepts, and values, but he can also choose to adopt different ways of thinking and acting.

Psychologists and sociologists study how people are defined by one another. A person's ideas, values, and ways of thinking are first shaped by her upbringing and continue to be affected by the people with whom she interacts and by the general culture and societal institutions. Existentialists view these influences from the individualistic standpoint of existential freedom. They claim that conflicts always occur between a person's definition of herself and other people's definitions of her. In using your existential freedom, you may try to define yourself, but other people always form conceptions of what you are and how you should behave. Other people's expectations and requirements for you affect you, and so there is a conflict between your control of yourself and these other influences on you.

Different existentialists have different theories of how individual freedom interacts with the social dimension of humans. They make different recommendations for the best ways to relate to other people. The most influential views are those of Sartre, Heidegger, and Buber.

SARTRE

Sartre claims that a person is directly aware of other people by experiencing himself as an object defined by other people. In experiencing yourself as something definite that other people judge and act upon, you are directly aware of other people's judgments. These judgments influence what you are, and so come into conflict with your existential freedom. Sartre claims that all people have a fundamental project to be totally in control of what they are. The unavoidable conflict between individual freedom and being defined by other people makes all personal relationships unsatisfying. In the words of one of Sartre's literary characters, "Hell is other people."

Sartre analyzed different ways of relating to other people in terms of his subject-object account of consciousness of others. In all interactions with others, a person is either a subject who defines, evaluates, and acts on other people as objects; or an object that is defined, evaluated, and acted upon by other people. Sartre claimed that the objective of many close, interpersonal relations, such as love and sexual interaction, was to capture the other person's consciousness. Through capturing the other person's subjectivity, you hope either to get him to define you as you want to be defined, or to prevent him from defining you in some negative way. Interpersonal relations are combative, because each person wants to capture the other person's ability to define him. Sartre hoped to be able to find some way out of the negative cycle of interpersonal relations. He hoped that if everyone focused on freedom, interpersonal relations could be more satisfactory, but he never managed to work out this proposal in detail.

HEIDEGGER

Heidegger claimed that people are always largely defined by the historical culture in which they exist. Becoming authentic is a matter of exploring the grounds for the world view and values that you have absorbed from your culture and committing yourself to carrying forward your heritage in some specific way. Interactions with other people take place largely through the cultural conceptions and roles that people share. Heidegger does not oppose these culturally defined interactions, but he thinks that an authentic person must be open to changes in them. While shared standards and roles are necessary for understanding and working with one another, an authentic person must adapt them to her specific projects and sometimes transform them. An authentic person does not do things unthinkingly just because everyone else acts that way, but rather seeks out the reasons for doing things and may contribute new reasons. Heidegger also suggests that authentic relations with other people encourage them to be authentic, too.

BUBER

Buber claimed that there are two main ways of regarding and treating other people. You may consider and interact with them as something defined and limited within the spatial, temporal, causal world. This is an I-It relationship. You relate to an It through concepts that define what people are like. You are treating others as Its whenever you try to discover into what prearranged categories they fit. You are also treating others as Its whenever you use them to accomplish your purposes or assume that you know their objectives. There is nothing wrong with I-It relations. Like Heidegger, Buber thinks that it is necessary that we interact with one another in an I-It way most of the time. However, a person loses something if she relates to others only in this way.

The second way of relating with others is an I-Thou relation. Buber describes this in somewhat mystical terms. The Thou is not defined or limited within a spatial, temporal, causal world. You relate to a Thou with your whole being. The relationship is reciprocal and occurs for its own sake. An I-Thou relation is not a matter of using someone for your purposes or of helping him accomplish what you take to be his purposes. Buber thinks of the I-Thou as a relating in which you are not limited by preconceived ideas, but rather encounter the other person directly as he is. I-Thou relations cannot endure permanently, but they keep your concepts of others open, flexible, and spiritual.

EXISTENTIALISM AND MORALITY

Existentialism is an ethic. It is concerned with the best way to live. As we considered in chapter 2, some philosophers have claimed that the best way to live is not always to treat others morally. Many existentialists share the view that our society's morality is not the best set of values for individuals. Most existentialists think that existential freedom is more important than Judeo-Christian morality. They think that individuals should not accept these moral standards unthinkingly. It is better to embrace your existential freedom and perhaps choose to treat other people immorally than to follow moral standards automatically. Since they consider existential freedom to be the ultimate value, they consider it to be better for people to risk being immoral in order to develop their freedom fully. Some existentialists, such as Kierkegaard and de Beauvoir, also think that embracing existential freedom will eventually lead you toward treating other people morally.

Most existentialists do not accept the idea that individuals are subject to objective moral requirements. They deny that there can be any moral standards that have the authority to dictate how you should live. You are free to accept, reject, ignore, or modify any supposed moral duty. Existentialists do not deny all objective values. They think that existential freedom is a value that is dictated by human existence. However, most think that there are not many other specific values that are built in to human existence. Most think that you cannot derive the necessity of being moral from the necessity of being free. Most oppose Kant's position on moral requirements. Kant argued that the value of rationality is dictated by human existence, and that being rational requires that you be moral (see chapter 5). Most existentialists deny that being free requires that you be moral. However, some existentialists, such as de Beauvoir, accept a basically Kantian position.

Nietzsche's Attack

Nietzsche is the most influential and violent critic of Judeo-Christian morality. He rejected both the otherworldly character and the leveling character of most modern moral thinking. Nietzsche claimed that humans are a part of the natural world, and that there is no evidence for anything otherworldly, such as God, souls, or eternal moral standards. Humans are just an advanced type of animal whose culture and values are formed and changed in response to many pressures. He also rejected the idea that all people are equally valuable. He claimed that from the standpoint of the natural world some people are obviously worth more than others. The preaching of equality in Judeo-Christian morality, democracy, and socialism attempts to level everyone down to the lowest common denominator.

Nietzsche made two major claims about values. One is that values are human creations in response to factors such as natural instincts, people's abilities and limitations, their natural environment, and the culture and behavior of the people around them. Throughout most of human history, values have been created for whole societies and people have been unaware of the creating process. They believed that prophets and leaders received the values from God or discovered them in some intellectual way. Since values are passed on in a culture from generation to generation, values may become unsuitable for the conditions of a later generation. People's beliefs, their dominant drives, or their environment may change, so that the inherited values may no longer fit the current members. Values are also passed from person to person. Specific values may be suitable for one person but unsuitable for another. Nietzsche proposed that moral values be examined for their suitability for a whole group of people and for individual people. He emphasized that "higher individuals" should consider whether the moral values that are generally taught in the culture really allow these individuals to prosper.

Nietzsche's second major claim is that people can be ranked according to natural factors. Some people have stronger drives or greater abilities than others. Nietzsche claimed that more talented and more motivated people were in some natural sense better and more valuable than less talented and less motivated people. He sometimes expressed this view in terms of "will to power." Will to power is the natural drive to be able to control things. Nietzsche claimed that will to power is the fundamental drive of living things. Those who have a stronger will to power are better in this basic way than those with a weaker will to power. Nietzsche thought that values that promote the development and increase of will to power, particularly its highest expression in creativity, are better than "herd moralities" that seek to make everyone equal. Nietzsche favored values that would promote strength and creativity.

De Beauvoir's Existential Morality

Simone de Beauvoir attempted to develop a morality that was based on Sartre's existentialism. She accepted the idea that people should explicitly recognize their existential freedom and not hide it from themselves through bad faith. She extended the idea that your freedom is valuable for you to the idea that the freedom of others is also valuable for you. Since your freedom operates in a social context, and other people contribute to this social context, you have to respect other people's freedom in order to maintain your own. You have to treat them as free beings. You cannot use other people simply as means to your ends, because that would restrict their freedom. In order to develop or increase your own freedom, you have to seek to liberate others. You can liberate others either by removing unnecessary restrictions on their freedom to act or by encouraging them to recognize their freedom of choice. The first approach commits you to overthrowing repressive governments and social structures. The second approach commits you to educating people to recognize that they need not accept the customs, values, and roles of their society. Since freedoms can come into conflict with one another, there is always some ambiguity in following existential morality.

Criticism of Existentialism

The most frequent objections to existentialism are that it depends upon and overvalues individual freedom. Some philosophers deny that individuals have the freedom to choose their own values and way of life. They claim that human behavior and thought are determined by many complex factors, including heredity, environment, early-childhood experiences, education, and culture. People may think that they are making free choices about their goals and values, but the results are really the causal outcomes of determining factors. These factors cause you to reflect or not to reflect at any given time and determine your thought processes of reflection. Existential freedom does not exist, according to these critics, and so it is a mistake to expect or require people to exercise it.

Other critics claim that existentialism considers individual freedom to be too important. These critics claim that other things are as important or more important than existential freedom. The will of God, objective moral standards, individual happiness, an ideal or just society, and the preservation of a culturally shared way of life have been considered by different ethical thinkers to be more important than individual freedom to choose your own values and way of life. It is better to pursue these other goals, they claim, than to develop your existential freedom. Some critics argue that existentialism produces alienation of the individual from her society. Existentialism cuts people off from their societal roots, which is bad for people. The anxiety that accompanies existential freedom is a sign of alienation rather than of authenticity.

Existentialism is a philosophy that emphasizes personal decisions about how to live. Although different existentialists consider the same questions to be important, there is not one specific set of existentialist answers. Existentialism emphasizes the importance of raising and thinking through questions about the meaning of life. It is by taking a stand on these issues that a person defines herself as a distinct individual.

Worrying about the meaning of life usually includes several concerns. Is there a divine plan or rational world order that governs everything that happens? Does objective goodness and value exist? Does your own individual life have some purpose? Can your life be significant if it has no noticeable effect on the universe? What does anything matter since you are going to die anyhow? Existentialists agree that humans should not try to fit themselves into some rational world order, that individual freedom and responsibility are valuable, and that the inevitability of death does not make your current life meaningless. However, different existentialists take different positions on other aspects of these issues. Albert Camus examined these concerns from the standpoint of absurdity. The feeling of absurdity arises from the confrontation of what people want and expect to find in the universe with what they actually find.

Individual freedom to choose your own goals, standards, and values is the basic concern of existentialism. Existential freedom requires that you not be completely causally determined to follow natural inclinations, societal customs and standards, or some combination of these. Existentialists think that people should recognize their fundamental freedom and make full use of it. Most existentialists think that all people are intrinsically required to exercise their freedom at all times. They disagree about whether a person is always defining everything about himself or rather defining some features of himself from the standpoint of other features that are currently unquestioned.

All existentialists claim that a person's choice of goals, standards, and values is to some degree unjustified. You have to commit yourself to things that are of vital importance to you without having a guarantee that you are choosing the best ones. Existentialists disagree about whether there are fixed options from which a person must choose her own position or whether she can create new options. They also disagree about the degree and type of influence that antecedent factors have on free choice.

Existential freedom includes a feeling of anxiety, because you have to stake your life on choices that define you but for which you do not have sufficient reasons. Many existentialists think that the experience of anxiety shows that people are free. Authenticity is being your own person or being responsible for what you are. Not being your own, inauthenticity, is tempting because of the anxiety that accompanies existential freedom.

Existentialists claim that relations with other people are always complicated because people are individually free. Conflicts always occur between a person's definition of himself and other people's definitions of him. Sartre claimed that interpersonal relations are combative, because each person wants to capture the other person's ability to define them. Heidegger claimed that interactions with other people largely take place through the cultural conceptions and roles that people share, but that being authentic requires openness to changes. Buber claimed that there are two ways to relate to others, as I-It or I-Thou, and that the I-Thou keeps our concepts of others open, flexible, and spiritual.

Existentialism is concerned with the best way to live. Most existentialists think that existential freedom is more important than Judeo-Christian morality. Most deny that individuals are subject to objective moral requirements. Although they accept the objective value of existential freedom, they deny that being free requires that you be moral. Nietzsche strongly attacked modern morality for its otherworldly assumptions and leveling character. He claimed that values are human creations that can be evaluated in terms of their fit with people's natural instincts, their abilities, their environment, and their human environment. He also claimed that more talented and more motivated people were intrinsically better than others. De Beauvoir attempted to develop an existentialist morality that was based on respecting and increasing the freedom of others in order to maintain and increase your own freedom.

The most frequent objections to existentialism are that it depends upon and overvalues individual freedom. Critics claim either that people cannot exercise existential freedom or that there are more important goals to pursue.

Selected Readings

de Beauvoir, Simone. T*he Ethics of Ambiguity.* B. Frechtman (tr.). Secaucus, NJ: Citadel, 1948.

Camus, Albert. *The Myth of Sisyphus.* J. O'Brien (tr.). New York: Vintage, 1955.

Macquarrie, John. *Existentialism.* Harmondsworth, England: Penguin, 1973.

Nietzsche, Friedrich. *On the Genealogy of Morals.* W. Kaufmann and R. Hollingdale (tr.). New York: Random House, 1967.

Raymond, Diane. *Existentialism and the Philosophical Tradition.* Englewood Cliffs, NJ: Prentice-Hall, 1991.

Sartre, Jean-Paul. *Existentialism.* B. Frechtman (tr.). New York: Philosophical Library, 1947.

Solomon, Robert. *From Rationalism to Existentialism.* New York: Harper & Row, 1972.

8

Abortion

*A*bortion has been one of the most hotly disputed ethical and political issues in recent years. People frequently have strong emotional commitments to one side or the other. Opponents claim that abortion is equivalent to murdering innocent babies. Defenders claim that a woman's right to control her own body requires that she have the choice of whether or not to carry a fetus for nine months. Ethics attempts to weigh the reasons for and against abortion and to determine whether there are specific conditions in which abortion is morally permissible.

ETHICAL, MORAL, AND LEGAL ISSUES

Abortion is the ending of a pregnancy before live birth. The major ethical, moral, and legal issues concern intentionally causing an abortion. A fetus is viable when it is able to survive outside the mother's womb. Many techniques of abortion directly kill the fetus, even though the separation of the fetus from the mother before it is viable would produce its death anyway. The time of viability changes with advances in medical techniques. With the most advanced medical techniques, fetuses five to six months after conception can now be kept alive outside of the mother's womb.

One important ethical issue is whether a pregnant woman should seek an abortion. Is it ever good for the pregnant woman to abort her fetus? Different theories of the best way to live (see chapter 2) may give different answers to this question. If abortion is always immoral and being moral is always the best thing to do, then it is best for the woman not to have an abortion. However, if being moral is not always the best way to live or if abortion is not always immoral, then an abortion may be the best course of action. Depending upon the specific facts of her case, it may be in a woman's selfish interest and self-interest to have an abortion. Her physical health, mental health, or general happiness may be increased by detaching herself from the fetus. Her ability to pursue the projects that she wants, her prospects of making creative advances in art or science, and her freedom to choose her own values may be increased. More of her informed wants, including wants concerning the welfare of people close to her, may be satisfied. Her close interpersonal relationships may be improved by detaching herself from the fetus. If any of these factors is what makes a person's life good, a pregnant woman would be wise to have an abortion in some circumstances.

Another major issue is whether abortion is ever moral. Abortion is a difficult moral issue because it frequently involves a conflict between the interests of the fetus and the interests of the pregnant woman. The moral status of the fetus makes a major difference for the morality of abortion. If abortion is killing an unborn child, abortion may be morally wrong. Is abortion really equivalent to killing a baby, or is it more like the surgical removal of a cancerous tumor? The rights and interests of the pregnant woman are also important moral factors. Does a woman's right to liberty mean that she always has the right to refuse to let the fetus use her body? Other factors, such as the value of a fetus's future life to the child it will become and the interests of other people who will have to support the child, vary from case to case, but are considered to be morally important by many moral thinkers. According to some moral theories, such as act utilitarianism (see chapter 7), the morality of abortion may vary from case to case.

There has been much dispute in recent years about whether abortion should be permitted or forbidden by law. Those who favor laws against abortion argue that such laws are necessary because abortion is a serious moral wrong, comparable to murder. Their arguments for making abortion illegal are basically the same as the moral arguments against abortion (see "Moral Arguments Against Abortion," page 111). Similarly, many arguments against making abortion illegal claim that abortion is not a serious moral wrong, so that it should not be forbidden by law. However, opponents of laws that prohibit or restrict abortion also use another argument. They claim that if the morality of abortion is a matter of dispute in society, society should not intervene in the involved people's decisions. If it is not obvious that abortion is immoral, society should allow the pregnant women, their families, and doctors to decide the difficult questions for themselves. Since there are major disagreements among informed, reasonable people about the morality of abortion, decisions about abortion should be private.

Roe v. Wade

Before 1973 medical abortion was illegal in most states, except when the mother's life or physical health was at risk. In 1973 the Supreme Court of the United States ruled in the *Roe* v. *Wade* decision that laws restricting abortion violated a woman's constitutional right to privacy. "We therefore conclude that the right of personal privacy includes the abortion decision, but that this right is not unqualified and must be considered against important state interests in regulation" (Justice Harry Blackmun, majority opinion). *Roe* v. *Wade* held that states may not make abortions performed during the first six months of pregnancy illegal, but that states may regulate and even forbid abortions in the last three months of pregnancy. "For the stage subsequent to viability the State, in promoting its interest in the potentiality of human life, may, if it chooses, regulate, and even proscribe, abortion except where it is necessary, in appropriate medical judgment, for the preservation of the life or health of the mother" (Justice Blackmun, majority opinion). Since 1973 there have been several legal challenges to this position, but the basic position of *Roe* v. *Wade* concerning the constitutional right to abortion has been maintained.

MORAL ARGUMENTS AGAINST ABORTION

Most arguments against abortion claim that it treats the fetus in an immoral way. They focus on what abortion does to the fetus. Another approach focuses on what the acceptance of abortion does to the attitudes of people in society.

The Right to Life

The most common argument against abortion claims that a fetus has a right to life because it is a person or a human being. All human beings have certain rights just by virtue of being human beings. According to this argument, all human beings have a basic right to life, and a fetus is a human being. Hence, a fetus has a right to life. Moral theorists differ about the exact nature of a right to life, but the basic idea is that a right to life places requirements on how other people may treat the being that has the right. Other people may not take away its life. They may not kill a being with a right to life except in special circumstances, such as when their self-defense requires it. The right to life may also impose some duties on third parties, such as the duty to defend the being with the right to life against those who would take away its life. If a fetus does have a right to life by virtue of being a human being, abortion would be immoral, except in special circumstances. Abortion would be either murder of an unborn baby or at least a serious violation of someone's rights.

The Value of Human Life

Another argument against abortion is that all human life is intrinsically valuable. There is a sanctity or dignity to human life, either because humans, as a species, are rational and moral beings, or because God has given this sacredness to human life. Since human life is ultimately valuable, no one should kill a living human if that can be avoided in some way. Since a fetus is a living human, abortion is morally wrong and should be forbidden.

Depriving a Fetus of Its Personal Future

A third argument against abortion is that it deprives a fetus of its future life as a person. This argument claims that what makes killing an adult or a child morally wrong is that it deprives the being of a future life. Killing it takes away a valuable future. The argument claims that a fetus has a future that is just like the future of an adult or a young child. If not aborted, the fetus will go on to have the experiences of a living person. To kill a fetus is to deprive it of its valuable future as a person. Since depriving someone of a valuable future is morally wrong, abortion is morally wrong.

Producing Sensitivity

One argument against abortion depends upon the results or consequences of abortion on people in society, including the women who have abortions. The acceptance of abortion would make people less sensitive to the value of human life. People would tend to generalize from the unimportance of fetal life to the unimportance of human life in general. If fetuses can be killed because of the burdens of supporting them until birth, why could not other burdensome humans be killed? If abortion were accepted, people would become more callous and less concerned about newborn infants, old people, the terminally ill, and other members of society. This decreased concern for the value of human life is a morally bad result. Hence, abortion should be forbidden, or at least restricted, in order to avoid this morally bad result.

THE MORAL STATUS OF THE FETUS

Most arguments about abortion concern the moral status of the fetus. People disagree about whether a fetus is a person, about whether it has a right to life, and about whether it has a personal future of which it can be unjustly deprived. Most opponents of abortion consider the fetus to have some important moral standing, so that moral arguments against killing apply to it. They think that a fetus is a type of being that deserves moral and legal protection, whereas a mosquito is not such a type of being. Many defenders of abortion consider the fetus, at least at early stages of development, not to have any important moral standing, so that it does not deserve to be protected by morality and law. Both sides recognize that a fetus develops throughout the nine-month period from conception to birth. Some defenders and some opponents of abortion consider the stage of development to affect the fetus's moral status.

The first three arguments against abortion depend upon the fetus's having a moral standing that is similar to babies and other people. Most people agree that newborn babies and other living humans must be allowed to continue living. Parents should not be free to kill their children, even if this would make the parents' lives better. Most people also agree that human tissue and human germ cells (sperm cells and unfertilized egg cells) do not have any special moral standing. A person is free to have living tissue, such as a mole or an appendix, removed from his body if he wants it removed for some reason. What is it about the fetus that is supposed to give it the moral status of a young infant, rather than the status of a mole? What features affect the fetus's moral standing? Several different features have been proposed.

Physical Appearance

For the first few days after an egg cell is fertilized by a sperm cell, a human fetus is only a microscopic group of cells. By the time of birth, a fetus has become a fully formed human baby. During the intervening period, the fetus develops all the biological features of a normal baby. Distinct arms, legs, trunk, and head develop fairly early in this process. Some opponents of abortion point to the physical appearance of fetuses that were aborted before viability as an indication that these fetuses were already living babies. They think that the noticeable human form of the fetus shows that it is an unborn infant, and so should have the moral standing of a baby that has been born. Critics of this position claim that mere physical appearance is not relevant to moral status. Something, such as a robot or monkey, may look like a baby without having the moral status of a baby.

Having a Soul

The idea that the soul is the life principle of the body is a very ancient one. A soul is supposed to be something that is distinct from the physical body and that makes it alive. The body is alive and can develop so long as the soul is present within it. If the soul departs, the physical body is left lifeless.

Many religions consider the soul to be a substance in which human mental properties exist. The soul underlies feelings and thoughts and is the basis for personal identity. God creates the soul and implants it in the body. There are different views about when a soul is implanted in a body. Some think that the soul is implanted at the moment an egg is fertilized, because they consider the soul to be necessary to animate and guide the biological growth of the fetus. According to this view, even abortions in the first few months of pregnancy kill a human with a soul. Others think that all biological development does not depend upon a soul. They consider the soul to be the mind—that which perceives, feels, and thinks. According to this view, the soul is implanted later in pregnancy at the time when mental activity begins. Abortions before the implanting of a soul do not kill a person, only human tissue. Critics claim that neither of these positions is correct, because there is no good evidence that souls exist at all.

Potentiality to Be a Person

A fetus will frequently develop into a baby, although many natural miscarriages occur. A baby will normally develop into a self-conscious person. From the moment of conception there are internal features that drive the fetus toward being a person. A fertilized egg has a complete genetic code that in favorable conditions will guide its growth into a fully formed baby. Thus, there is a natural goal for the fetus. The fetus is defined by its potentiality to be a person. The fetus is intrinsically directed toward being a person. The making actual of its potentiality will change the fetus into a person.

Both sides of the abortion debate usually accept the idea that a fetus has the potentiality to be a person. However, they draw from this different conclusions about the moral status of the fetus. Opponents of abortion frequently argue that since a fetus is potentially a person, and a person has a right to life, a fetus has a right to life. They claim that a fetus's intrinsic directedness toward personhood gives it full moral standing from the moment of conception. Defenders of abortion frequently argue that there is a big difference between the potentiality to be a person and actually being a person now. Individual human cells might someday be stimulated so as to grow into the clone of a person. This potentiality to become a person does not give to each cell now the moral standing of a person.

Formed Brain and Nervous System

Modern science has discovered that communication between different parts of the body depends upon a working nervous system and that mental experiences depend upon a working brain. Without a properly functioning brain, people can not perceive, feel, or think. Without a properly functioning nervous system, the brain receives no information about what is happening in other parts of the body and cannot control muscular reactions and bodily motions. In light of these facts, some people think that a fetus becomes a person and acquires full moral standing only when its brain and nervous system have formed. These are formed by about the twelfth week of pregnancy, although they continue to develop after this. According to this view, abortions that occur before the brain and nervous system are formed do not kill a living person, but after their formation the fetus deserves protection.

This position has been criticized from both directions. Some critics claim that a fetus is a person from the moment of conception. Other critics claim that a formed brain and nervous system alone are not sufficient. They claim that a brain that functions to produce conscious experiences is necessary for being a person.

Noticeable Physical Movement

During the fourth month of pregnancy, women usually begin to feel movements of the fetus within them. This time of "quickening" has sometimes been considered to be the time at which the fetus becomes alive. The fetus is considered to be alive because it engages in noticeable physical movement, rather than just growth. Some religious thinkers consider "quickening" to be the time at which a soul is implanted. Critics claim that mere physical movement, whether noticeable or not, does not establish something's moral standing.

Viability

A fetus is viable when it is able to survive outside the mother's womb. Some consider viability to be the point at which a fetus becomes an independent human being, rather than being tissue that is part of the mother. Before viability, a fetus is wholly dependent upon the pregnant woman for its nutrition and life. In this respect the fetus is like a part or organ of a living being, rather than like a complete living being. Some consider the fetus's inability to survive on its own to show that the fetus is not a being separate from the woman, and so should not have the moral standing of an independent person. According to this view, abortion before viability is not immoral, but abortion after viability is immoral. A fetus acquires full moral standing only when it is able to live separate from the woman.

Critics of this position point out that the time of viability changes with advances in medical techniques for keeping a fetus alive outside the womb. They claim that external circumstances, such as the availability of medical techniques, cannot determine the moral status of the fetus. Some critics also note that for many years after birth children are still totally dependent on other people to feed and care for them.

Being a Self-Conscious Person

Developed humans share many mental and bodily features with other animals. Both humans and other animals can perceive their environment, feel pain and hunger, and act from desires. However, after the first few years of life, normal humans have many mental capacities and abilities that other animals do not have. Normal humans plan ahead and act on their plans, have some ideals for their behavior (such as being moral or "cool"), have a sense of their own past, are able to solve new and complex problems, are able to communicate through a language, have complex conceptions of who they are, and have complex emotions. Some thinkers consider some combination of these characteristics to be necessary for being a full-fledged person. A living thing is a person only if it has some combination of these mental capacities and abilities. Living things that are not persons can be closer to or further from being persons. The more a living being's mental capacities and abilities are similar to those of persons, the closer it is to being a person.

Some moral theorists think that personhood is important because only persons have full moral standing. They claim that persons have full moral standing that other animals do not have, because persons have these special mental capacities and abilities. Persons, but not fish, chickens, or cows, have rights to life and liberty, and there is a special value to life as a person. According to this theory that only self-conscious persons have full moral status, fetuses never have full moral standing. In the early stages of development, fetuses do not even have a well-formed brain and nervous system, so that they are very far from personhood. As the fetus progresses, it becomes somewhat closer to personhood. However, even just before birth, the fetus's mental capacities and abilities are less developed than those of an adult chicken. Hence, abortion is never a serious moral wrong, because fetuses are not persons with full moral standing.

Critics of this position point out that babies are not full-fledged persons according to this theory either. This theory would appear to allow infanticide, the killing of unwanted or defective infants, as well as abortion. Defenders of the position claim that babies are more like persons and that they can be put up for adoption so as not to impose a burden on their biological mothers.

RIGHTS AND INTERESTS OF THE PREGNANT WOMAN

Pregnancy involves both a fetus and a woman. The rights and interests of the pregnant woman as well as those of the fetus must be taken into account in evaluations of abortion. A pregnant woman is a full-fledged person and has full moral standing. If a fetus has little moral standing and is not a person, a pregnant woman's rights and interests will be the decisive moral factors. Even if a fetus has full moral status, however, a pregnant woman's rights and interests might still make abortion morally permissible in some circumstances.

The Woman's Right to Life

If all human beings or all self-conscious persons have a right to life, a pregnant woman has a right to life. This right requires that other people not kill her, and it allows her to defend herself against attack. It may also require third parties to help defend her from attack, and it at least allows them to help her. In some cases the medical condition of a pregnant woman is such that continuing the pregnancy will probably kill her. Although the fetus is not intentionally trying to kill her, the fetus's continued life will probably cause her death. Many moral thinkers, even those who consider the fetus to have a right to life, claim that in such a case a woman's right to life makes it morally permissible for her to have an abortion. Morality allows her to preserve her own life and to defend herself by detaching herself from the fetus. If morality allows the woman to defend herself in this way, it should also allow doctors to help the woman defend her life by performing the abortion.

The Woman's Right to Liberty

Many people think that all persons have a right to liberty. They think that morality requires that people be allowed to control their own bodies and actions. No one should be a slave who is forced to work for others. A woman's right to liberty seems to include her right to control the use that is made of her body. With respect to pregnancy, a woman seems to have the right either to allow the fetus to develop within her or to refuse to let the fetus use her body. A woman should not be forced to have her body used against her will by the fetus. This right seems to apply whether or not the fetus has full moral standing. Even self-conscious persons who need the use of your body to keep them alive cannot rightfully force you to sustain them. If someone wanted to be connected by tubes to your internal organs for nine months in order to survive an accident or illness, you would have the right to refuse him. Similarly, a woman has the right not to suffer the burdens of pregnancy.

If a fetus has full moral standing, how a woman became pregnant in the first place seems to affect her right to refuse the fetus the use of her body. If she became pregnant involuntarily, such as through rape or a failure of birth control, she seems to have the right to end the pregnancy that started without her consent. She did not voluntarily bring into existence a fetus whose continued life was totally dependent upon the use of her body. However, if she chose to become pregnant and if the fetus has full moral standing, she may not have the right to change her mind later. Once she has voluntarily brought into existence a fetus with full moral standing, she seems to be obligated to keep it alive until it can live on its own.

OTHER CONSIDERATIONS

Real cases in which abortion is considered always involve many specific circumstances. According to some moral theories, the morality of abortion may vary from case to case, depending upon these specific circumstances.

The Welfare of the Fetus

The welfare of the fetus is one factor that varies from case to case and may affect the morality of abortion. Most of the moral arguments against abortion claim that it treats the fetus in an immoral way. People tend to assume that a fetus's interests are best served by allowing it to develop and to be born. However, there are large differences between specific cases. In some extreme types of case, it may be obvious that the fetus's interests are best served by not forcing it to endure its future life. If a fetus has some physical defect that will make its future life short and very painful, abortion would seem to benefit the fetus. The fetus's future life would be of no value to the fetus. If the fetus were somehow able to decide the issue for itself, it would prefer not to be born just to suffer for a few years.

There are many other, less extreme, types of cases in which a fetus's future is likely to be very difficult and somewhat painful. If a fetus will develop into a child with mental, emotional, or physical defects, its future seems to be of less value to it than a future as a normal person would be. A child with Down syndrome, autism, or extensive paralysis will have a hard life without special care. Although it is difficult to be precise about these judgments, a woman and her family may have good reason to judge that it is better for the fetus not to be born. Factors outside the fetus itself also affect the quality of its future life. Its parents or family may be likely to abuse the child that a fetus will become. Extreme poverty or warfare may make a fetus's future life likely to be very hard. Knowing the conditions in which the child would have to grow up, a woman and her family some- times judge that it is better for the fetus not to be born.

Some opponents of abortion think that the value of its future life to the fetus is not morally important. They claim that the value of human life to God is the decisive moral factor. Only God should decide who will con- tinue to live and who will die. This response assumes that God is the source of morality and that people know what God wants in these cases.

Bringing a baby into the world affects people other than the mother and the fetus. If a baby is not put up for adoption, the mother will usually have to provide most of the care in the early years. However, other members of the family may be strongly affected. They may have to provide food, shel- ter, care, and other things for the baby, and frequently for the mother. The benefits, burdens, and dangers to other people will vary from case to case. In extreme cases in which the family is already barely able to survive, the addition of another child may threaten everyone else's life. Such condi- tions, which existed in our society in the past and that still exist in some parts of the world, may make abortion morally acceptable. According to consequentialist theories of morality that consider the affect of an action on the welfare of all people, abortion in the most extreme circumstances would be morally justified, because it would increase the overall welfare of people. According to utilitarianism, abortion would be morally justified in *any* circumstances in which it produced more overall happiness than not having an abortion would produce. Utilitarianism, even rule utilitarianism (see chapter 7), considers abortion to be moral in many circumstances, because it takes into account the welfare of other people and of the pregnant woman, as well as the welfare of the fetus. Poor countries that want to limit their populations, such as China and India, frequently appeal to the general welfare of people in the society in order to encourage abortions.

Killing vs. Letting Die

Many surgical methods of abortion involve destroying the fetus before removing it from the woman's womb. The doctor who performs the abortion kills the fetus directly, rather than just letting it die outside the womb if it is not viable. Some moral theories, such as the traditional Catholic position, claim that it is immoral for a doctor to kill a fetus directly, even in order to save the woman's life. While it might be morally permissible to let a fetus die in order to save the woman's life, a doctor and anyone else may never kill an innocent human life. Killing is an intentional action in which the intention is to make someone die. Letting the fetus or the mother die is not acting to save their lives. According to many moral theories, not acting to save someone's life is less morally serious than killing that person. Hence, if a fetus has full moral standing and letting die is much less serious than killing, morality may require a doctor to allow both a mother and a fetus to die, rather than to kill the fetus directly.

Abortion is the ending of a pregnancy before live birth. Different theories of the best way to live may give different answers to the question whether it is ever good for the pregnant woman to abort her fetus. Having an abortion may be in her individual selfish interest and self-interest, and it may be morally acceptable. Abortion is a difficult moral issue because it frequently involves a conflict between the interests of the fetus and the interests of the pregnant woman. The Supreme Court ruled in the Roe v. Wade decision that laws restricting abortion violated a woman's constitutional right to privacy.

Frequent moral arguments against abortion are that abortion violates a fetus's right to life, that it does not respect the intrinsic value of human life, and that it unjustly deprives a fetus of its valuable future life as a person. A different type of moral argument against abortion is that the acceptance of abortion would make people less sensitive to the value of human life in general.

Most arguments about abortion concern the moral status of the fetus. Is it the sort of being that deserves moral and legal protection? Since a fetus develops over time, what features might give a fetus full moral standing? Different features that develop at different times have been proposed: the physical appearance of a human, having a soul implanted by God, having the potential to develop into a person, having a formed brain and nervous system, moving in a noticeable way, and viability. An opposing view is that fetuses never have full moral standing, because they never have the mental capacities and abilities of a person.

The rights and interests of a pregnant woman must also be respected. If a fetus has little moral standing, the woman's rights and interests will be the decisive moral factors. Even if a fetus has full moral standing, a woman's right to life allows her to protect herself and her right to liberty may allow her to refuse to let the fetus use her body against her will.

The welfare of the fetus is one factor that varies from case to case and may affect the morality of abortion. In cases in which a fetus's future life will be short and very painful, the fetus's interests may be best served by not forcing it to endure its future life. In less extreme cases, women and their families may judge that it is better for the fetus not to be born. Another factor that varies from case to case is the effect of bringing a child into the world on other people. Utilitarianism claims that abortion would be morally justified in any circumstances in which it produced more overall happiness than not having an abortion would produce. Some moral theories claim that doctors may let the fetus or the woman die, but may not directly kill an innocent human being.

Selected Readings

Cohen, Marshall, ed. *The Rights and Wrongs of Abortion*. Princeton: Princeton University Press, 1974.

Feinberg, Joel, ed. *The Problem of Abortion*, 2nd ed. Belmont, CA: Wadsworth, 1984.

Noonan, John. *How to Argue About Abortion*, New York: Free Press, 1979.

Tooley, Michael. *Abortion and Infanticide*, New York: Oxford University Press, 1983.

9

Sexism

Sexual interactions are some of the most important influences in our lives. Sexual interactions include, of course, romantic attachments; but the sex of others—our children, our parents, our colleagues, our friends—shapes our interactions with them. Notice the difference in the way people dress little girls and little boys. The influence of sex in our lives is so profound and pervasive that many people never even consider the possibility that these sexual interactions might be sexist. But a glance at other time periods or other cultures reveals that the sexes can interact differently and raises the question: How ought the sexes interact?

WHAT IS SEXISM?

An act, practice, or attitude is sexist when it creates unjustified differences between the sexes or exploits irrelevant differences between the sexes. People are sexist when they knowingly perform a sexist act, support a sexist practice, or have a sexist attitude. Sexism is the view that sexist acts, practices, or attitudes ought to be encouraged. One can perform a sexist act, support a sexist practice, or have a sexist attitude without knowing that the act, practice, or attitude is sexist. In that case, one might not be sexist. As the use of the pejorative terms "unjustified" and "irrelevant" indicates, to call an act, practice, or attitude sexist implies that it is immoral. Sexist acts, practices, and attitudes are immoral because they harm one sex. For example, refusing to allow women to vote harms them by dramatically reducing their role in the political process. Sexism can also harm someone in her personal life. A husband who thinks that women should be seen and not heard might cause his wife frustration and unhappiness.

The phrases "creates unjustified differences" and "exploits irrelevant differences" require comment. Unjustified differences between the sexes can be created by society. Some think that the way little girls are raised in our society causes women to be more passive than men and that there is no justification for creating this difference. Others disagree and hold that the greater passivity of women is either natural, not created by society at all, or that the creation of this difference is justified by natural differences between the sexes. Turning to "exploit irrelevant differences," some think that if someone refused to hire someone as an accountant because she was a woman, he has exploited an irrelevant difference between the sexes. Features are relevant in some contexts and irrelevant in others. Height is relevant if one is hiring a basketball player but irrelevant if one is picking an accountant. Many think that sex, like height, is irrelevant when it comes to accountants. The debate over sexism is a debate over what the differences between the sexes are, over whether the creation of sexual differences is unjustified, and over what differences are relevant in various contexts.

There is wide agreement that certain practices are sexist. It is clear that denying women the right to vote or to own property is sexist. Similarly, the view that one may beat one's wife has few defenders. But there is wide disagreement about other practices. Some think that encouraging girls to take home economics and boys to take shop is sexist, while others disagree. Some think that traditional families—families in which the father goes to work while the mother stays home with the kids—are sexist, while others stoutly defend them.

FOUR QUESTIONS ABOUT SEXISM

Debate on this issue is often hampered because people fail to distinguish four related but distinct questions about sexism.

The answers we give to any one of these questions may affect our answers to the others. But running them all together leads to confusion. We will not consider possible answers to these questions until later in this chapter. At this point, we need to note simply that these are the questions that need to be answered if we are to resolve the disputes surrounding sexism.

What is the Place of Sex in Our Society? We have a great many unnoticed assumptions about the sex of those around us. We assume that nurses are women and doctors are men. We assume that plumbers are men and maids are women. These assumptions may be perfectly appropriate, but, appropriate or not, the fact that we make them shows that the distinction between the sexes is an important feature of our lives.

The importance of sexual distinctions is hard to exaggerate. We treat people differently depending on whether they are male or female. For example, women and men wear their hair differently. They sit, walk, and hold themselves differently. They wear different clothes. We announce our sex to those around us by conforming to the patterns our society associates with our sex. The importance of these patterns can also be seen in our reactions to those who do not conform to the patterns. For example, men who walk and talk like women are a bit of shock and some people find them offensive. The importance of sexual distinctions is also seen in the different expectations people have of men and women. Many people expect women to have a greater concern about family life than men. They expect women to put family before career, and men to put career before family. Our language also shows that sex is important to us. We have different pronouns ("he" and "she") for referring to people of different sexes.

That sexual distinctions are important in our society is not denied by anyone. Many, but not all, also think that female patterns are disadvantageous and male patterns are advantageous. For example, when walking home late at night, the fact that one can tell by clothing, hair, and gait whether a person is a woman or a man is beneficial for men and harmful for women. Being recognized as a man makes one less likely to be attacked. Being recognized as a woman makes one more likely to be attacked. Many also think that being recognized as a woman makes it less likely that one's views will be taken seriously at a business meeting, while being recognized as a man has the opposite effect. Some, following Simone de Beauvoir (1908-86), think that our language (as well as other languages) treats women not only differently, but also as if they were deviations from the norm. For example, we use "he" when we do not know the sex of someone, and when describing someone we assume that the person in question is a man unless it is specified that the person is a woman.

How Did Sex Come to Have This Place in Our Society?

In answering this question, thinkers have distinguished sex from gender. Being a man or a woman is partly a matter of sex and partly a matter of gender. Sex refers to those differences between women and men that are biological in origin. That men have penises and women do not is a matter of sex. Gender refers to those differences between women and men that are sociological in origin. That women wear dresses and men do not is a matter of gender. While there are cases such as these in which the sex/gender distinction is very clear, there are also cases in which the origin of a feature is a matter of dispute. For example, some think that men are naturally more aggressive than women. In other words, they think that the aggressiveness of men is a matter of sex. Others disagree and hold that the greater aggressiveness of men is a product of the way boys are raised—a matter of gender.

Everyone agrees that being a man or a woman is partly a matter of sex and partly a matter of gender. But there is a great deal of debate about which is more important. The debate over how sex came to have the place it does in our society is a debate over the relative importance of sex and gender. Some think that the different treatment of women and men in our society is primarily a matter of sex—a reflection of natural differences. Others think that the different treatment is primarily a matter of gender—a reflection of society.

What Would a Nonsexist Society Be Like?

This is a question of ideals. Ideals are important because we guide our actions by them. If we feel that our society meets our ideals, then we will not try to change it. On the other hand, if we feel that our society falls short of our ideals, then we will be motivated to change it. There are three competing ideals of a nonsexist society.

SEXUALLY STRATIFIED

In a sexually stratified society people care about the differences between women and men, and one sex occupies a place subordinate to the other. For example, if in a particular society husbands control whether or not their wives work and only men occupy important social positions, then the society is sexually stratified, with women in the subordinate place. Many think that our society is currently sexually stratified. While many argue that a sexually stratified society is a sexist one, some think that the natural differences between men and women imply that sexual stratification is moral, and so not sexist. Recall that a practice is sexist when it creates *unjustified* differences between the sexes or exploits *irrelevant* differences between the sexes. Some think that the natural differences between men and women justify the differences found in a sexually stratified society, and therefore such a society is not sexist.

SEXUALLY BLIND

In a sexually blind society people are indifferent to whether someone is a man or a woman. People treat the differences between women and men the way we currently treat the differences between those who have a mole on their left leg and those who do not. We do not care whether someone has such a mole. It is obvious that in a sexually blind society all hiring decisions would be made without considering the sex of the applicant—just as all current hiring decisions are made without considering whether or not the applicant has a mole. But this ideal would require more changes than one might think at first glance. For example, if a sexually blind society is our ideal, then we ought to be bisexual. Only bisexuals can be indifferent to whether their romantic partners are women or men. By definition, both heterosexuals and homosexuals prefer to be with one sex rather than another.

SEXUALLY DIVERSE

In a sexually diverse society, people care about the differences between men and women just as they do in a sexually stratified society. The difference between a sexually diverse society and a sexually stratified one is that in a sexually diverse society neither sex is subordinate to the other. Instead, everyone regards the differences between the sexes as something to be celebrated. This ideal can be better understood by considering our attitude toward different cuisines. We have preferences about cuisines. Some people like Chinese food while others prefer Italian. But we also think it is good to have a diversity of cuisines. People praise a city for having many different sorts of restaurants, even though they do not like the style of cuisine served in some of these restaurants. We think that cuisine preferences are purely personal. We do not think that society ought to encourage some cuisines and discourage others. No cuisine is subordinate to any other. Defenders of the sexual-diversity ideal think that in the ideal society people would have preferences concerning sex like those we currently have about cuisines. They might prefer to have a boy or a girl or prefer to have a man or a woman as a romantic partner, but no sex would be thought of as inferior to the other.

If Our Society Is Sexist Now, What Ought We Do to Eliminate This Sexism?

There are many ways to change a society. They range from very heavy-handed methods, such as making certain behaviors illegal through less coercive methods such as offering tax incentives, to very mild methods such as putting advertisements on television. One's judgment about these measures will be affected by many things. For one, if one thinks sexism is a very serious problem, then one would be more likely to support using coercive methods to get rid of it. It is also important to consider how effective any particular measure is. A very coercive method that will have little effect on sexism is unlikely to be supported by anyone. So while those who think we need to change our society to make it less sexist agree that a combination of these methods is necessary, they disagree about which combination of methods is best. Some think we ought to ban pornographic materials because they encourage the subordination of women. Others think that this has too high a cost in freedom of speech (see chapter 12). Some think that we ought to have affirmative action in favor of women, while others disagree (see chapter 10). Most think that while this is not a matter in which laws are appropriate, changing the way we raise our children is crucial to making society less sexist. For example, they think we ought to stop giving different toys to girls and boys.

THE BASIC ARGUMENT FOR EQUAL TREATMENT

Arguments concerning sexism begin with the claim that equals ought to be treated equally. In this context, "to be treated equally" means to be treated in the same way. The idea that equals ought to be treated equally has very deep roots in our culture. It goes back at least as far as Aristotle (384–322 B.C.) and is key to the argument against racial inequality (see chapter 10). But as it stands, the claim has little content, for it does not specify what makes two people equals. This is the problem of determining what differences are relevant. If there exists a relevant difference between two people, then they are not equals and we are not obligated to treat them equally. In some cases it is clear whether a difference is relevant or not. For example, if someone hired only blond people to work on an assembly line, this would clearly violate the requirement that equals be treated equally. Whether someone is blond or not has absolutely no bearing on whether she would be a good assembly-line worker. But in the case of men and women, the question of whether there are any relevant differences is hotly disputed.

The basic argument for equal treatment of the sexes couples the claim that equals ought to be treated equally with the claim that there are no relevant differences between women and men.

1) Unless there is a relevant difference between two groups of people, they ought to be treated in the same way.

2) There are no relevant differences between women and men.

3) Therefore, women and men ought to be treated in the same way.

This argument is clearly flawed because, as we noted above, whether one is a man or a woman is very important in our society, and this means that being a woman or a man is relevant in many contexts. Premise 2 is false. For example, if one were hiring a construction-crew chief and there were a long history of only men doing the job, it might very well be that many men on the construction site would not work as well if their boss were a woman. If one were the owner of the construction company and wanted to increase profits, the reaction of fellow workers would certainly be a relevant difference between potential female crew chiefs and potential male crew chiefs.

THE REVISED ARGUMENT FOR EQUAL TREATMENT

Many think there is something very wrong with allowing the views of the men on the construction site to count as a relevant difference between women and men. If one thinks that the attitudes of these men are sexist, then to allow these attitudes to count as a relevant difference allows sexist attitudes to justify a sexist practice. Moreover, many point out that it is no fault of the potential women crew chiefs that the men have these attitudes. They argue that were it not for attitudes such as these, women would be just as good crew chiefs as men. They think that by nature women are able to be just as good crew chiefs as men. Therefore, the following revised argument suggests itself:

1) Unless there is a relevant *natural* difference between two groups of people, they ought to be treated in the same way.

2) There are no relevant *natural* differences between women and men.

3) Therefore, women and men ought to be treated in the same way.

This argument draws a distinction between natural and nonnatural differences between women and men. In this context, "natural" refers to biological. So natural differences between men and women are those differences created by the biological differences between them. "Nonnatural" refers to those differences that are a product of society. As noted above, this distinction is usually marked by referring to the natural differences as matters of sex, and to the nonnatural differences as matters of gender.

Socialization and Sexual Roles

As we just saw, one reason for revising the basic argument for equal treatment is that allowing nonnatural differences between the sexes to justify treating men and women differently seems to allow sexist attitudes to justify a sexist practice. Another reason for revising the basic argument is that many think that nonnatural differences between women and men are wrong in and of themselves. These people attack the sexual socialization of men and women. Socialization is the process by which people come to accept and embody attitudes, beliefs, and characteristics of their society. Learning to use the right hand when shaking hands is an example of socialization. Sexual socialization is the process by which people come to embody the attitudes, beliefs, and characteristics associated with their sex in their society. While some object to sexual socialization, others argue that it is a good response to the natural differences between men and women. They point out that socialization can be a good response to natural facts. For example, socializing people to shake hands with the right hand is a good response to the fact that people have two hands, and it is awkward to shake hands with someone if they are using the opposite hand.

Sexual socialization creates differences between women and men that do not naturally exist. For example, many think that the reason there are many men and few women auto mechanics is that, from a very early age, boys are told that they ought to care about cars and girls are told they ought not to care about them. Boys are given trucks to play with, while girls are given dolls. Another example of this is the fact that there are many more male than female mathematicians despite the fact that (at least at first glance) there seems to be no natural reason that men should be better at math.

Sexual socialization creates sex roles. Sex roles are career and life-style patterns which, because of sexual socialization, are associated with men or with women. Many think that sexual socialization and sex roles are morally objectionable because of their effect on people's freedom of choice. For example, suppose that a certain woman finds that she has a nat-ural mechanical talent. However, she was given dolls, not trucks, as a child and took home economics instead of shop so that others would not make fun of her. She will find that she is at a disadvantage when competing with men (who played with trucks and took shop) for jobs as an auto mechanic. Those who object to sex roles are quick to point out that they harm men as well as women. For example, some men find that they enjoy taking care of children. But society puts more pressure on men to go out and work than it does on women. Men who want to be house husbands may find that people make fun of them or tell them that they are wasting their lives. Society's sex roles restrict the opportunities of those, whether man or woman, whose natural talents and desires run counter to the pattern society expects.

THE CONSERVATIVE VIEW

Conservatives do not object to the first premise of the revised argument for equal treatment. They acknowledge that unless there is a relevant nat-ural difference between two groups of people, they ought to be treated in the same way. But they think that the second premise of the argument is false—they think that there are many relevant natural differences between women and men. Not only do they think that there are relevant natural dif-ferences, but they think that these differences imply that women ought to be subordinate to men, that we ought to have a sexually stratified society. Conservatives think that most of the differences between men and women are a product of sex, not gender.

Conservatives see many natural differences between men and women. They point to such obvious things as the fact that women can bear children and men cannot. Women can nurse children and men cannot. Women menstruate and men do not. Women's bodies have a higher percentage of fat and water than men's do. Men are physically stronger than women and women are more physically flexible than men. Women have a lower center of gravity than men do. They think that women have less sex drive than men. They argue that the hormonal differences (for example, the different levels of testosterone) and differences in the brains of men and women make women more passive, more practical, and less inclined toward abstract subjects like math, physics, and philosophy. They also think that women have a stronger natural maternal need—a need to care for someone—than men.

Conservatives argue that these differences imply that women ought to do different things than men. These differences show that women were designed by God or evolution to care for children and that they have personalities suited to this task. So women ought to stay home and take care of children, while men ought to pursue careers in the aggressive business world. Women ought to study psychology, not math; English, not philosophy. They also think that these differences imply that women ought to be subordinate to men. So conservatives think that the ideal society is sexually stratified. Recall that in a sexually stratified society people care about the difference between men and women and one sex is subordinate to the other. Conservatives think a sexually stratified society is not sexist because they think that there are natural and relevant differences between the sexes. They argue that because men are naturally more aggressive, stronger, and better at high-paying jobs than women, women ought to be subordinate to men—to care for children, cook, clean, and in general take care of the home so that men can do their jobs well. They are quick to add that to say that women ought to be subordinate to men does not mean that it is fine for men to beat women or that the roles women ought to occupy are unimportant. Rather, they think that the role of raising children and taking care of the home is a very important one.

The Argument from Efficiency

Conservatives offer two arguments for the view that the natural differences between women and men imply that women and men ought to do different things and women ought to be subordinate to men. The first is the argument from efficiency. Conservatives argue that treating women and men equally will lead to people doing jobs for which they are naturally unsuited. For example, if men are naturally not good at taking care of children, and women are naturally not good at business, then it would be inefficient for men to stay home and take care of children while women work in the business world. Both jobs will be done less effectively than they would be if they were done by those who are naturally better at them. Conservatives think that the differences between traditional male and female roles are a good response to the natural differences between men and women and to the fact that efficiency is an important societal goal. Therefore, they think society ought to be sexually stratified.

The Argument from Frustration

Apart from the societal problems that conservatives think treating women and men in the same way will cause, they also think that it will tend to make both women and men frustrated and unhappy. They argue that since women are naturally better than men at caring for children, we ought to encourage them to care for children by doing things like encouraging them to study home economics. They think that if girls choose to take shop or, in general, to work toward a career in business, they are going to be frustrated and unhappy when they discover that, because of the natural differences between men and women, they do not succeed in business competitions against men. Similarly, if boys choose to take home economics and work toward being a house husband, they will be frustrated because they will not be as good at caring for children as women are. Conservatives cite this as an additional reason that society ought to be sexually stratified.

THE LIBERAL VIEW

Until comparatively recently, the conservative view has been dominant. It has been defended by such philosophers as Aristotle and Immanuel Kant (1724–1804). But currently, while there are still plenty of conservatives around, another view, the liberal view, is dominant. One of the most famous and influential defenses of the liberal view is John Stuart Mill's *The Subjection of Women*. Liberals like Mill (1806–73) were responding to the dominant conservative view. Their view is best approached by looking at their attacks on the conservative view.

Liberals and Natural Differences

Liberals begin by claiming that conservatives have greatly exaggerated the number of natural differences between the sexes. They claim that because of sexual socialization, differences between women and men appear to be natural when they are not. They point to examples of women who have succeeded in nontraditional roles and to different cultures as evidence that the current sex roles are a matter of gender—not sex. They point to women such as Catherine the Great of Russia and Queen Elizabeth I of England as counter-examples to the view that women cannot succeed in politics. They point to matriarchal cultures as counter-examples to the view that women are naturally more passive than men. They point to the many successful women who have decided to pursue a career in business as counter-examples to the view that women naturally have more of a maternal need than men do. And they point to successful women mathematicians and philosophers to support their claim that women are not naturally inferior to men at these tasks. They argue that the fact that there are fewer women mathematicians and more women who raise children is a product of sexual socialization. Liberals go on to claim that if this sexual socialization were eliminated, we would gradually come to have equal numbers of househusbands and housewives, equal numbers of female and male mathematicians.

Of course, liberals do not claim that there are no natural differences between men and women. They recognize that women can bear children and men cannot, women can nurse children and men cannot. They also acknowledge that men are physically stronger than women and women are more physically flexible than men. But liberals claim that these differences, while natural, are irrelevant in a modern society. For example, they claim that whether a person can bear children or not is irrelevant to the question of whether they would be a good mathematician or not. They think that the fact that one can nurse children is, given the availability of baby bottles, irrelevant to the question of whether one will be good at raising children.

Liberals also argue that even if there were natural and relevant differences between women and men, there would be no need for sexual socialization to reenforce them. For example, if women really were naturally worse at math than men, then women would not do as well as men on math tests graded by professors who did not know whether they were grading a man's or a woman's test. Sexual socialization is redundant if there really are natural and relevant differences between the sexes. Liberals acknowledge that women do not currently do as well as men on math and other tests. But they think that this is the result of the sexual socialization of women and those who grade the tests.

Liberals and Sexual Tendencies

Liberals also point out that even if conservatives are right and there are great many relevant and natural differences between men and women, these differences are only tendencies. For example, it is true that men tend to be physically stronger than women. But it is not true that every man is stronger than every woman. Some women can bench-press more than some men. Even if there is a general tendency for women to be better at raising children than men are, there are some men who are better at it than some women. Therefore, liberals argue, socializing to reenforce these natural sexual tendencies will lead to those women who are bad at raising children doing it anyway, and to those men who are good at raising children doing something else.

At this point the liberals turn the conservatives' arguments from efficiency and frustration back against them. They argue that sexual socialization to reenforce natural sexual tendencies will be inefficient because it will cause the people who are exceptions to the natural tendency to do jobs for which they are not naturally suited. Liberals also argue that reenforcing natural tendencies will make those people who are exceptions to the tendencies feel frustrated, inadequate, or weird. If women are socialized to think that women are good at and ought to raise children, then those women who are exceptions to the natural tendency will feel frustrated if they try to raise children. If, on the other hand, these women decided to go against sex roles, do what they are naturally good at, and pursue a career instead of having children, then they are likely to feel that they are unfeminine, inadequate, or weird.

The Argument from Efficiency

Liberals think that the conservatives' argument from efficiency is flawed because it relies on the claim that there are natural and relevant differences between men and women. They then go on to make an efficiency argument of their own. They argue that since there are no differences between the sexes that are both natural and relevant, it is inefficient to waste the talents of half the population. Since women are naturally as good at everything as men, socializing them to do only a few things and to be subordinate to men deprives society of all the good ideas women would have if they were free to choose to do whatever they wished.

Liberals and the Ideal Society

Most liberals think that the ideal society is a sexually diverse one. Recall that a sexually diverse society is one in which people care about the differences between men and women, but, rather than one sex being subordinate to the other, everyone regards the differences between the sexes as something to be celebrated. These liberals think that since there are no relevant natural differences between men and women, both sexes should be completely free to choose whatever sort of life they wish. Of course, different people will choose different sorts of lives. These liberals think that we should celebrate these differences.

For example, these liberals note that women tend to have higher voices than men. They will also point out that there are exceptions to this rule. They think that both men and women ought to be free to develop their singing voices as they wish without any pressure from society to sing higher if they are women or lower if they are men. These liberals then argue that we might notice that more women are in the soprano section of the chorus while more men are in the bass section. But, while there is a natural difference between men and women, this difference is not relevant to the question of who sings better. Neither higher nor lower voices are better than the other. But the combination and interplay of high and low voices is beautiful. The difference between high and low voices is something to be celebrated.

Other liberals draw a different conclusion concerning the ideal society from their view that there are no natural and relevant differences between the sexes. They argue if there are no natural and relevant differences between the sexes, then we ought not to care whether a person is a man or a woman. Any difference that currently exists between women and men is either an example of sexual socialization (in which case we ought to work to eliminate it) or is irrelevant (in which case there is no reason to notice it). These liberals think that the ideal society is sexually blind, a society in which people are indifferent to the sex of others.

Problems with the Liberal View

There are two main problems with the liberal view. Some attack the view because they think that it has not been effective in reducing sexism. These critics point out that the liberal view has been dominant for the last twenty years and women still earn less than men in the same job, still are socialized to be subordinate to men, still face barriers to advancement in business, and still are underrepresented in politics. Liberals respond that twenty years is not very long to remove the effects of a conservative view that was dominant for at least 2,000 years.

Another problem with the liberal view is that it seems implausible to claim that there are absolutely no natural and relevant differences between men and women. Conservatives and others argue that liberals have not adequately demonstrated that things like the fact that women can become pregnant and men cannot is either nonnatural or irrelevant. This criticism is the starting point for two other views on sexism—the progressive view and the radical view.

THE PROGRESSIVE VIEW

The progressive view is of very recent origin. It was the publication in 1982 of Carol Gilligan's *In a Different Voice* that caused many to see that the liberal view was not the only alternative to the conservative view. Progressives agree with conservatives about one fundamental thing—that there are relevant and natural differences between the sexes. So, like conservatives, they reject the second premise of the revised argument for equal treatment.

Progressives and conservatives often point to different features as natural and relevant differences. For example, progressives do not usually argue that women are naturally worse at math or that they are naturally more passive. Rather, they point out that women can become pregnant and men cannot. Progressives think that this simple fact has important ramifications. For example, if women and men are to have equal career opportunities, then the fact that women can get pregnant and men cannot means that women and men will need to have different medical-leave policies. Progressives also point out that the fact that men tend to be physically stronger than women means that when a man and a women quarrel, women will tend to lose physical battles and so find the possibility of physical violence more threatening than men will. Men will therefore tend to use or threaten physical violence more often than women will.

To take a more positive example, progressives argue that it is natural and relevant that women can experience childbirth and men cannot. Progressives argue that experiencing (or even the possibility of experiencing) childbirth tends to make women more connected to others than men are. They think that because women have the possibility of experiencing a physical connection between two people, women tend to be more appreciative of all the nonphysical connections between people. Progressives think that women will be more likely to see and appreciate the importance of the emotional connections between people. They also think that women are more inclined to see the fact that people require help from others if they are to obtain the things (for example, food, clothing, and shelter) necessary to live.

While progressives agree with conservatives that there are some natural and relevant differences between men and women, they disagree strongly with the conservative claim that these differences imply that society ought to be sexually stratified, with women subordinate to men. Rather, they support sexual diversity as a societal ideal. They think that there are natural differences between men and women, but we must not use these differences to justify the oppression of women. Instead, as some liberals do, they think that we should appreciate the differences between the sexes without letting one sex dominate the other. The different strengths and weaknesses of women and men, like the different voices in a chorus, ought to be combined to form the best society.

Sex Roles and Sex Correlations

Progressives frequently distinguish sex correlations from sex roles. Recall that sex roles are career and life-style patterns which, because of sexual socialization, are associated predominantly with men or with women. Progressives, like liberals, object to sex roles. But they and those liberals who support a sexually diverse society do not object to sex correlations. Even if, as progressives hope, all sexual socialization and so all sex roles are eliminated, if there are natural differences between the sexes, then it may be the case that more women than men will be good at some tasks, and more men than women will be good at other tasks. For example, women tend to have a lower center of gravity than men. Having a lower center of gravity makes one better on the balance beam. This means that even if there is no sexual socialization and all judging of balance-beam competitions is perfectly unbiased, women will still tend to do better than men. In this case, doing well on the balance beam is a sex correlation—not a sex role. Sex correlations are differences in the number of a particular sex that succeed at a particular task that are the result of natural differences between the sexes—not sexual socialization. Sex roles are the product of gender, while sex correlations are the product of sex. Progressives think that there is nothing wrong with sex correlations. In other words, they think that there is nothing wrong with differences between men and women as long as the differences in the numbers of women and men who do well at a particular task are exclusively the product of natural differences and not the product of either sexual socialization or biased judging.

Problems with the Progressive View

Liberals attack the progressive view on the same grounds that they attacked the conservative view. Both conservatives and progressives think that there are natural and relevant differences between the sexes, and liberals deny this. Another problem with the progressive view is that since progressives think that a sexually diverse society is the ideal one, they also think that there is nothing wrong with sex correlations. Some argue that while the distinction between sex roles and sex correlations is clear in theory, it is very difficult to make in practice. It is very hard to tell whether a particular difference in the performance of women and men is the result of sexual socialization or the result of natural differences. Given this difficulty, some worry that allowing sex correlations will allow sex roles to continue to exist. For example, some worry that allowing sex correlations like those discussed in the balance-beam case will perpetuate stereotypes of women and so help maintain sex roles—such as the role of raising children. This objection is most forcefully made by those who hold the radical view.

THE RADICAL VIEW

Radicals, like progressives and conservatives, think that there are natural and relevant differences between the sexes. They tend to point to the same differences that progressives do. Radicals differ with progressives in that they do not see the natural and relevant differences between men and women in a positive light. Progressives think that there are natural and relevant differences between the sexes and that these differences ought to be celebrated. But radicals think women are enslaved by their sex.

Radicals emphasize the harmful effects of the natural differences between men and women. For example, they point to the fact that women can become pregnant and men cannot and argue that being pregnant is a debilitating condition. It makes one sick, unable to run, and prone to dramatic mood swings. It also causes an extraordinarily painful experience—childbirth. Radicals make similar arguments about women's inferior physical strength and inability to run as fast as men. So radicals agree with conservatives that women are naturally inferior to men.

But while conservatives and progressives think that natural and relevant differences ought to be respected, radicals argue that just because something is natural does not mean that we ought to respect it. They point out that people do all sorts of things which are not natural to correct or improve on nature. For example, houses are not natural. We are born unprotected from the elements. But that is no reason to remain unprotected. We can improve on nature by building houses. Radicals do not hold that everything that is unnatural should be encouraged. They acknowledge that interferences with nature can be wrong. For example, using powerful chemicals to kill mosquitoes might be wrong because of its effect on the ecosystem. Radicals think that we must evaluate each interference with nature individually without presuming either that interferences with nature are a good or a bad idea. Some interferences with nature are good (for example, houses), and some are bad (for example, powerful chemicals to kill mosquitoes).

Radicals think that women are naturally inferior to men and that we should use our technology to remove the natural disabilities of women. So they support using reproductive technology to free women from the necessity of bearing children. They support using technology so that the natural weakness and slowness of women will not prevent them from entering any profession. Radicals acknowledge that we do not currently have the technology to remove all the bad effects of being a woman. But they think that we have made some progress with things like contraceptives and can hope to make more in the future. For example, they think one day science will enable people to have children without gestation in a woman. Radicals think that when this is possible and common, women will be free from a disability, pregnancy. The radical view is indeed radical, for it would have us eliminate the family as we know it. Mother and father would be replaced by any number of parents who might be of any sex.

Radicals, like liberals and progressives, object to sex roles. But unlike progressives, they also object to sex correlations. As we saw above, some think that allowing sex correlations will allow sex roles to continue to exist. So radicals think that the ideal society will be sexually blind. Recall that in a sexually blind society no one cares about the sex of others. Radicals think it will require lots of technological advances before such a society is possible and they, like progressives and liberals, think sexual socialization and the sex roles that go with it will be hard to eliminate. But they think that this is the ideal we should be striving to reach.

Problems with the Radical View

As is to be expected with any view called "the radical view," many people have raised strenuous objections. Many reject the radical view that the ideal society is sex-blind. They point out that in a sex-blind society everyone is bisexual. If no one cares about the sex of their romantic partners, then everyone is bisexual. Some object to this view because they think that bisexuality and homosexuality are immoral. Others object to the view because, while they do not think bisexuality is immoral, they do not think homosexuality or heterosexuality is immoral either. These people think that no matter what sex one is, there is nothing wrong with choosing a partner of either sex.

Another problem with the radical view relates to their rejection of sex correlations. To eliminate sex correlations, some point out, one would have to eliminate all activities that one sex is better at than the other. To return to an example discussed above, one would have to get rid of balance-beam competitions because, given their lower center of gravity, women will tend to be better at this than men. More important, bearing children is a sex-correlated activity because only women can do it. To eliminate all sex-correlated activities would eliminate many of the activities many women and men find intensely satisfying. Many women report that childbirth, though painful, is one of the most wonderful experiences of their lives. To eliminate sex-correlated activities would be to deprive people of these satisfying experiences.

Another objection to the radical view focuses on the link between natural and morally right. This objection admits that there is no necessary connection between something being natural and its being right or wrong. But, the objection continues, whether something is natural or not may have an indirect effect on whether it is right or not because natural differences may cause people to be happy in certain sorts of societies and unhappy in others. Whether people are happy in a certain sort of society is certainly relevant to the question of whether that sort of society is the ideal one. So, objectors point out, the fact that people want to go through the experience of having children the old-fashioned way is a strike against the radical view's contention that the ideal society is sex blind. In a sex blind society people might be unhappy because they could not have children in this way.

SEX AND OTHER DIFFERENCES

Throughout this chapter we have been speaking as if there were features common to all men and features common to all women. We have ignored the fact that the people who are women and men are not just women and men. In other words, we have ignored the differences within the sexes in focusing on the differences between the sexes. But, of course, all women are not alike in every way. Some women are black, some are white, and some are Asian. Some women are heterosexual, some are homosexual, and some are bisexual. Some women are poor, while others are rich. Some have physical disabilities, while others do not. The same is true of men.

Sexual inequality may be experienced differently by women of different races, sexual orientations, classes, or abilities. A black woman is doubly disadvantaged in our society. She is disadvantaged because of her race and because of her sex. Methods that might be effective against sexism directed at white women might be ineffective against sexism directed at black women. For example, designing a computer training course to include examples and issues of interest to white middle-class women may be effective in getting more white middle-class women to work in this area. But examples and issues of interest to white middle-class women may not be of interest to working-class black women, and so the redesigned course may not be effective in encouraging working-class black women to enter this profession. The intellectual separation of sex, race, sexual orientation, class, and ability into different chapters of books must not lead us to overlook the fact that, because real people embody all these characteristics at once, these factors interact in subtle and complex ways.

An act, practice, or attitude is sexist when it creates unjustified differences between the sexes or exploits irrelevant differences between the sexes. The various views about sexism often turn on different theories of what differences are unjustified and irrelevant. There is broad agreement that such things as denying women the right to vote are sexist. There is also a great deal of disagreement over whether such things as encouraging girls to study home economics and heterosexuality are sexist.

Sex is very important in our society. We all announce our sex in the way we dress, walk, and talk. We treat our male and female friends differently. Many people feel that women are oppressed by our society. They point to the fact that women earn less money than men, that women's clothing is not as practical as men's, that women are more frequently the victims of physical violence, and that there are fewer women than men in political offices and corporate board rooms.

There is a great deal of debate about the source of these differences. Some think that they are the result of natural differences between the sexes, while others think that they are the product of sexual socialization. The term "sex" is used to refer to differences between men and women that are the result of natural biological differences, and the term "gender" is used to refer to differences between men and women that are the result of sexual socialization. There is also a great deal of debate about what a nonsexist society would be like. Some think it would be sexually stratified, while others think it would be sexually blind, and still others think it would be sexually diverse.

The central argument of the sexism debate is the argument for equal treatment. This argument begins with the premise that unless there is a rel-

evant and natural difference between two groups of people, these groups ought to be treated in the same way. The second premise of the argument is that there are no natural and relevant differences between women and men. The conclusion is that women and men ought to be treated in the same way.

There are four main positions in the sexism debate: the conservative view, the liberal view, the progressive view, and the radical view. Conservatives, progressives, and radicals all agree that there are natural and relevant differences between the sexes, while liberals think that there are none. Conservatives think that the natural differences between men and women imply that women ought to be subordinate to men. They support a sexually stratified society. Progressives think that we ought to acknowledge the differences between the sexes but that neither sex should be subordinate to the other. They support a sexually diverse society. Radicals think that the natural differences between men and women harm women, and therefore we must use technology and change society to eliminate these differences. They support a sexually blind society. Liberals, holding to the view that there are no natural and relevant differences between the sexes, sometimes support a sexually diverse society and sometimes support a sexually blind one.

Selected Readings

de Beauvoir, Simone. *The Second Sex* (several good translations).

English, Jane. *Sex Equality*. Englewood Cliffs, NJ: Prentice-Hall, 1978.

Frye, Marilyn. *The Politics of Reality*. Trumansburg, NY: The Crossing Press, 1983.

Gilligan, Carol. *In a Different Voice*. Cambridge, MA: Harvard University Press, 1982.

Mill, John Stuart. *The Subjection of Women* (several editions are available).

Schlafly, Phyllis. *The Power of the Positive Woman*. New Rochelle, NY: Arlington House, 1977.

10

Racism and Affirmative Action

Our nation has a long history of racism. Slavery was legal and an integral part of the economy until 1868, and it is only thirty years since racial segregation was made illegal. This racism has had a profound effect on our society and on the way we as individuals see members of other races. Overt racism is now almost universally condemned. There are very few who continue to argue that blacks are naturally inferior to whites. But there remains a great deal of debate over how racist our society currently is, and over how we ought to respond to the effects of past and current racism.

WHAT IS RACISM?

An act, practice, or attitude is racist when it creates unjustified differences between races or exploits irrelevant differences between races. People are racist when they knowingly perform a racist act, support a racist practice, or have a racist attitude. Racism is the view that racist acts, practices, and attitudes ought to be encouraged. One can perform a racist act, support a racist practice, or have a racist attitude without knowing that the act, practice, or attitude is racist. In that case, one might not be racist. The parallels between the definition of racism and the definition of sexism are obvious (see chapter 9). The definition of racism, like the definition of sexism, contains the pejorative terms "unjustified" and "irrelevant," so calling an act, practice, or attitude racist implies that it is immoral. Racist acts, like sexist acts, are immoral because they harm people. The physical harms of practices like slavery are obvious. But pervasive everyday slights, such as teachers not calling on members of a certain race, or people giving members of a certain race disdainful looks, may damage the self-confidence of those who are the object of these more subtle forms of racism. The effects of subtle racism can be very powerful.

The phrases "creates unjustified differences" and "exploits irrelevant differences" have the same sense in the definition of racism that they have in the definition of sexism. The subtle slights mentioned above may cause the members of one race to have less self-confidence than the members of another race, even though there is no good reason, no justification, for this difference in self-confidence. If I refused to hire a black person to teach philosophy because he is black, I would be exploiting an irrelevant difference. The color of one's skin is not relevant to the job of teaching philosophy.

In this country bringing up the issue of racism immediately leads people to think of whites and blacks. But this is only one form of racism. Even in this country there has been and continues to be racism against Asians, Native Americans, and Hispanics. In other countries, such as Japan, whites are the focus of racist beliefs. In Africa, racism exists between different tribal groups. In this chapter we will focus on the racism of whites against blacks. Applying conclusions based on the analysis of this example of racism to other examples of racism must be done with care.

Three Types of Racism

We can distinguish three different types of racism: overt racism, covert racism, and unintentional racism. Overt racism occurs when a racist act, practice, or attitude explicitly uses race. Segregation of schools as it existed in the South was an example of overt racism. Laws stated explicitly that blacks had to go to certain schools and not others. Covert racism occurs when an act, practice, or attitude does not explicitly use race but is nevertheless designed with the intent to create unjustified differences between the races or to exploit irrelevant differences between the races. When overt school segregation became illegal, many cities attempted to enact laws that were covertly racist. For example, they drew school district lines so that all blacks were in one district and all whites were in another. Unintentional racism occurs when an act, practice, or attitude has the effect of creating unjustified differences between the races or of exploiting irrelevant differences between the races but the people involved in the act, practice, or attitude do not intend (or perhaps even realize) this effect. In a town with racially divided housing patterns, drawing school district lines to maximize the number of children who can walk to school might have the unintended effect of creating segregated schools.

PARALLELS BETWEEN RACISM AND SEXISM

One can go through a debate over racism that is almost exactly parallel to the debate over sexism. Here we will do this briefly and presuppose familiarity with chapter 9.

Four Questions About Racism

Just as there are four related but distinct questions concerning sexism, there are four parallel questions concerning racism. The answers to these questions are clearer in the case of racism than they are in the case of sexism.

WHAT IS THE PLACE OF RACE IN OUR SOCIETY?

Race, like sex, is important in our society. We notice and care about the race of those around us. This can be seen in our different reactions to people depending on their race. Some whites treat blacks as inferior beings. Other whites are nervous around blacks either because they feel some sort of guilt for past and current racism or because they are afraid of blacks. Race, like sex, disadvantages some and gives advantages to others.

But while both race and sex are important in our society, they are not important in the same way. For example, many people seek a special sort of approval from members of one sex that they do not seek from the other sex. Heterosexual men seek the approval of women—partly because women are female. But whites do not usually seek the approval of blacks in this way. Many people of both sexes think that a certain sort of segregation of the sexes is appropriate. Few object to bathrooms segregated by sex. But most people object to bathrooms segregated by race. The differences between the place of race and sex in our society are many and complex.

HOW DID RACE COME TO HAVE THIS PLACE IN OUR SOCIETY?

Some used to argue that the place of blacks in our society was determined by natural differences between the races. They argued that blacks were naturally inferior to whites. This view is false. Race has the place it does in our society because of society. The socioeconomic positions and attitudes of blacks and whites have been formed by slavery, the Civil War, legal and overt racism, differences between European cultures and African cultures, and many other sociological factors.

WHAT WOULD A NONRACIST SOCIETY BE LIKE?

As with sexism, there are three possibilities: racially stratified, racially blind, and racially diverse. In a racially stratified society people care about the differences between the races, and one race occupies a place subordinate to the other. There was a time when people defended this ideal of society, but hardly anyone does today. In a racially blind society people are indifferent to the race of others. In a racially diverse society people care about the differences between the races but no race occupies a subordinate place. Almost everyone agrees that the ideal society would be racially blind.

Failing to distinguish racial blindness from cultural blindness can cause confusion. Races are sometimes associated with cultures. In our society most blacks belong to a common culture. But races are not necessarily correlated with cultures. Africa shows us that not all blacks are members of the same culture. Almost everyone thinks that the ideal society is racially blind but culturally diverse. A culturally diverse society is one in which people care about the differences between cultures but no culture occupies a subordinate place. Sometimes people object to a racially blind society on the grounds that this sort of society does not allow cultural differences. But a racially blind society does allow for cultural diversity.

IF OUR SOCIETY IS RACIST NOW, WHAT OUGHT WE DO TO ELIMINATE THIS RACISM?

As we noted when discussing sexism, there are many ways to change a society. We could make certain behaviors illegal, give tax incentives, or run ad campaigns. Also, as before, the methods one favors will be determined by one's views on the effectiveness of the various methods and the seriousness of racial problems. One method of changing society has generated a great deal of debate and will be the focus of this chapter—affirmative action.

The Argument for Equal Treatment as Applied to Race   Arguments concerning racism, like arguments concerning sexism, begin with the claim that equals ought to be treated equally. As before, "to be treated equally" means to be treated in the same way. And, as before, the claim does not tell us much unless combined with a theory of when people are equals—a theory about relevant differences. The basic argument for equal treatment with respect to race combines the claim that equals ought to be treated equally with the claim that there are no relevant differences between races.

1) Unless there is a relevant difference between two groups of people, they ought to be treated in the same way.

2) There are no relevant differences between people of different races.

3) Therefore, people of different races ought to be treated in the same way.

The basic argument for equal treatment of the races has the same problem that the basic argument for equal treatment of the sexes does—whether one is black or white, like whether one is a man or a woman, is very important in our society. If one were hiring a construction-crew chief and there were a long history of only whites doing the job, it might very well be that many whites on the construction site would not work as well if their boss were black. If the attitudes of the whites are racist, then to allow these attitudes to count as a relevant difference allows racist attitudes to justify a racist practice. Moreover, most think that by nature blacks are able to be just as good crew chiefs as whites. Therefore, revision of the basic argument seems necessary.

1) Unless there is a relevant natural difference between two groups of people, they ought to be treated in the same way.

2) There are no relevant natural differences between people of different races.

3) Therefore, people of different races ought to be treated in the same way.

The revised argument again draws the distinction between natural and nonnatural differences; and, as before, "natural" refers to biological differences, while "nonnatural" refers to those differences that are a product of society.

Four Views on Racism

It is possible to be a racial conservative, a racial progressive, a racial radical, or racial liberal. A racial conservative is someone who thinks that there are relevant natural differences between races and that these differences imply that some races are naturally inferior to others. A racial progressive is one who thinks that there are relevant natural differences between races and that we ought to celebrate these differences. A racial radical is one who thinks that there are relevant natural differences between races and that we ought to use technology to eliminate these differences. A racial liberal is someone who thinks that there are no relevant natural differences between races. For most of human history racial conservativism was the dominant view. This is the view upon which American slavery was based. But racial liberalism is clearly correct. There are no relevant natural differences between races. The natural differences between races, such as eye shape and skin tone, are not relevant when it comes to social stratification.

WHAT IS AFFIRMATIVE ACTION?

Affirmative action programs are programs that explicitly use race in hiring and admissions in order to reduce the effect of past and current racism. There are three features of affirmative action that need to be emphasized. First, to be an affirmative-action program, the purpose of the program must be to reduce the effects of racism—not increase the income and power of the racial majority. Second, rather than being based on the belief that one race is superior to another, affirmative action is based on the belief that explicit use of race in hiring and admissions is the best way to change society so that it reflects the fact that no race is superior to any other. Third, affirmative action is not imposed by a dominant social group on a subordinate one. It is not imposed by socially dominant blacks on socially subordinate whites.

These three features of affirmative action make the term "reverse discrimination" misleading. As we shall see, affirmative action does indeed raise serious moral problems. But the term "reverse discrimination" suggests that the only difference between affirmative-action programs and racism against blacks is that the racial positions are reversed. This is inaccurate. Reverse discrimination would be an accurate term to use if blacks become socially dominant in our society and, because of a belief that blacks were superior to whites, started programs that explicitly used race in hiring and admissions in order to keep whites in a socially inferior position. There is no harm in using the term "reverse discrimination" if we keep reminding ourselves of its misleading connotations. But perhaps it is safer to avoid the term.

Three Types of Affirmative Action

There are three types or levels of affirmative action. The first type of affirmative action occurs when a school or firm makes active efforts to find members of one race and encourage them to apply for open positions. For example, a firm that has historically hired few blacks might advertise job openings in magazines that circulate widely in the black community. The second type of affirmative action occurs when a school or firm considers all applicants from all races for all positions but gives a certain amount of preference to applicants of a certain race. For example, suppose that a school uses a numerical scale to rank applicants. It assigns a certain number of points to tests scores, interview performance, and so forth. The affirmative-action program would involve giving a certain number of points to black applicants. The amount of preference they give might vary. The lowest possible form of preference would be to use race only to break ties. In theory, the preference could be so strong that all black applicants were guaranteed admission. The third type of affirmative action occurs when a school or firm sets aside a certain number of positions for members of a certain race. This type of affirmative action is a quota system. For example, if a firm reserves 20 percent of jobs for blacks, then they have a quota affirmative-action program.

The second and third types of affirmative action are usually called "preferential treatment programs" to distinguish them from the first type of affirmative action. Very few people object to the first type of affirmative action and we will not consider it further. Hereafter "affirmative action" will refer, as it usually does in popular debate, to preferential treatment programs. Some people think that there is no important difference between the two different sorts of preferential treatment programs, while others think there is. Those who argue that there is no important difference point out that the effects are the same. Given statistical data, it is easy to set the preference level in the second type of affirmative-action program to admit or hire a predetermined number of people of a certain race. If one does not get the number of blacks one wants, one simply raises the number of points assigned to blacks. Those who argue that there is an important difference between the second and third types of affirmative action think that while the effect may be the same, the two types of programs are procedurally different. In the second type of program, each applicant is compared individually to all other applicants. In the third type of program, members of the various races are only compared against other members of their race. Those who defend the second type of affirmative action but object to the third think that this procedural difference is important.

Active Nondiscrimination

Active nondiscrimination programs are another possible way to make our society less racist. Active nondiscrimination programs are programs that do not use race explicitly in hiring and admissions, but instead make an active effort to: 1. ensure that all current hiring and admissions is completely race blind; 2. find those who perform racist acts; and 3. punish these people severely. A college that had an active nondiscrimination program might ensure that those who make admissions decisions do not know the race of applicants, check the grading of professors to ensure that it is not racist, and punish racist professors severely.

THE ARGUMENT AGAINST AFFIRMATIVE ACTION

The principal argument against affirmative action is simple and powerful—it is the revised argument for equal treatment. Affirmative-action programs treat different races differently. According to the revised argument for equal treatment, treating two groups of people differently is wrong unless there is a relevant natural difference between them. As we noted above, there seems to be no relevant natural differences between people of different races. Therefore, they ought to be treated in the same way, and affirmative action is wrong. The arguments in favor of affirmative action are attempts to show that despite this powerful case against affirmative action, it is morally required. There are two arguments for affirmative action: the argument from social utility, and the argument from compensation.

THE ARGUMENT FROM SOCIAL UTILITY

This argument is also simple. Our society is not now racially blind. Our society ought to be racially blind. Affirmative action is the best way to make our society racially blind. The best way to make society racially blind is to consider race for a while. This is no more paradoxical than the fact that adding boiling water to cold water will bring the water to room temperature faster than merely leaving the cold water to sit in a room. Active nondiscrimination will either not make our society racially blind, or will not do so fast enough. Therefore, our society ought to have affirmative-action programs.

Four Ways Affirmative Action Would Lead to a Racially Blind Society

First and most obviously, affirmative action will move minorities from the inferior social positions they now typically occupy to higher social positions. Affirmative action in law schools will create more black lawyers. Second, proponents of affirmative action argue that it will create role models for minority young people. When a black lawyer walks down the street and gets into a BMW, she sends a message to all the young black people who see her that they can succeed as she has. Third, affirmative action would improve services to minorities. For example, black doctors serve black people better than white doctors do. Blacks are more likely to go to and be forthright with a black doctor. Black doctors understand the social environment of blacks better and will therefore be able to treat black patients better than white doctors would. Finally, proponents of affirmative action argue that racial intolerance decreases when members of different races work together. They argue that racism is usually the product of ignorant stereotypes and that putting blacks and whites together causes them to see that these stereotypes are false. Since affirmative action will increase the interaction between races, it will contribute to the breakdown of racial stereotypes.

Objections to the Argument from Social Utility

No one denies that our society shows the effects of our racist history. But many argue that affirmative action is not the best way to make society racially blind.

AFFIRMATIVE ACTION IS INEFFICIENT

Some who object to affirmative action argue on the grounds that it is inefficient. They point out that if certain races are given preferential treatment in hiring and admissions, then some people who are not the best qualified for jobs will receive them. A black person with slightly less mathematical training might be hired as an accountant over a white person with slightly more. This will mean that firms will not produce things as efficiently.

This objection seems to have a serious flaw. The argument from social utility claims to show that we have a moral obligation to have affirmative-action programs. Most people think that we ought to do morally obligatory acts even if they are inefficient. Installing pollution-control devices might be inefficient. But if installing these controls is morally obligatory (perhaps they are necessary to avoid poisoning people), then they ought to be installed whether they are efficient or not. So if affirmative action is morally obligatory, the fact that it would make society less efficient is not a good reason to oppose it.

AFFIRMATIVE ACTION WILL NOT LEAD TO A RACIALLY BLIND SOCIETY

Many argue that affirmative action will not make society racially blind. They have four reasons for thinking this.

Reinforces Stereotypes Those opposed to affirmative action argue that far from breaking down racial stereotypes, it actually encourages them. They argue that affirmative action will cause blacks to be placed in jobs for which they are not as well qualified as whites. Suppose a firm has an affirmative-action program and some of the blacks hired would not have been hired had it not been for the program. The blacks will be, on average, less well qualified for the jobs. Because of this, on average the blacks will not do as well as the whites. People who see this and do not know that the blacks were hired under an affirmative-action program might very well note that blacks are not performing the jobs as well as whites and mistakenly infer that blacks are naturally inferior to whites. Proponents of affirmative action respond that this objection only shows the need for educational programs to keep people from making this mistaken inference.

Harms Black People Opponents of affirmative action argue that these programs harm black people in three ways. First, they decrease blacks' job skills by reducing incentives for them to work hard and depriving them of the difficult work experiences that make people better workers. Opponents argue that blacks will not work as hard at school and on the job because they know that, because of affirmative-action programs, they will have an easier time getting into schools, getting jobs, and getting promotions. This will mean that their jobs skills will be inferior to those of white people. Opponents also argue that affirmative-action programs will lead white people, responding to the lower qualifications of black students and employees, to coddle blacks and encourage them to take easy courses and easy jobs. This deprives them of the difficult experiences necessary for acquiring good job skills. Proponents of affirmative action respond that blacks already have plenty of incentives and difficult experiences—more than white people do. The second harmful effect of affirmative action is the demoralizing of blacks. Suppose that black people are admitted to a difficult school under an affirmative-action program. They will be less qualified than the white people and will therefore be more likely to flunk out. This could greatly damage the self-confidence of these black people. The same effect could occur if firms hire black people for positions they are not qualified to fill. Finally, opponents of affirmative action argue that it harms blacks by leading them to doubt their own worth. Suppose that, under an affirmative-action program, a particular black person is hired at a law firm. This black person may never know if he was hired because he is the most qualified for the job or because he is black.

White Resentment   Opponents also argue that affirmative action will not lead to a racially blind society because it causes white people to resent black people. White people who do not get into schools or do not get certain jobs because of affirmative action programs may come to resent the blacks who do get these positions. This could lead to interracial tension and racial polarization. Proponents of affirmative action point out that the same was said of attempts to desegregate schools. Desegregation did in fact cause many whites to resent "uppity" blacks. These proponents argue that making society racially blind will obviously make those who benefit from racism unhappy. But this is no objection to affirmative action.

Benefits the Well Off   Finally, some think that affirmative action will not lead to a racially blind society because the benefits of the programs go to those members of the minority who need it the least. For example, affirmative-action programs at prestigious colleges do nothing for those blacks who drop out of high school. Rather, they benefit the daughters and sons of blacks who are already well off and have the resources to give their children a good education. Proponents of affirmative action respond that a comprehensive system of affirmative action will benefit all blacks. Having affirmative action only at prestigious colleges would primarily benefit well-off blacks. But if there are affirmative-action programs in all schools—elementary schools, high schools, community colleges, state universities, and private colleges—then all blacks will benefit.

THE POWER OF ACTIVE NONDISCRIMINATION

Opponents of affirmative action claim that active nondiscrimination is a better alternative. Because affirmative action has the problems just discussed, active nondiscrimination is more likely to make our society racially blind. They sometimes argue that real, active nondiscrimination has not been tried. Immediately after overt racism was made illegal, affirmative-action programs began. At the very least we ought to try active nondiscrimination programs before considering affirmative action.

Empirical Data

Proponents of affirmative action argue that the effects cited by its opponents either do not occur or are weaker than the effects they point out. Opponents of affirmative action argue that the effects cited by its proponents either do not occur or are weaker than the effects they point out. Both sides in the debate have spent a lot of time outlining *possible* positive and negative effects of affirmative action without citing the empirical studies that would seem to be necessary to determine what the total effect of the programs is. This is because very few of these studies have been done. It may be that we cannot evaluate the social utility argument until we have more information.

Social Utility and the Revised Argument for Equal Treatment

Whatever the effects of affirmative action, the argument from social utility has a crucial weakness. It does not respond to the case against affirmative action. Let us suppose that affirmative-action programs will lead to a racially blind society. Opponents of affirmative action still argue that these programs are wrong because they fail to treat equals equally. And many think that the revised argument for equal treatment is more powerful than the argument from social utility. This is usually expressed by saying that even if affirmative action would lead to a racially blind society, it would do so by violating a right to equal treatment that follows from the revised argument for equal treatment. They then argue that we cannot violate rights even to achieve worthwhile social goals. This powerful criticism of the argument from social utility is the reason that many proponents of affirmative action argue for their view using another argument—the argument from compensation.

THE ARGUMENT FROM COMPENSATION

Karen steals Juan's CD player. It seems that we ought to make Karen compensate Juan by returning the CD player (or giving him its cash value if it is no longer possible to return the CD player) and that we ought to punish her for the theft. The following principle seems plausible:

People who do immoral actions ought to be punished and made to compensate those hurt by these actions.

Let us call this the direct-compensation principle. Two points about the principle need to emphasized. First, the principle requires that the person compensated be the person who was harmed by the immoral action. Karen ought to compensate Juan and no one else. Second, the principle requires that the person who does the compensating be the person who performed the immoral action. Karen, and no one else, ought to compensate Juan.

But the revised argument for equal treatment implies that the direct-compensation principle is false. Recall that the first premise of the revised argument for equal treatment is:

Unless there is a relevant natural difference between two groups of people, they ought to be treated in the same way.

Notice further that there is no natural relevant difference between Karen and some other person—Aiju—who had nothing to do with the theft of Juan's CD player. So the revised argument for equal treatment implies that we ought to treat Karen and Aiju in the same way. This clearly seems mistaken.

The Modified Argument for Equal Treatment

The problem is that while there are no relevant *natural* differences between Karen and Aiju, there clearly is a relevant difference between them—Karen stole Juan's CD player and Aiju did not. The revised argument for equal treatment clearly needs to be modified to allow for holding people accountable for their actions. The example of Karen, Juan, and Aiju suggests the following modification of the first premise of the revised argument for equal treatment:

Unless there is (a) a relevant natural difference between two groups of people or (b) a relevant difference created by the actions of one of these groups, they ought to be treated in the same way.

The relevant difference between Karen and Aiju is not natural; rather, it is created by Karen's actions—stealing Juan's CD player. Let us refer to the latest argument for equal treatment as the modified argument for equal treatment.

The direct-compensation principle and the modified argument for equal treatment suggest an argument for affirmative action. Many proponents of affirmative action point out that white people have done a great many wrongs to black people. Among many other things, white people have enslaved black people, segregated them into unequal facilities, and refused to let them have certain jobs. According to the direct-compensation principle, white people ought to compensate the black people who were harmed by these immoral actions. Proponents of affirmative action argue that it is the best way for white people to compensate black people.

Making white people compensate black people through affirmative-action programs does not violate the modified argument for equal treatment because this argument does not require us to treat people who have acted differently in the same way. White people enslaved black people, but black people did not enslave white people, so white people have acted differently than black people. Therefore, treating white people differently than black people does not violate the modified argument for equal treatment. Race is not usually relevant, but when it is *white* people who have done immoral things to *black* people, then race is relevant.

The direct-compensation argument for affirmative action is clearly flawed. The problem stems from the compensation principle. As we noted, this principle requires that the person who does the compensating be the person who performed the immoral action. But the white people who wronged black people are not the white people hurt by affirmative action. The direct-compensation argument might justify a program in which those who voted for and supported segregation compensated black people. But affirmative action hurts young white people who may not have even been alive when overt racism was legal and supported by many white people. Making young white people compensate black people seems parallel to making Aiju compensate Juan for the loss of his CD player.

Indirect Compensation

In response to this problem, proponents of affirmative action have turned to a slightly different version of the argument from compensation. Karen gives Juan's CD player to John as a birthday present. John is unaware that he is receiving stolen goods. If he discovers that the CD player is stolen, he ought to return it. This example indicates that:

> People who benefit from the immoral actions of others ought to compensate those hurt by these actions.

This principle is a supplement to, not a revision of, the direct-compensation principle. The compensation principle is accurate as it stands. Let us call this principle the indirect-compensation principle.

This new principle suggests a modification of the compensation argument for affirmative action. White people in the past performed a great many immoral actions that damaged blacks. Proponents of affirmative action argue that today's white people continue to benefit from these immoral actions and that today's black people continue to be hurt by them. They then argue that, just as John ought to give the CD player back to Juan (even though John did nothing wrong), today's white people ought to give economic and social resources back to today's black people (even if today's white people have done nothing wrong). They argue that the best way to give these economic and social resources back is through affirmative-action programs.

Proponents of affirmative action argue that today's white people receive two primary benefits from the past immoral actions of white people. The first is the extra economic resources that they currently have and would not have if their ancestors had not exploited black people. The great-grandsons and great-granddaughters of people who amassed resources because they enslaved blacks or hired black people at lower wages than white people continue to benefit from those resources, just as today's Rockefellers continue to benefit from the fortune amassed by earlier Rockefellers. The second, and probably greater, continuing benefit that proponents of affirmative action point to is the reduced competition for coveted social positions. They argue that today's white people benefit from past racism because past racism causes today's black people to start out with fewer socioeconomic resources and less self-confidence than they would have had in the absence of racism. Therefore, they do not compete with white people for coveted social positions as much as they would if there had been no racism.

Objections to the Argument from Compensation

While the indirect-compensation argument for affirmative action seems to resolve the objections raised against the direct-compensation argument, it has been subject to a number of attacks.

THE MODIFIED ARGUMENT FOR EQUAL TREATMENT

The indirect-compensation argument seems to violate the modified argument for equal treatment. Recall that the first premise of this argument is:

Unless there is (a) a relevant natural difference between two groups of people or (b) a relevant difference created by the actions of one of these groups, they ought to be treated in the same way.

While there is a relevant difference between past whites and past blacks created by the actions of past whites, there is no relevant difference between today's whites and today's blacks created by the actions of today's whites or today's blacks. Between today's whites and today's blacks, there is neither a relevant natural difference nor a relevant difference created by the actions of today's whites or the actions of today's blacks. So, opponents of affirmative action argue, while it would be fine to treat past whites differently than past blacks, it is wrong to treat today's whites differently than today's blacks.

Proponents of affirmative action might then point out that the modified argument for equal treatment also implies that we ought not treat John differently than someone else—Brian—who did not receive Juan's CD player. Between John and Brian there is neither a relevant natural difference nor a relevant difference created by the actions of John or Brian. It seems clear that we ought to be able to treat John differently than Brian—we ought to make John compensate Juan, but it would be wrong to make Brian compensate Juan. It would appear that the modified argument for equal treatment requires refinement.

But it is not clear what sort of refinement is required. One might suggest:

Unless there is (a) a relevant natural difference between two groups of people or (b) a relevant difference created by the actions of people, they ought to be treated in the same way.

Here the requirement that the relevant difference be created by the actions of one of the two groups of people being compared is dropped. This would allow us to treat John and Brian differently. While there is no relevant difference between them created by their actions, there is a relevant difference between them created by the actions of another person—Karen gave the CD player to John, not to Brian.

But this refinement seems to have the same problem as the basic argument for equal treatment. Recall the construction-crew chief example. If one were hiring a construction-crew chief and there were a long history of only whites doing the job, it might very well be that many whites on the construction site would not work as well if their boss were black. This is a relevant difference between black and white potential crew chiefs created by the actions of other persons—the prejudiced actions of white construction workers. But, as we saw before, if one thinks that the attitudes of the whites are racist, then to allow the actions that stem from these attitudes to count as a relevant difference allows racist attitudes to justify a racist practice.

It seems clear that the modified argument for equal treatment requires further refinement. It also seems clear that this refinement ought to allow us to treat John and Brian differently, but not allow the owner of the construction company to treat black and white potential crew chiefs differently. It is not clear how to refine the argument to make this distinction.

INFINITE DURATION

Some argue that if one accepts the argument from indirect compensation, then one is committed to affirmative action programs existing forever. If the children of yesterday's white people must compensate the children of yesterday's black people, then the children of today's black people will have to compensate the children of today's white people for the benefits they receive because of today's affirmative-action programs. And, the objection continues, this process will never end, as each generation ought to transfer back the benefits they received from the previous generation.

This argument is clearly flawed. John ought to give the CD player back to Juan. For a compensation process of infinite duration to begin, it would have to be the case that Juan ought to compensate John for the loss of the CD player. But that does not seem to be true. John ought to compensate

Juan, and the compensating ends there. According to the indirect-compensation principle, people who benefit from the *immoral* actions of others ought to compensate those hurt by these actions. But, if the indirect-compensation argument is correct, compensating black people for damages done by earlier white people is not an immoral action. Therefore, black people are not benefiting from an immoral act, and so they owe no compensation.

AFFIRMATIVE ACTION REQUIRED FOR ALL ETHNIC GROUPS

Opponents of affirmative action argue that if the indirect-compensation argument for affirmative action is a good argument, it implies that affirmative-action programs are required for all ethnic groups that have been the object of racism in our society. They then point out that groups such as the Irish, the French, the Italians, and the Chinese were at one time the object of racism. So, they argue, the consistent defender of affirmative action must work for affirmative action for these groups. They take this to be ridiculous.

Proponents of affirmative action respond in three ways. First, they argue that the oppression directed at the Irish was nothing like the oppression directed at blacks. Blacks were held in slavery and killed by the millions. Blacks were subject to massive overt legal racism and the Irish were not. Second, they point out that the indirect-compensation argument implies that compensation is necessary only when descendants of the victims of past racism continue to be affected by the past racism. They then claim that the descendants of the victims of past racism against the Irish are not currently affected by the racism against their ancestors. Finally, they accept the view that *if* a racial group was the object of racism and *if* this racism has current effects, then this racial group deserves an affirmative-action program. Proponents of affirmative action argue that while some members of other racial groups (for example, the Japanese) may be entitled to direct compensation for more recent wrongs done to them, the only racial groups that meet these conditions and so qualify for affirmative action under the indirect compensation argument are blacks, Native Americans, and Hispanics.

DISTANT BENEFITS

Opponents of affirmative action claim that the indirect compensation principle is too strong. They point out that it contains no restriction on how long ago the immoral action took place. They argue that because it lacks this restriction it implausibly implies that the descendants of the Crusaders ought to compensate the descendants of the people harmed by the Crusades. Opponents then claim that the immoral actions of whites occurred too long ago for today's blacks to be compensated. Proponents of affirmative action respond that there is no need for any restriction—indeed, any restriction would make the principle false. They claim that the amount of time that has elapsed since the immoral action took place is irrelevant. Of course, the more time passes, the greater the chance that past immoral actions have no current effects. This, according to the proponents of affirmative action, is why the descendants of the Crusaders do not owe compensation of the descendants of those harmed by the Crusades.

PROPORTIONAL REPRESENTATION

Some opponents of affirmative action argue that if one accepts affirmative action for blacks, then one is committed to having affirmative-action programs until all racial groups are represented in all professions in proportion to their representation in society. Let us assume that 11 percent of the people in our country are black. Opponents of affirmative action argue that if one thinks that we ought to have affirmative action in colleges until 11 percent of new college graduates are black, then one must favor affirmative action for blacks in Italian restaurants until 11 percent of owners of Italian restaurants are black. They take this to be an impossible task, and one we should obviously not try to undertake.

Proponents of affirmative action respond that their view does not have these implications. They claim that this objection confuses race and culture. Affirmative action, they argue, is an attempt to compensate people for past racism—not an attempt to wipe out all cultural differences. Differences between cultures do not trigger affirmative action. So, while college affirmative-action programs ought to continue until 11 percent of new college graduates are black, affirmative action in, for example, lending to restaurant owners should continue only until 11 percent of restaurants are owned by blacks. Proponents assert that it quite likely that most Italian restaurants will be owned by Italians, and most soul-food restaurants will be owned by blacks. They think that there is nothing wrong with this because it reflects a cultural, not a racial, difference.

INDIVIDUAL MERIT

Opponents of affirmative action also object to the programs because they assert that everyone ought to be admitted and hired only on the basis of individual merit and not treated as a member of a group. They argue that considering anything besides individual merit is immoral. Proponents of affirmative action think that this is false. They point out that most colleges consider many things besides individual merit when admitting students and claim that this is perfectly appropriate. Colleges consider financial ability. They cannot admit exclusively on the basis of individual merit because that might result in so many students who cannot pay their bills that the college goes bankrupt. Many colleges also give preference to students from certain geographic areas and admit only a certain percentage of science students. Proponents of affirmative action argue that this point also applies to hiring. Rita discovers that she needs extra help in her record store. Rather than hiring the best-qualified person, she hires her friend James. He is not the best qualified, but Rita likes him. This does not seem immoral, so, proponents of affirmative action argue, it is not true that everyone ought to be admitted and hired only on the basis of individual merit.

EMPIRICAL DATA

A final objection often raised by those opposed to affirmative action is very similar to one we considered when discussing the argument from social utility. This objection begins by reminding us that the principle of indirect compensation requires that compensation be given by the people who currently receive the benefits of past immoral action to the people who are now being harmed by past immoral action. It then continues with the claim that not all blacks are harmed by past racism, and not all whites are benefiting from it. Moreover, the objection continues, we cannot tell which blacks are being harmed and which whites are benefiting.

Proponents of affirmative action respond that it is clear that all blacks are harmed by past discrimination and all whites are benefited by it. They argue that this objection is thinking of specific benefits and harms—such as cash, cars, and CD players. But, they argue, the character of the benefits and harms of racism are more subtle than this. The benefits are, as we noted above, general economic resources and less competition. The harms are less general economic resources and damage to self-confidence. They argue that all blacks cannot help but be harmed and that all whites cannot help but benefit from these sorts of harms and benefits.

WOMEN AND AFFIRMATIVE ACTION

In this chapter we have focused on racial affirmative action. But many proponents of these programs also argue that they ought to be extended to women. They argue that women have suffered and continue to suffer from sexism in a way analogous to the way blacks have suffered. Women were subject to overt legal sexism. For example, at one time married women could not own property and no women could vote. The structure of the arguments for and against sexual affirmative action is parallel to the structure of the arguments for and against racial affirmative action. The picture is complicated because, as we saw in chapter 9, there is more debate about the place of sex in the ideal society than there is about the place of race in the ideal society. Space does not permit an extended analysis of sexual affirmative action, but we should note that analogies between sex and race, while often enlightening, must be done with a watchful eye turned to the differences between sex and race.

An act, practice, or attitude is racist when it creates unjustified differences between races or exploits irrelevant differences between races. There are three types of racism. Overt racism occurs when a racist act, practice, or attitude explicitly uses race. Covert racism occurs when an act, practice, or attitude does not explicitly use race but is nevertheless designed with the intent to create unjustified differences between the races or exploit irrelevant differences between the races. Unintentional racism occurs when an act, practice, or attitude has the effect of creating unjustified differences between the races or of exploiting irrelevant differences between the races, but the people involved in the act or the practice do not intend this effect. There are many parallels between racism and sexism, but drawing conclusions from these parallels must be done with care. There are also important differences between race and sex.

Most of the debate concerning racism now focuses on the methods for achieving a racially blind society. Two methods have been suggested. Affirmative-action programs are programs that use race explicitly in hiring and admissions in order to reduce the effect of past and current racism. Active nondiscrimination programs are programs that do not use race explicitly in hiring and admissions, but instead make an active effort to: 1. ensure that all current hiring and admissions is completely race blind; 2. find those who perform racist acts; and 3. punish these people severly.

There are three types of affirmative action. The first type of affirmative action occurs when a school or firm makes active efforts to find members of one race and encourage them to apply for open positions. The second type of affirmative action occurs when a school or firm considers all applicants from all races for all positions but gives a certain amount of preference to applicants of a certain race. The third type of affirmative action, the quota system, occurs when a school or firm sets aside a certain number of positions for members of a certain race. The third type of affirmative action is a quota system.

The principle objection to affirmative action is that it violates the revised argument for equal treatment. There are two main arguments for affirmative action: the argument from social utility, and the argument from compensation. The argument from social utility asserts that affirmative-action programs are the best way to achieve a racially blind society. The two principle objections to this argument are the empirical claim that affirmative action will not create a racially blind society, and the claim that the argument does not respond to the fact that affirmative action violates the revised argument for equal treatment. There are two versions of the argu-

ment from compensation. According to the direct version, white people owe compensation to black people for the wrongs that white people did to black people. The direct version fails because the people who wronged black people are not the people hurt by affirmative-action programs. According to the indirect version of the argument from compensation, today's white people owe today's black people compensation because today's white people receive the benefits of past racism. It is not clear whether this argument for affirmative action violates the argument for equal treatment.

Selected Readings

Blackstone, William, and Robert Heslep. *Social Justice and Preferential Treatment.* Athens, GA: University of Georgia Press, 1976.

Bowie, Norman. *Equal Opportunity.* Boulder, CO: Westview Press, 1988.

Cohen, Marshall, Thomas Nagel, and Thomas Scanlon. *Equality and Preferential Treatment.* Princeton, NJ: Princeton University Press, 1977.

Goldman, Alan. *Justice and Reverse Discrimination.* Princeton, NJ: Princeton University Press, 1979.

Gross, Barry. *Reverse Discrimination.* Buffalo, NY: Prometheus Press, 1977.

11

Poverty and Affluence

As you read this, there are people dying of hunger. Some are in the developed countries of North America and Europe, but most are in the developing countries of Africa and Asia. Everyday you, and almost everyone else in the developed countries, spends enough to keep a person in the developing world alive for a year. What, if anything, ought you and the rest of us in the developed countries do to aid those who are dying of hunger? Some think that we have a moral obligation to give a great deal of our wealth to those who are dying in the developing countries, while others argue that we have no such obligation.

THE NATURE OF EXTREME POVERTY

When one thinks of extreme poverty, images of starving children spring to mind. Advertisements for charitable organizations and pictures on the nightly news show us people who are quite literally dying of hunger. But there are millions of people who do not make the nightly news because their plight, while as grave, does not lend itself to dramatic pictures. People do not usually die of hunger. Rather, people who are extremely poor are consistently malnourished and lack shelter from the elements. They die of diseases that people who have adequate food and shelter easily resist— diarrhea, chicken pox, and flu. And while many die because of extreme poverty, many more live with and have their lives ruined by it. The effects of even temporary hunger are enormous. Consider how you are affected if you go without food for even thirty-six hours. The long-term malnutrition that comes with extreme poverty causes high infant mortality, brain damage, and chronic illness. These in turn destroy families and ruin the ability of people to enjoy productive and happy lives.

Wealth in this world is unequally distributed. Some are very rich while others are very poor. The rich—those in the top 20 percent of wealth—share 80 percent of the world's resources. The poor—those in the bottom 20 percent of wealth—share 1 1/2 percent of the world's resources. Almost everyone in the developed countries is a member of the rich. Most of those we call "poor" in the United States are among those whose wealth is in the top 20 percent. This disparity in wealth has dramatic consequences. People in developing countries are frequently malnourished and sometimes face catastrophic famines, while most of those we call "poor" in the developed countries not only have food and shelter but have cars and cable TV. In this chapter, "poor" will refer to those who are extremely poor—those who are in the bottom 20 percent of wealth. "Extreme poverty" will refer to the sort of poverty currently being experienced by the extremely poor. "Rich" will refer to those, almost everyone who is reading this book, who are in the top 20 percent of wealth.

The transfer of resources from the rich to the poor has dramatic affects. A VCR costs about $300. And many (perhaps even most) people in rich countries have VCRs. While $300 is not an insignificant sum of money in rich countries, its value in these countries is dramatically less than it is in developing countries. In some developing countries $300 is more than three times the *average* annual income. And unequal income distribution in most developing countries means that the majority of people make less than the average. The very high incomes of a few pull the average up. So it seems that by giving up such seemingly insignificant things as VCRs, people in rich countries could quite literally save the lives of millions of people at little cost to themselves.

DEVELOPMENTALISM

Developmentalists think that people in rich countries have strong and extensive moral obligations to give to the poor, to help developing countries develop. Different developmentalists have different views about the precise nature of what we in the rich countries ought to do. For example, some argue that we ought to give food. Others argue that direct food assistance does not improve the long-term chances for development and that we ought instead to give education, technical assistance, and/or encourage political change.

The basic argument for developmentalism was put forward by Peter Singer (1946–   ) in his seminal article "Famine, Affluence and Morality."

(This article can be found in *World Hunger and Moral Obligation*. See the Selected Readings section for details.) Singer's argument is:

1) If we can prevent something bad without sacrificing anything of comparable moral significance, then we ought to do it.
2) Suffering from extreme poverty is bad.
3) There is some extreme poverty we can prevent without sacrificing anything of comparable moral significance.
4) Therefore, we ought to prevent some extreme poverty.

The phrase "comparable moral significance" is deliberately vague. Developmentalists wish to avoid resting their case on either Kantianism or utilitarianism (see chapters 4 and 5). In this way they hope to convince both rich Kantians and rich utilitarians that they have an obligation to help the poor. Kantianism and utilitarianism have different theories about what makes something have moral significance. Utilitarians think that the moral significance of an act depends only on the act's effect on happiness. Kantians think that an act's moral significance turns, at least in part, on the intrinsic features of the act. For example, many Kantians think that it is important to respect and encourage people's autonomy. But when it comes to actual cases, Kantianism and utilitarianism often counsel the same action. Suppose you are sitting by a wading pool sipping a drink. A toddler walks by, trips, falls into the pool, and knocks herself unconscious. To save her life all you have to do is set down your drink, reach down, and pick her out of the pool. If you do not do this, she will die. The only cost of saving her would be wetting your arm. Many utilitarians think you ought to save the toddler because it maximizes happiness. Many Kantians think you ought to save her because her death would end her possibility of becoming an autonomous person. But both think you ought to save her. Using the terms from the developmentalist's argument, both utilitarians and Kantians think your getting your arm wet is less morally significant than the child's life. To determine exactly what is of moral significance would require resolving the debate between Kantianism and utilitarianism, but by using the overlap of the theories, developmentalists hope to reach powerful conclusions without entering this debate.

The developmentalist's argument is a simple one, and this simplicity has profound implications. The argument does not contain any reference to how far away those in extreme poverty are, whether they are in one's country, or whether others could help them. The simplicity of the argument is deliberate—developmentalists do not think any of these factors is relevant. Most of us find poverty close to us more moving than poverty that is far away. People like to give to charities that spend their money locally.

Organizations hoping to get us to give to poor people far away attempt to bring the poor "closer to us" by showing us dramatic pictures and asserting that poverty that is far away affects us. Developmentalists think that the preference to give to those close to us is mere sentimentality. They think that the location of a poor person has no effect on our obligations to help. Similarly, people are more likely to give to the poor in their own country before they give to the poor in other countries. Again, developmentalists assert that there is no good reason to prefer to give to the poor in one's own country over the poor in other countries. Finally, developmentalists assert that whether others could help the poor is irrelevant. If others are not helping the poor, then whether they *could* help the poor is irrelevant. My obligation to help the poor is not diminished because others are refusing to help. Indeed, if others helped, then poverty would be that much less serious and my obligations would diminish.

The implications of the developmentalist's argument are profound. If it is correct, then most of us in the United States (and most of the people who could afford to buy this book) ought to make radical changes in the way we live our lives. Most of us have closets full of clothes we rarely wear. Yet we continue to buy more clothes either to dress in style or simply to cheer ourselves up after a bad week. It seems clear that dressing in style and cheering ourselves up are not nearly as morally significant as the lives of those in extreme poverty. So we ought not to buy these clothes and send this money to help the poor. The same seems to be true of tickets to basketball games, CD players, meals at fancy restaurants, house plants, many books, and new drapes. Look around the room where you are now sitting. How many of the things in it are as morally significant as a person's life?

As we noted above, most of the extremely poor live outside the developed world. But there are some extremely poor people in the developed world. The homeless people you pass on the street fall into this group. Further, there is a large group of people living in the developed world whose situation is not as grave as those who are extremely poor, but is very serious nevertheless. One need only drive through certain parts of certain cities or through certain rural areas to see poverty which, while not extreme as we have defined it, is very serious indeed. In this chapter we will focus on the disparity between the extremely poor in developing countries and the rich in the developed world. But the developmentalist's argument implies that the rich in the developed world have serious moral obligations to the extremely and nonextremely poor in the developed world. You might consider what the arguments concerning extreme poverty overseas imply about the poor who live closer to our homes.

NEO-MALTHUSIANS

Some of those who reject the developmentalist argument are called "neo-Malthusians." Those who hold this position take their name from Thomas Robert Malthus (1766–1834). Malthus held that population growth always outruns economic growth and so extreme poverty is inevitable. Neo-Malthusians acknowledge that economic growth in the 200 years since Malthus wrote has outpaced population growth. But they argue that this will not be so in the future. They believe that assisting the poor only causes population increases that will eventually overtax the resources of a country. When this happens, extreme poverty will result. And, because assistance has caused population growth, this extreme poverty will cause more deaths than earlier extreme poverty would have caused. Therefore, they think the best course of action right now is to cut off aid and allow some extreme poverty now in order to prevent more extreme poverty later. So neo-Malthusians think that people in rich countries do not have a moral obligation to give to poor countries.

Different neo-Malthusians have different reasons for thinking that assisting the poor will only cause population increases and more extreme poverty. Many of them point out that there is a finite amount of natural resources on this planet. Population growth means that these resources must be shared by more and more people. Economic growth, they argue, also causes people to use natural resources at a faster rate. When these resources run out, extreme poverty will result. Other neo-Malthusians think that political factors cause extreme poverty. They argue that when rich countries give to poor countries, the aid is not used effectively because political structures in poor countries are corrupt and/or inefficient. So the aid only serves to prop up corrupt governments. Other neo-Malthusians think that it is cultural factors that cause population growth. They point out that in poor countries people tend to have strong religious and cultural preferences to have large families. So, giving aid will only allow them to act on these preferences, have more children, and so cause more extreme poverty.

Triage

Neo-Malthusians argue that we ought to triage poor countries. Triage is a way of treating wounded soldiers. Wounded arriving at hospitals are divided into three groups. Those with nonlife-threatening injuries are given only minor first aid to stabilize their situation. Those whose injuries are so severe that they cannot be saved or can be saved only by occupying many doctors for a long time are left to die. The time and energy of the staff are therefore concentrated on the third group of soldiers—those with injuries that are serious enough to be life-threatening, but not so severe that they cannot be saved at all or could be saved only with massive assistance. This procedure dramatically increases the number of wounded soldiers who survive.

Neo-Malthusians think that rich countries ought to use triage in giving assistance to poor countries. Some poor countries currently have the natural and social resources to develop without assistance. (Perhaps Korea and Singapore were in this category twenty years ago.) Rich countries ought not to give these poor countries assistance. Other poor countries are so poor in natural resources or have such serious political and/or cultural problems that they will not develop even if rich countries assist. Neo-Malthusians think that we ought not to waste our assistance on these countries. In other words, people in these countries ought to be allowed to die of extreme poverty now so as to avoid more extreme poverty later. Finally, some poor countries are in the middle group. They will not develop on their own but will develop if given assistance. Neo-Malthusians argue that we ought to give our assistance to these countries.

The Lifeboat Analogy

Neo-Malthusians often use a lifeboat analogy to defend their view. They argue that countries are like three groups of lifeboats on a sea. All the lifeboats can hold 100 people. The rich lifeboats have 60 people in each, and the number of people in these boats is not growing. The poor lifeboats have 90 or 95 people in each, and this number is rising rapidly. These boats will soon exceed capacity and swamp. All aboard will drown. The other group of lifeboats have 75 or 80 people in each. The number of people in these boats is rising, but measures are being taken that will stabilize the number of people in these boats before they swamp. People jump out of the poor lifeboats and swim to the rich lifeboats. They ask to be pulled into the rich lifeboats. This is analogous to asking for aid. Neo-Malthusians argue that if the people in the rich lifeboats take in people from the poor lifeboats, then the rich lifeboats will swamp and sink just as the poor lifeboats will. So, those in the rich lifeboats ought not pull in the poor. They ought to pull in a few people from the third group of lifeboats if that will assist these lifeboats in their efforts to stabilize the number of people in their lifeboats.

Objections to Neo-Malthusianism

Many objections have been raised against neo-Malthusianism. First, many think that the lifeboat analogy is flawed. They argue that a better analogy, given the difference in wealth between the rich and the poor, would be to picture the rich in luxury liners, while the poor are in lifeboats. Thinking of the rich and the poor in lifeboats falsely gives the impression that there is not much difference in the resources of the rich and poor. Another reason that some have thought that the lifeboat analogy is flawed is that in normal lifeboats people are not responsible for being in one lifeboat or another. When a ship is sinking, people in real lifeboats merely get in one of the available lifeboats. But the rich, some argue, benefit from and are partially responsible for the poor being in lifeboats. Rich countries have repeatedly intervened economically and politically in poor countries in ways that, according to many, benefit the rich at the expense of the poor. So, some argue that if we wish to make the lifeboat analogy accurate, we must imagine the rich throwing some people into the sea. Surely, in that case the rich ought to pull in the poor—that is, the rich ought to assist the poor.

Second, many think that the neo-Malthusian's assertion that assisting the poor will only cause population increases and more poverty is false. Many think that population increases do not cause poverty but that poverty causes population increases. They point out that population growth was very high in those countries that are currently rich before they were rich. Population growth slowed dramatically when these countries became rich. They theorize that in poor countries unskilled labor is valuable, so it is good to have many unskilled children to help support the family. But in rich countries skilled labor is valuable. For one's children to be skilled, one must educate them. But educating a child is expensive so one cannot educate many children. In rich countries it is economically better to have a few more-educated children than many less-educated children. In poor countries it is economically better to have many less-educated children than a few more-educated children. Therefore, development decreases population growth.

Another reason for thinking that assisting the poor will not cause population increases and more extreme poverty is that the currently rich countries were once poor and made the transition to economic growth and population control. So we know it can be done. And those countries that are currently poor have an advantage that the currently rich countries did not have when they were becoming rich—the benefit of doing something that others have done before. Poor countries do not have to reinvent the wheel. They can examine the history of rich countries to figure out the best way to develop.

Finally, many argue that even if all the neo-Malthusian's claims about population control are correct, this only shows that rich countries ought to give a different kind of aid—not that they have no obligation to give aid. If it is true that the root cause of extreme poverty is not lack of food but population growth, then rich countries ought to assist poor countries in controlling their populations. If the neo-Malthusians are correct, we ought to send birth-control devices, not food and not nothing. But this response to the neo-Malthusians does show that developmentalists have important lessons to learn from neo-Malthusians. Neo-Malthusians point out that helping the poor may not be as straightforward as the developmentalist's argument might originally lead one to believe. The best way to help the poor may not be by sending food or even tractors. It may well be that the best way to help the poor is to work for social, political, and economic changes in poor countries. Neo-Malthusians have pointed out that we cannot give assistance without looking at the social, political, and economic context. For example, it might be more beneficial for poor countries if rich countries stopped sending food and cut back on farm subsidies to farmers in rich countries. These subsidies drive down the world price of food products and so mean that farmers in poor countries do not get as much money for the food they produce. It might also be better for rich countries to support family-planning clinics and preventative medical treatment so that those in the poor countries have both more children who survive to adulthood and the means to reduce the number of children they have.

OTHER OBJECTIONS TO DEVELOPMENTALISM

Neo-Malthusians are not the only ones who object to developmentalism. The driving force behind many of the following objections is the same—the conviction that developmentalism is too demanding. As we noted above, if the argument is correct, then most of us in the United States ought to make radical changes in the way we live our lives. We ought to stop buying new clothes, tickets to basketball games, CD players, fancy meals, and so forth. The developmentalist's argument implies that moral demands are much more pervasive than most of us thought they were. But, developmentalists point out, the simple fact that the developmentalist argument implies that we ought to make profound changes in our lives is no objection to the argument. That is, after all, exactly what the developmentalist intends to show us. We can hardly object to the developmentalist's argument on the grounds that it proves what it intends to prove. If we are going to reject the conclusion, we must examine the argument and show that it is flawed.

Moral Subjectivism

Both developmentalists and neo-Malthusians believe that moral absolutism is true. Recall from chapter 3 that moral absolutism is the view that there is one set of objective moral standards that applies to all people at all times. Developmentalists think that the claim "Suffering from extreme poverty is bad" is part of this set of objective moral standards. As we saw in chapter 3, some people are moral subjectivists. They think that moral standards are always a matter of personal opinion, individual emotions, or societal customs. Subjectivists would reject the moral absolutism implicit in both developmentalists and neo-Malthusians. For example, a subjectivist might argue that what is morally correct is determined by what is thought to be morally correct in a society. They then might go on to claim that, because of this, we have no moral obligations to people in other societies. Developmentalists and neo-Malthusians would respond with the arguments in favor of moral absolutism discussed in chapter 3.

Rich Will Become Poor

Some object to developmentalism on the grounds that if rich countries gave a great deal of resources to poor countries, this would damage the economies of the rich countries so that they would no longer be able to assist poor countries. Consider an analogy. I work as a truck driver and you are a poor person. I am assisting you. I decide to sell my truck and give you the large sum of money that I would get for it. If I do that, I lose my job and become poor myself. Now I can no longer assist you. Therefore, I ought not sell my truck and give you the proceeds. Developmentalists respond that they never claimed that rich countries should give so much that they destroy their capacity to give. Extending the analogy, I ought to help you, but not so much that I destroy my ability to keep helping you. Similarly, developmentalists argue that rich countries could certainly give a great deal more than they are currently giving without becoming poor countries.

Government Responsibility

Some respond to the developmentalist's argument by arguing that while it is true that the governments of rich countries ought to increase dramatically the amount of assistance they give to poor countries, individuals have no moral obligation to assist poor countries personally. They claim that assisting the poor is the government's responsibility—not theirs. They often go on to claim that personal giving to private organizations that are assisting the poor only lets governments avoid their responsibility. Therefore, we have no obligation to help the poor personally.

Developmentalists respond that it is not true that helping the poor is *only* the government's responsibility. Certainly, they claim, governments ought to help the poor, but private individuals ought to do so as well. They return to the wading-pool analogy. Developmentalists claim that it is absurd to suppose that it is only the government's responsibility to help others, so you have no obligation to reach down and pull the toddler out of the wading pool. Of course, the government has an obligation to help those in need, but so do individuals. Developmentalists also argue that individuals refraining from giving to help the poor does not force governments to take on this responsibility. Rather, they argue that if individuals are not giving to help the poor, governments are likely to conclude that citizens do not think helping the poor is very important, and so they will not help the poor either. Of course, in many cases governmental action will be more effective than individual action. Therefore, in some cases what individuals ought to do to help the poor is to contribute to efforts to lobby for increased governmental assistance to the poor. But, as with the neo-Malthusian objection, this objection may only indicate how we ought to help the poor—not that we have no obligation to help the poor.

Moral Capacity

A sophisticated version of the claim that developmentalism is too demanding is the assertion that the argument would require people to do things that they cannot do, things that are beyond their moral capacities. This objection notes that most people think that "ought" implies "can." In other words, most people think that if it is true that a person ought to do something, then it must be true that he can do that thing. Suppose Corinne and Malcolm are standing at the base of a burning skyscraper. They see that several people are trapped on the fifteenth floor and will burn to death. Malcolm turns to Corinne and says: "You ought to fly up there and save those people." Corinne would be very puzzled. Since she cannot fly up to the fifteenth floor, it cannot be true that she ought to fly up there. One can only have a moral obligation to do those acts that one can do. Those making this objection to developmentalism then argue that ordinary people cannot make the radical changes in life-style that developmentalism claims we have a moral obligation to make. It is physically impossible for Corinne to fly and save the people in the burning building and, they claim, it is psychologically impossible for most people to give up things like sports tickets, fashionable clothes, fancy cars, and so forth. Since ordinary people cannot do this, it is not true that they ought to do this.

Developmentalists acknowledge that some things are psychologically impossible. It may well be that certain people find certain acts, such as speaking to large groups, literally psychologically impossible. And developmentalists agree that people cannot have an obligation to do psychologically impossible things. But developmentalists claim that the radical life-style changes they advocate are not beyond the psychological capacities of most people. Of course, ordinary people would not like it, but there are many things we do not like (for example, paying taxes) that are perfectly possible. Developmentalists also point out that some people have made the life-style changes they propose. They think that the reason more people have not made these changes is that most people do not realize that they have a moral obligation to make them. They argue that if people were taught from the time they were small that they had this obligation (as they are taught that they have an obligation to refrain from murdering people), then many people would find it relatively easy to live in this way.

No Identifiable Person

In most cases when one's action harms another it is very easy to identify the person harmed. If you fail to pull the toddler out of the wading pool, then it is one identifiable toddler who is harmed. When you hit someone, there is one identifiable person who is harmed. But suppose you buy a VCR. Someone is harmed—the person who would have been helped by your sending that money to help the poor. But it is hard, perhaps impossible, to identify that person. We cannot tell which persons in Africa would have been helped by your assistance. Some argue that since we cannot identify who is harmed by buying the VCR, we have no obligation not to buy the VCR. Developmentalists argue that this is false. They point out that the same is true of polluters in Los Angeles. Suppose Margaret owns a factory in Los Angeles that emits large amounts of air pollutants. We know that this pollution harms someone, but it is difficult, if not impossible, to determine who is harmed. But that does not mean that Margaret has no obligation to refrain from polluting.

No Intention to Harm

There is a difference between buying a VCR and the typical killing of someone. When you buy a VCR you do not intend to harm anyone, but in the typical case of someone killing someone else the killer intends to harm the victim. This is clearly an important difference, and some object to the developmentalist's argument on the grounds that since you do not intend to do anything wrong in buying a VCR, you do nothing wrong in buying it. Developmentalists acknowledge the importance of intentions, but they think that intentions are important only in the evaluation of people, not of acts. Suppose Margaret knows that her factory pollutes and has designed it that way because she enjoys hurting people in this way. Suppose that Deirdre owns a factory in New York that pollutes just as much as Margaret's. But Deirdre does not know that her factory is polluting and so does not intend to harm anyone. Clearly Margaret is a much worse person than Deirdre. But, developmentalists argue, the action they should perform at this point is the same—stop polluting. So while the fact that you do not intend to harm anyone in buying a VCR does mean that you are not an immoral person for buying it, it does not mean that you do not have an obligation not to buy it.

Care for Our Own

The developmentalist's argument implies that we ought not buy VCRs, sporting tickets, fancy clothes, and so forth for ourselves. It also seems to imply that we ought not to buy these things for our children, friends, and family. Some argue that there is nothing wrong with giving some moral preference to our friends and family, and so the developmentalist's argument is too strong. Some argue that it is morally permissible to give gifts to one's own child even if another child would like or benefit more from the gift. So, this objection to the developmentalist argument claims, it is permissible for us to help our own friends and family before we help poor people we do not know or care about.

Recall that the phrase "comparable moral significance" in the developmentalist's argument is deliberately vague. Some think that helping one's own child is of more moral significance than helping another's child. But others disagree.

Developmentalists do not take a position in this disagreement. But they do assert that even if helping one's own child is more morally significant than helping another's child, we must consider the nature of the need of the two children as well as whose children they are. Developmentalists think it is clear that keeping your own child from becoming poor is of (at least) comparable moral significance to keeping another's child from becoming poor. And doing other things for our children (such as providing them with a good education) might or might not be of comparable moral significance to saving another's child from extreme poverty. But they think that providing one's own child with video games or fashionable clothes is clearly not morally as important as saving another's child from extreme poverty. Developmentalists acknowledge that we may give *some* preference to our own children, but we may not give as much preference as that. So, developmentalists argue, this objection at best slightly reduces the obligation we have to help the poor—it does not eliminate it.

We Did Not Cause Poverty

Some object to the developmentalist's argument on the grounds that we did not cause the poor to be poor, so we have no obligation to help them out of poverty. Those who make this argument object to one of the crucial moves made at the beginning of the developmentalist's argument. Recall the toddler example. Developmentalists assumed that it was clear that you have an obligation to pull the toddler out of the wading pool. But some argue that since you did not cause the toddler to fall in, you have no obligation to pull the toddler out. These objectors claim that one has a moral obligation to help others only if one caused them to be in need of help. They often argue that the reason one has an obligation to help others only if one caused them to need help is that it is unfair for one's freedom to choose the sort of life that one finds fulfilling to be abridged because of the existence of situations that one did not cause. It is unfair for my freedom to do things I find fulfilling (like keeping large sums of money) to be abridged just because there is poverty that I did nothing to cause.

Developmentalists have two first responses to this argument. The first is the denial of the claim that one has a moral obligation to help others only if one caused them to be in need of help. They think that someone who did not pull the toddler out of the water would reveal herself to be a moral monster. They think that while one's freedom to choose the sort of life that one finds fulfilling is morally important, it is not nearly as morally important as another's life. The second developmentalist response is to claim that the rich caused the poor to be poor. They point to the frequent intervention by rich countries in poor countries in order to advance the economic interests of rich countries. Rich countries, they argue, have frequently been economic imperialists. Even today, they claim, rich countries arrange the international economic situation to help rich countries and hurt poor countries. This second response rests on the principles of direct and indirect compensation that we discussed in chapter 10. Rich countries now ought to help poor countries either because in the past they caused the poor countries to be poor (thus triggering an obligation of indirect compensation) and/or because they are currently causing poor countries to be poor (thus triggering an obligation of direct compensation). Most developmentalists think that rich countries have both an obligation of indirect compensation and an obligation of direct compensation.

Fair Shares

Some object to the developmentalist's argument on the grounds that all any one person is obligated to do is to contribute her fair share to the project of eliminating poverty. Determining precisely what a particular person's fair share is would be very difficult and would require that we know a great deal about that person's particular situation. Many think that the more rich ought to contribute more than the less rich. Many think that those who have benefited more from extreme poverty or done more to cause extreme poverty ought to contribute more than those who benefited or did less. But whatever this fair share is, many argue that all one is morally obligated to give is one's fair share. Let us simplify a bit and suppose that if everyone who is rich gave $2,000 per year to the poor, extreme poverty would be eliminated in a short period of time. If we pretend, again to simplify, that a fair share is an equal share, then $2,000 per rich person per year is a fair share of the costs of solving the problem of extreme poverty. On these assumptions, those who make the fair-shares objection argue that all a rich person is obligated to give to the poor is $2,000 per year.

Developmentalists respond to the fair shares argument by agreeing that *if* every rich person were giving $2,000 per year, *then* it would be true that all any particular rich person would be obligated to give is $2,000 per year. But, developmentalists argue, it is not true that every rich person is giving $2,000 per year. Therefore, those rich people who do give ought to give more than $2,000 per year. But those who make the fair-shares objection argue that this allows the immoral actions of other rich people to hurt the rich who are giving their fair share. It is not the fault of the rich who are giving a fair share that other rich people are not meeting their obligations. We are all obligated, they argue, to do our fair share to solve grave moral problems. But we are not obligated to do more than that. Otherwise, the rich who fail to give a fair share are hurting not only the extremely poor, but the rich who are obligated to give more than their fair share, because some rich people are not giving a fair share.

Even if the fair-shares objection is correct, it only limits the scope of the obligation that the rich have to the poor. It does not fully refute the developmentalist's argument because we are still obligated to give our fair share, and our fair share will almost certainly be more than we are giving now. The force of the fair-shares objection is further weakened if we consider the developmentalist's use of the direct- and indirect-compensation principles. Those who make the fair-shares objection assert that the rich who give ought not owe more, ought not be hurt, because other rich fail to give their fair share. But developmentalists point out that the rich who give their fair share ought not benefit from the fact that some other rich people are not giving their fair share. Suppose that a rich person who gives her fair share works at a VCR factory or an expensive private college and so benefits from the fact that other rich people are not giving their fair share. According to the indirect-compensation principle, she ought to give more help to the poor who are being hurt by the rich buying more VCRs or sending their children to more expensive colleges because they are not giving their fair share to help the poor. Most rich people benefit economically from the fact that not many rich people give much to help the poor. So even if the fair-share objection is correct, it seems to imply a position very close to developmentalism—we ought to give our fair share plus any benefits we gain because others are not giving their fair share.

Many people are living in extreme poverty. They have radically inadequate food, clothing, and shelter. Some die of hunger and many millions more die from diseases that they would have survived if they had adequate food and shelter. Besides causing death, extreme poverty causes brain damage and chronic illness. It destroys families and ruins the ability of people to enjoy normal lives. Wealth in this world is not equally distributed. Some are very rich while others live in extreme poverty. 20 percent of the people in the world share 80 percent of the world's resources while another 20 percent share 1 1/2 percent. The rich have money to spend on being fashionable, fancy meals, sporting events, video games, and thousands of other diversions. The extremely poor do not have enough to buy minimal food, clothing, and shelter. Transferring resources from the rich to the poor has dramatic effects. The $300 that buys a VCR in the United States would feed 100 people for a year in Africa.

Developmentalists think that people in rich countries have strong and extensive moral obligations to give to the poor. Developmentalists claim that if we can prevent something bad without sacrificing anything of comparable moral significance, then we ought to do it. They think that suffering from extreme poverty is bad and that there is some extreme poverty we can prevent without sacrificing anything of comparable moral significance. Therefore, they think we ought to prevent some extreme poverty. The phrase "comparable moral significance" is deliberately vague to avoid assuming either Kantianism or utilitarianism. The developmentalist's argument does not contain any reference to how far away those in extreme poverty are, whether they are in one's country, or whether others could help them. Developmentalists do not think any of these factors is relevant. If they are correct, then most of us in the United States ought to make radical changes in the way we live our lives. We ought not to buy many of the clothes, sporting-event tickets, CD players, fancy meals, and so forth that we currently do, and we ought to use the money we save to help the poor instead.

Neo-Malthusians object to developmentalism on the grounds that assisting the poor only causes population increases that will eventually overtax the resources of a country. When this happens, more extreme poverty will result. And, because assistance has caused population growth, this extreme poverty will cause more deaths than earlier poverty would have caused. Therefore, they think the best course of action right now is to cut off aid and allow some extreme poverty now in order to prevent more extreme poverty later. So, neo-Malthusians think that people in rich countries do not have a moral obligation to give to poor countries. Developmentalists respond that population growth does not cause extreme poverty—extreme poverty causes population growth. They also respond that, with the assistance of rich counties, poor countries can make the transition to being rich countries. Finally, they respond that even if the neo-Malthusians are correct, their view only implies that the rich ought to give to population-control programs and not to food programs—not that the rich have no obligation to give at all.

Many others objections have been made against developmentalism. Some argue that developmentalism implies that the rich should make themselves poor. Others argue that the rich do not have an obligation to give to the poor because this is the government's responsibility, because it is beyond the moral capacity of most rich people to give to the poor, because no identifiable person is harmed by a rich person's not giving to the poor, because the rich do not intend to harm the poor, because the rich ought to care for their families and friends, because the rich are not responsible for the poverty of the poor, or because the rich are obligated only to give a fair share. In most cases developmentalists seem to have plausible responses to these objections. In other cases, it seems that the objections only limit the scope of the developmentalist's argument instead of refuting it.

Selected Readings

Aiken, William, and Hugh LaFollette (eds.). *World Hunger and Moral Obligation.* Englewood Cliffs, NJ: Prentice-Hall, 1977.

Brown, Peter, and Henry Shue (eds.). *Food Policy.* New York: Free Press, 1977.

Lucas, George, and Thomas Ogletree (eds.). *Lifeboat Ethics.* New York: Harper & Row, 1976.

Luper-Foy, Steven. *Problems of International Justice.* Boulder, CO: Westview Press, 1988.

O'Neill, Onora. *Faces of Hunger.* London: George Allen and Unwin, 1985.

12

Pornography and Censorship

A trip to the local convenience store would enable you to find pornographic materials. In this country pornographic materials are distributed by the millions. Many people favor censoring pornography. They think that pornography is morally repugnant and that it harms people. But others argue that, whether one wants to buy it or not, it ought not be censored. They claim that any censorship of pornography would be an immoral restriction on our liberties.

DEFINITIONS OF PORNOGRAPHY

The debate on this issue is muddied by a lack of clear definitions of the key terms—pornography, obscenity, and erotica. The root of this problem is that the courts have accepted definitions that differ from those used in ordinary language.

Ordinary Definitions

To call something "obscene" is to say that it is extraordinarily offensive, indecent, or repulsive. The term is not necessarily associated with sexuality. One who says "When I traveled to India, I realized that the wealth of the United States is obscene" may not be saying something true, but she is using all her terms properly. Many people think that graphic depictions of extreme violence are obscene. But obscenity is frequently associated with sexuality. Obscene language is frequently language that refers to sexual conduct in offensive ways.

Pictures or descriptions are sexually explicit when they contain detailed or graphic depictions or descriptions of sexual acts or organs. Not everything that is sexually explicit is obscene. The most obvious examples of this are the sexually explicit pictures found in medical books. Let us use the term "clinically sexually explicit" to refer to sexually explicit materials, like those found in medical books, which are neither obscene nor sexually interesting. "Erotica" refers to sexually explicit, but not obscene, pictures or descriptions which, unlike clinically sexually explicit materials, are sexually interesting. Consider the works of Rodin. They are certainly sexually explicit. They often depict naked people, and sometimes these people are engaged in sexual acts. Part of the reason that Rodin's works are so powerful is that they are sexually interesting. Like many great works of art, Rodin's sculptures tell us about human experiences. Sometimes the human experience that Rodin is focusing on is sexual attraction. Therefore, part of the interest of some of Rodin's works is their sexual nature. In contrast, clinical pictures of sex organs are not sexually interesting. They are interesting in the same way that pictures of kidneys and veins are interesting— they help us treat disease.

"Pornography" refers to sexually explicit material that is obscene. So erotica, by definition, is not pornographic. Pornography is obscene and erotica is not. All pornography is obscene, but not all obscenity is pornographic. Things that are obscene but not sexually explicit are obscene but not pornographic. The person above who traveled to India claimed that the wealth of the United States is obscene (extremely offensive, indecent, or repulsive), but it would be a misuse of language to claim that the wealth of the United States is pornographic. It may be very difficult to determine whether certain material is erotic, pornographic, or clinically sexually explicit. Someone might think that Rodin's works are obscene and therefore examples of pornography, not erotica. Someone might think that the pictures in medical books are sexually interesting but not obscene and therefore erotic. But this is not a problem with the definitions—it merely shows that people differ about what they find sexually interesting and/or offensive. Unless otherwise noted, we will use the definitions of pornography, obscenity, erotica, and sexually explicit presented in this section instead of the legal definitions presented in the next section.

Legal Definitions

Legal definitions of the terms "obscene," "pornographic," and "erotic" differ from ordinary definitions of these terms. The definition of these terms is crucial because the Supreme Court has ruled that obscene materials are not protected by the First Amendment to the United States Constitution. In other words, the legal right to free speech does not extend to obscene materials. In *Miller v. California* (413 U.S. 15), the Court held that a work is obscene when:

1) the average person, applying contemporary community standards, would find that the work, taken as a whole, appeals to the prurient interest and;

2) the work depicts or describes, in a patently offensive way, sexual conduct that is specifically defined by law and;

3) the work, taken as a whole, lacks serious literary, artistic, political or scientific value.

This definition requires several comments. First, note that, according to this definition, all obscenity is sexual. For something to be obscene it must depict or describe sexual conduct. Depictions or descriptions of extreme violence, no matter how graphic, cannot be legally obscene. Most people would think that some depictions of violence could be obscene in the ordinary sense. Second, according to this definition something can be pornographic but not obscene. For example, the Court has ruled that materials such as *Playboy* are not obscene. These are the main ways that the legal definitions differ from the ordinary ones. Third, the phrase "taken as a whole" means that in determining that a work is obscene one must not look only at a part of it. One must examine the entire work. Something that seems offensive if viewed by itself might not seem offensive if viewed as part of a larger work. Fourth, "patently" means completely and obviously. In other words, for a work to be obscene it must be completely and obviously offensive. Fifth, a prurient interest is an obsessive interest in things one ought not be interested in. Sixth, the phrase "specifically defined by law" means that the law that prohibits obscene materials must clearly list the sexual conduct that cannot be depicted. The law cannot merely prohibit offensive depictions.

Some have argued that this definition contains phrases that are so vague that it is impossible to determine what materials fall under the definition. Most of the criticism has focused on the phrases "average person," "community standards," "patently offensive," and "lacks serious literary, artistic, political or scientific value." Critics of this definition, including some Justices of the Supreme Court, think that these terms are drastically vague. Who is the average person? Is the average person the owner of a store selling pornographic materials, the minister of a local church, the professor of literature at a local college, the mechanic at a local garage, or the manager of a local department store? What makes any one of these people any more average than any of the others? What community is the relevant one? Many cities contain several communities. What makes something patently offensive? Presumably some of the people buying the material in question do not think it is offensive. Finally, how are we to determine whether a work has serious literary, artistic, political, or scientific value? Merely raising these questions is no attack on the definition, for these questions might have answers. But the critics go on to claim that these questions cannot be answered in any nonarbitrary way. Defenders of this definition think that they can answer these questions.

CENSORSHIP AND LIBERTY-LIMITING PRINCIPLES

Censorship occurs when the government places a legal prohibition on the distribution of pictures or descriptions. In the United States, some materials are censored. For example, pornographic pictures of children and certain rap songs are censored. Cigarette ads are also censored—they cannot be shown on television. Censorship is controversial because it reduces our liberties. If materials are censored, it is illegal to sell, buy, or display these materials, and this means that people do not have the liberty to do these things. Censorship is a governmental activity. Neither refusing to buy material nor urging others not to buy it is censorship. Many people oppose censorship, refuse to buy pornographic materials, and urge others not to buy it. This is a consistent position. Indeed, many who oppose the censorship of pornography hope that society will change so that the demand for pornography will dry up and it will no longer be produced.

Liberty-Limiting Principles

Censorship is one sort of governmental restriction on liberty. Four principles have been suggested as justifications for governmental restrictions on liberty.

THE HARM PRINCIPLE

The harm principle states that the government may prohibit an act if it is an act in which one person harms another person. For example, according to the harm principle, the governmental prohibition of murder is justified because murder harms someone else—the person murdered. The same is true of laws against theft, rape, speeding, and polluting. There is wide agreement that this principle is true. It is the only noncontroversial liberty-limiting principle.

THE OFFENSE PRINCIPLE

The offense principle states that the government may prohibit an act if it is an act in which one person offends another person. For example, according to the offense principle, the law against public nudity is justified because public nudity offends people. The offense principle also seems to be the justification for laws against public indecency. If one ate feces in public, one might well be convicted of public indecency. Some argue that the offense principle is false. They argue that if one is offended by certain public acts, one has only to turn one's head or walk away.

LEGAL PATERNALISM

According to the principle of legal paternalism, the government may prohibit an act if it is an act in which one person harms herself. For example, the justification for requiring people who ride motorcycles to wear helmets seems to be that if they do not, they greatly increase their risk of harming themselves. Legal paternalism is controversial. Many argue that if a person wishes to risk his own body, this is nobody's business but his.

LEGAL MORALISM

According to the principle of legal moralism, the government may prohibit an act if it is an act which, while it harms or offends no one, is immoral. Legal moralism appears to be the justification for the laws that prohibit private oral sex between mutually consenting adults. This act, because it is private, offends no one. It also harms no one. So it seems the only reason that the government can have for prohibiting oral sex is the view that oral sex is immoral. Legal moralism is the most controversial of the four liberty-limiting principles. Many, perhaps most, reject this principle. In many states the rejection of legal moralism has led to the repeal of statutes against oral sex.

Legal moralism and the offense principle are easily confused. The oral-sex example illustrates the possible confusion. Some people say that they are offended by people performing private consensual acts of oral sex. They then argue that they are also offended by nudity, and so the reason they wish to prohibit these acts is the same as the reason they wish to prohibit public nudity. But this argument seems to use the word "offend" two different ways. When people say that they are offended by nudity, it is clearly not the nudity itself they find offensive. After all, they are nude themselves every morning when they change clothes. They are offended by seeing others nude. But when people say they are offended by acts of oral sex that they do not even see, what they mean is that they are offended by the immorality of the act. In this chapter we will keep the offense principle and legal moralism distinct by stipulating that the term "offend" refers only to acts that one has experienced. So one cannot be offended by acts that one does not witness.

THE HARM PRINCIPLE

Perhaps the most common arguments for and against censoring pornographic materials are based on the harm principle. One common argument against censoring pornography is the no-harm argument. This argument begins with the claim that the only true liberty-limiting principle is the harm principle. Then it is held that pornography does not harm anyone. From these two claims it follows that we ought not to censor pornography. The most common argument for censoring pornographic materials is the harm argument. This argument begins with the claim that the harm principle is *a* true liberty-limiting principle. (As we shall see later, defenders of censorship of pornography also think that there are other true liberty-limiting principles.) It continues with the assertion that pornography harms people. If the harm principle is true and pornography harms people, then it follows that censoring pornography is permissible. Clearly a crucial issue that divides those who favor censoring pornography from those who oppose it is the issue of whether pornography causes harm.

Causation

There are two steps to showing that one thing causes another. First, one must show that the two things are correlated. Two things are correlated if one is present when the other is present and absent when the other is absent or the two things rise and fall together. Humidity and rain are correlated and so are the numbers on a digital thermometer and the temperature for the air. Increased humidity occurs at the same time as an increased chance of rain. The numbers on a thermometer rise as air temperature rises, and they fall as air temperature falls. But merely showing that two things are correlated does not show that one causes the other. First, mere correlation does not tell us which thing is causing the other. One cannot conclude from the fact that the numbers on the thermometer are correlated with air temperature that the rising numbers cause the air temperature to rise. Rather, the increased air temperature causes the numbers to rise. Second, correlation between two things may mean not that either of the things causes the other, but that both of them are caused by some third one. The light on my porch and the light in my entryway are correlated. When one is on, the other is also on; and when one is off, the other is off. But neither light causes the other to be on. Both lights are hooked to a single light switch, and this single switch causes both lights to go on and off.

Traditional Conservatives and Harm

Traditional conservatives who favor censoring pornography have argued that it causes a wide variety of harms. These include sexual violence, the breakdown of families, venereal disease, marital infidelity, births out of wedlock, the disappearance of love, and the end of civilization. Defenders of censoring pornography do not argue that pornography is the only cause of these harms. Rather, they think pornography is one cause among many. Establishing that pornography causes any of these harms is very difficult because there are a great many factors that might cause any one of the harms. It is more plausible that pornography causes some of these harms than it is that it causes others. Few think it is likely that there is even a correlation between pornography and the disappearance of love or the fall of civilization. Most people also think that, while increased pornography may be correlated with venereal disease, marital infidelity, and births out of wedlock, it is much more likely that larger societal changes (for example, the availability of birth control and the abandonment of Victorian moral beliefs) have caused both an increased use of pornography and these three other things. In other words, just as the single light switch causes the two lights to be correlated, larger societal changes cause increased pornography, more venereal disease, reduced marital fidelity, and increased births out of wedlock.

Most of the debate concerning the possibility that pornography causes harm has, therefore, focused on the question of whether increased availability of pornography causes an increase in sexual violence. Two presidential commissions appointed to determine whether pornography causes sexual violence have reached opposing conclusions. A commission appointed by President Nixon concluded that pornography does not cause sexual violence. A commission appointed by President Reagan concluded that pornography does cause sexual violence. Many have argued that the Reagan commission's findings are flawed because, rather than attempting to run scientific studies, they based their conclusion on the testimony collected at a series of public forums. The Nixon commission, on the other hand, did use scientific studies. Defenders of the Reagan commission argue that public testimony is more reliable than scientific studies done by academics.

All the above-noted difficulties with determining whether one thing causes another apply to the question of whether pornography causes sexual violence. Even if a correlation between pornography and sexual violence could be established, it might be that both are caused by the same societal forces that caused reduced marital fidelity. As we noted above, correlation does not tell us which thing is causing the other. So even if one could show that there is a correlation between pornography and the desire to be sexually violent, it might be that a desire to be sexually violent causes a desire to view pornography, rather than pornography's causing a desire to be sexually violent. Many have argued that any possible correlation between pornography and sexual violence is the result not of pornography causing a desire to be sexually violent, but of a desire to be sexually violent (perhaps because of early childhood experiences) causing a desire to view pornography. Since one thing might have two completely different causes, this possibility is perfectly compatible with there being a group of people who have no sexually violent desires but enjoy looking at pornography.

Harms Must Outweigh Benefits

Those who oppose censorship of pornography argue that those who favor it need to show more than the fact that pornography causes *some* harm. They argue that it must be shown that censoring causes less harm than allowing pornography. They point out that it is clear that drinking causes harms—drunk driving and increased violence toward others. But the Prohibition experience shows us that the harms of banning alcohol are greater than the harms of allowing it. Similarly, it may be that banning pornography would cause a black market and/or bring very high enforcement costs. In other words, to show that censoring pornography is justified, one must show not merely that pornography causes harm, but that the harms outweigh the benefits and that the enforcement costs are not too high.

Benefits of Pornography

This last argument is often coupled with the claim that, even if pornography causes some harm, it also has benefits. Some argue that pornography benefits society by invigorating stale sexual relations, aiding in normal sexual development for sexually repressed people, and allowing a harmless pleasure. Some studies indicate that couples who occasionally use pornography have better sexual relations. Some argue that, far from causing increased sexual violence, pornography causes a decrease in sexual violence. Some studies indicate that pornography reduces sexual tension that might otherwise lead to violence. If this is true, censoring pornography would cause more sexual violence. Those who make this argument often point out that sexual violence in Denmark decreased when the government stopped censoring pornography.

Feminists and Harm

Recently a group of feminists has taken up the harm argument for censoring pornography. These feminists agree that the harm principle is a true liberty-limiting principle. (Some hold that it is the only true liberty-limiting principle.) They, like the conservatives, argue that pornography causes harm. But the harm they point to is different from the harms that conservatives have traditionally cited. These feminists argue that pornography harms women by causing sexist attitudes. They point out that the vast majority of pornography is offensive because of the way it depicts women. In most pornographic works, women are shown as subservient, enjoying pain, and in general as mere objects to be used to give men pleasure. These feminists argue that pornography is one of many factors in our society that causes women to be seen as objects and as inferior to men. They also argue that pornography perpetuates myths such as the view that women enjoy being raped and that when women say "no" they mean "yes." They then argue that these attitudes and myths are part of the cause of all the harms of sexism—inferior pay, lack of access to high-paying jobs, unequal family relationships, and so forth (see chapter 9). Feminists who make this argument for censorship often also agree with conservatives that pornography causes sexual violence. These feminists have drafted legislation that bans pornographic materials that demean or degrade women. (This legislation has passed in some cities but been struck down by the courts.) They do not wish to ban erotica because they believe that, just as the main reason pornography is offensive is because of the way it portrays women, the main reason erotica is not offensive is that it does not depict women in offensive ways.

Those making this feminist argument for censoring pornography face the same problems with establishing a causal link that traditional conservatives face. In particular, many people, and a majority of feminists, think that it is much more likely that sexist attitudes cause a desire to see pornography than it is that a desire to see pornography causes sexist attitudes. Moreover, many think that a desire to see pornography and sexist attitudes are both caused by larger societal forces. Those who object to this feminist argument for censorship also point out that it seems to justify a great deal more than censoring pornography. Pornography is not the only thing that demeans or degrades women. Indeed, one might argue that because pornography is generally thought of as wrong, its effect on societal attitudes is not nearly as powerful as the demeaning images of women in advertisements that are thought to be perfectly appropriate. Beer ads may have more of an effect on attitudes toward women than pornography. Some political speech and art also demean women. Some argue that the feminist argument for censoring pornography implies that we ought to censor advertisements, political speech, and art. They take this to be a serious problem with the feminist argument. But some feminists accept this implication of their view. They agree that we ought to censor all these things. In response to this claim, those who object to the feminist argument for censoring pornography often refer to the slippery-slope arguments that we will discuss at the end of this chapter.

Child Pornography

There is one sort of pornography that has very few defenders—photographic child pornography. Photographic child pornography is sexually explicit and obscene photographs of children engaged in sexual conduct. Photographic child pornography is to be distinguished from descriptive child pornography—sexually explicit and obscene descriptions of children engaged in sexual conduct. Almost everyone agrees that the government may censor photographic child pornography because making this sort of pornography requires taking pictures of children engaged in sexual conduct, and many studies have shown that children are psychologically harmed by engaging in sexual conduct. Therefore, according to the uncontroversial harm principle, the government may prohibit this action. This argument does not apply to descriptive child pornography because producing this sort of pornography does not require that children engage in sexual conduct.

THE OFFENSE PRINCIPLE

Recall that the no-harm argument against censoring pornography relied on two claims: 1. that pornography causes no harm; and 2. that the harm principle is the only true liberty-limiting principle. We have examined the first claim, and now we turn to the second. Those who make the no-harm argument assert that the offense principle, the principle of legal paternalism, and the principle of legal moralism are all false. Those who argue for censoring pornography often argue that one or more of these principles is true.

Some use the offense principle to argue for censoring pornography. They argue that pornography, like public eating of feces, is offensive and that the government may prohibit acts that offend people. Those who argue against censoring pornography have two responses. The first is to deny the offense principle. They claim that the government ought not to prohibit actions merely because they are offensive. The main argument for this claim is that people who find behavior offensive do not have to look at it. They can turn their heads or leave. Those who defend the offense principle reply that this is too simplistic an answer. If pornography is allowed, it will be advertised. One will see magazine covers in stores and signs outside of the book shops that sell pornography. One cannot simply turn one's head because one may come across pornography suddenly, or pornographic signs may be very common in places where one is forced to go.

The second response to the offense-principle argument for censoring pornography grants that the offense principle is a true liberty-limiting principle. But, those who oppose censorship argue, the offense principle only justifies prohibiting acts that offend. The mere existence of pornography does not offend even if the way it is advertised does. So all the offense principle seems to justify is the regulation of the advertising of pornography. For example, governments might make laws saying that the only way one may advertise pornography is with black block letters on small white signs that say *Pornography Available Here*. One might also prohibit the display of pornographic materials in stores. One would then have to ask to see them.

LEGAL PATERNALISM

Some argue that, even if pornography does not cause any harm to others, it harms the people who buy it. They claim that people who use pornography have emotional problems, as well as difficulty loving others and making friends. They then claim that legal paternalism is a valid reason for the government to prohibit actions, and therefore the government may prohibit pornography. This argument relies on the claim that pornography causes harm to the people who use it. Here again we have all the causal issues that were discussed earlier. Even if it could be shown that viewing pornography and emotional trouble were correlated, we would still need to show that the viewing is not caused by the emotional trouble and that there are no larger societal forces that cause both the emotional trouble and the desire to view pornography.

Further, many people reject legal paternalism altogether. They argue that even if it is true that pornography harms the people who decide to view it, this is their decision. If it affects no one but them, then no one else ought to prohibit them from doing it. The basic argument behind the rejection of legal paternalism is the view that people ought to be able to determine for themselves what they will do with their lives. The harm principle implies that the government may keep people from interfering with the lives of others, but when it comes to actions that affect only the person who does the action, many feel that the government ought to leave people free to make their own decisions.

LEGAL MORALISM

The final liberty-limiting principle is legal moralism. Those who favor censoring pornography often rely on this principle. They argue that, even if pornography harms no one and is regulated so that it offends no one, the government ought to prohibit it simply because it is immoral. They argue that showing pictures of nude people involved in sexual acts is immoral on its face. Those who claim that pornography is immoral often use religion-based arguments to support their views. For example, some think that God has commanded us to be modest and have sex only with those to whom we are married. Others claim that pornography is immoral because it separates sex from love, and encourages lust. They claim that sex ought not be separated from love and that lust is immoral.

There are again two responses to the legal-moralism argument for censoring pornography. First, many deny that pornography is immoral. They reject religion-based arguments for moral views. They argue that there is nothing inherently immoral about pornographic materials. Pornography is merely sexually explicit materials that offend many people. It would certainly be wrong to force people to view it. But, many claim, there is nothing wrong with viewing it privately or selling it to people who wish to buy it. Even if pornography does depict the separation of sex and love, there is nothing immoral about that. While most people prefer to love those with whom they have sex, opponents of censoring pornography argue that there is nothing immoral about having or depicting sex separated from love. As for lust, many people argue that it is a perfectly natural and appropriate human emotion—nothing to be ashamed of at all.

The second response to the legal-moralism argument for censoring pornography is the denial of legal moralism. Many people object to legal moralism on the grounds that the government ought not be in the business of choosing a moral code and requiring people to follow it. Unless a moral code and the conduct that goes with it harm others, the government ought to remain neutral between moral views. People ought to be allowed to follow what they perceive as the correct moral code and to persuade others to follow them. But the government ought not to try to enforce one moral code over others. In response, defenders of legal moralism argue that, to create a genuine nation with a community spirit, the government must be allowed to prohibit actions which, while harmless and inoffensive, do not conform to the moral views accepted in a society. They argue that it is very important for the members of a nation to feel as if they are part of a community. A nation is not merely a collection of people who live in the same area, but a community of people who have a sense that they share certain values. These shared values, defenders of legal moralism claim, create a feeling of belonging that is central to human happiness. Those who attack legal moralism respond that this is just a nice way of saying that the government must be allowed to prohibit action that is harmless merely because some people hold a certain moral view. They worry that minorities and people who have atypical life-styles will have their rights violated by a pervasive government.

SLIPPERY-SLOPE ARGUMENTS

Besides the arguments we have already considered, there are two other common arguments against censoring pornography. Both are slippery-slope arguments. A slippery-slope argument is an argument that if we do some seemingly appropriate act, then we will inevitably do some other clearly inappropriate act. For example, someone might argue that, while there is nothing wrong with a single nuclear power plant, if we allow one to be built, then we will inevitably allow many to be built, and many nuclear power plants would be too great a risk. Slippery-slope arguments ought to be examined with great care because the slopes are frequently not as slippery as might be thought by people who use slippery-slope arguments. In other words, we must be sure that someone who proposes a slippery-slope argument really has shown that if we do the first act, we cannot stop and will inevitably do the second.

Vagueness

There are two slippery-slope arguments against censorship of pornography. The first focuses on the vagueness in the legal definition of the term "obscene." As we noted above, many claim that the current legal definition of "obscene" contains such vague phrases as "average person," "community standards," and "serious literary value." Moreover, those who make this argument claim, this is not merely a problem with this particular legal definition of "obscene," but with all possible legal definitions of the term. They claim that any accurate definition will contain vague terms. A vague definition means that it will be impossible to determine nonarbitrarily whether a particular work is legally obscene. Therefore, they claim, if we prohibit some pornographic materials because they are legally obscene, we will be unable to prevent nonarbitrarily the prohibition of some nonobscene material. For example, when considering whether a certain song that deals with sexual subjects is obscene, the court will have only a vague definition to work with and will therefore declare materials to be obscene when they are not. Moreover, the vagueness will mean that people will not be able to predict whether they will be prosecuted for publishing certain pictures or descriptions, and this will have a chilling effect—it will keep people from publishing anything that might be thought to be legally obscene under the vague definition. For example, certain artists might change the lyrics of songs because, while they do not believe the lyrics are legally obscene, they cannot, given a vague definition, be sure that the lyrics will not be declared obscene by a court.

Abuse of Authority

Another slippery-slope argument against the censorship of pornography focuses on the fact that, even if "obscene" could be defined with sufficient precision, censorship has a long history of being abused by authorities. If we allow censorship of pornography, then the censors will abuse their authority and censor nonpornographic material. In the past, people who had the power to censor works used that power not merely to prohibit obscene works, but to suppress unpopular ideas and prop up corrupt governments. Some fear that if we allow censorship in this country, this sort of abuse will occur here. A prosecutor might abuse her power and attempt to censor nonpornographic material. She might think that works defending communism are so offensive that they are obscene. Given the costs of defending oneself, convictions are not necessary to have a chilling effect. Even the possibility of being prosecuted for publishing obscene materials will keep people from publishing material. Defenders of this second slippery-slope argument point out that in the 1950s, during the McCarthy persecutions of real and supposed Communists, people in this country attempted to censor political views. They argue that this shows that, even today, the danger of abuse of power is real.

Those who defend the censorship of pornographic materials argue that these slippery-slope arguments are flawed. As for vagueness, they often claim that we all know pornography when we see it, even if we cannot give it a precise definition. Concerning the abuse of authority, defenders of censorship acknowledge that this is a danger. But they claim that with the safeguards we have built into our legal system (for example, appeals and the freedom to vote), it is not a large danger. They point out that many other countries censor not only pornography, but political speech, without hampering a free political debate. For example, in France and Germany it is illegal to publish racist material. (For a discussion of racism, see chapter 10.)

The key terms in this debate—obscenity, pornography, and erotica—are defined differently in the courts and in ordinary usage. In ordinary usage, "obscene" refers to something that is extraordinarily offensive, indecent, or repulsive. The term is often but not necessarily associated with sexuality. Pictures or descriptions are sexually explicit when they contain detailed or graphic depictions or descriptions of sexual acts or organs. Not everything that is sexually explicit is obscene. Clinically sexually explicit material is neither obscene nor sexually interesting. "Erotica" refers to sexually explicit but not obscene pictures or descriptions that are sexually interesting. "Pornography" refers to sexually explicit material that is obscene.

The legal definition of obscenity was established in Miller v. California. The Supreme Court held that a work is obscene when:

1) *the average person, applying contemporary community standards, would find that the work, taken as a whole, appeals to the prurient interest and;*
2) *the work depicts or describes, in a patently offensive way, sexual conduct that is specifically defined by law and;*
3) *the work, taken as a whole, lacks serious literary, artistic, political, or scientific value.*

According to the legal definition, but not according to the ordinary definition, all obscenity is sexual, and something can be pornographic but not obscene.

Censorship occurs when the government places a legal prohibition on the dissemination of pictures or descriptions. In the United States, some materials are being censored. Censorship is controversial because it reduces liberty. Censorship is a governmental activity, so neither refusing to buy material nor urging others not to buy it is censorship. Four principles have been suggested as justifications for governmental restrictions on liberty. The harm principle states that the government may prohibit an act if it is an act in which one person harms another person. The offense principle states that the government may prohibit an act if it is an act in which one person offends another person. According to the principle of legal paternalism, the government may prohibit an act if it is an act in which one person harms herself. According to the principle of legal moralism, the government may prohibit an act if it is an act which, while it harms or offends no one, is immoral.

The most common arguments for and against censoring pornographic materials are based on the harm principle. There is wide agreement that the harm principle is true. Therefore there is wide agreement that if pornography causes harm to people other than those who buy pornography, then the government may prohibit it. Traditional conservatives argue that pornography causes sexual violence, the breakdown of families, venereal disease, reduced marital fidelity, births out of wedlock, the disappearance of love, and the end of civilization. Some, but not all, feminists argue that pornography harms women by causing sexist attitudes.

It is very hard to determine whether pornography causes harm to others. First, it is difficult to determine whether there is a correlation between pornography and any harm. Second, even if a correlation is established, this does not show that pornography causes the harm. The desire to do the harm might cause the desire to view pornography, or both pornography and the harm might be caused by larger societal forces. Those who oppose censoring pornography also argue that, to justify censoring pornography, one must show not merely that pornography causes harm, but that the harms outweigh benefits and that enforcement costs are not too high. They also argue that pornography benefits society by invigorating stale sexual relations, aiding in normal sexual development for sexually repressed people, allowing a harmless pleasure, and causing a decrease in sexual tension that might otherwise lead to sexual violence.

The offense principle is used to argue for censoring pornography. Pornography is offensive and the government may prohibit acts that offend people. Those who argue against censoring pornography respond that the offense principle is false. Moreover, all the offense principle seems to justify is a set of regulations of the advertising of pornography to keep it from offending people. Legal paternalism is also used to argue for censorship of pornography. It is claimed that pornography harms the people who use it. Those who oppose censoring pornography deny that pornography harms the people who use it and argue that the principle of legal paternalism is false. Finally, some defend censoring pornography on legal-moralist grounds. They argue that the government may prohibit pornography because it is immoral. Some respond that pornography is not immoral and that the principle of legal moralism is false.

There are two slippery-slope arguments against censoring pornogra-

phy. The first slippery-slope argument begins with the claim that any accurate definition of obscenity will contain vague terms. A vague definition means that it will be impossible to determine nonarbitrarily whether a particular work is legally obscene. Therefore, they claim, if we prohibit some pornographic materials because they are legally obscene, we will be unable to prevent nonarbitrarily the prohibition of some nonobscene material. According to the second slippery-slope argument, if we allow censorship of pornography, then the censors will abuse their authority and censor nonpornographic material.

Selected Readings

Devlin, Patrick. *The Enforcement of Morals*. New York: Oxford University Press, 1965.

Feinberg, Joel. *Offense to Others*. New York: Oxford University Press, 1985.

Hart, H. L. A. *Law, Liberty, and Morals*. Stanford, CA: Stanford University Press, 1963.

Holbrook, David. *The Case Against Pornography*. New York: Library Press, 1973.

Lederer, Laura. *Take Back the Night: Women on Pornography*. New York: William Morrow, 1980.

Wendell, Susan, and David Copp. *Pornography and Censorship*. Buffalo, NY: Prometheus Press, 1983.

13

Friendship

All normal people have some idea of what a friend is. They probably have some friends or have had friends in the past. They can recognize when one person is the friend of another person, even if they have not thought much about the nature of friendship. Most people also want to have friends. They consider having friends to be a good thing, and they may try to improve their friendly relationship with someone. To try to improve a friendly relationship presupposes that you have some idea of what would make someone more your friend or less your friend. Ethicists have tried to specify the nature of friendship, to understand its ethical importance, and to determine whether it is consistent with more general moral duties.

THE NATURE OF FRIENDSHIP

Most people think that having friends is a good thing, and some philosophers claim that having friends is an important part of a good life. Aristotle claimed that no one would choose to live without friends, even if he had all other goods. What is it to have friends? The term "friend" is sometimes applied to anyone with whom a person has a friendly relationship. Acquaintances with whom you get along well are sometimes called "your friends," even when these relationships are not very close, important, or permanent. There may be no sharp dividing line between friendly acquaintances and real friends, but most people think that there is an essential nature of friendship that real relationships can approximate to a greater or lesser extent. The essential nature of friendship is to be a close, important, and long-lasting relationship, so that friendly relationships with acquaintances are friendships only to a limited degree. Some people are more your friends because your relationship with them is a more full-fledged instance of the nature of friendship than your relationship with some other people is. A friendly acquaintance can become more your friend by a change in the relationship so that it more closely approximates the essential nature of friendship.

One-Sided Versus Mutual

Being a friend of someone can be a one-sided or a mutual relationship. Manuel may be a friend of Julius, without Julius being a friend of Manuel. In a one-sided friendship, one person receives the affection and care of the other but does not respond in the same way. Julius may not particularly like Manuel or look out for Manuel's interests, but Manuel may very much like Julius and do everything that he can for Julius. Completely one-sided relationships usually do not last very long, but there are degrees of one-sidedness. There frequently are long-lasting relationships in which each person cares about the other, but one person cares much more than the other person does.

Ethicists have focused their attention on mutual friendships. Most people think that mutual friendships are better than one-sided friendships, so that in trying to describe the best type of friendship, ethicists have described mutual friendships. They have usually included mutuality in the nature of friendship. Defined in this way, a one-sided relationship is not a friendship, but something else, such as an infatuation or a case of benevolence. In the remainder of this chapter, we will consider only mutual friendships.

Characteristics of Friendship

Friendship can be considered to be love between friends. Friendship differs from other forms of personal love, such as the love between parents and children and the love between members of a family. Friendship has many of the same features as romantic love (see chapter 2), except that it does not usually include any urge toward sexual union. Like lovers, friends tend to share each other's views. A person is affected by his friends' values, interests, and outlook on the world. You are much more likely to consider something to be interesting, valuable, or important if your friends do. Hence, friends partly transform each other psychologically, but this normally occurs to a lesser degree than in romantic love. There is usually more independence from your friend or friends than from your lover. People frequently have many friends simultaneously, so that the influence of each friend is more limited. Friends are much more likely to live separately and to spend less time with each other than lovers do. Like romantic lovers, friends usually consider themselves to be equal with each other. In contrast with the love between parents and children, even between parents and adult children, one friend does not have or claim any authority over the other. In their business relations or roles in an organization, one friend may have some authority over the other, but not in their friendship.

The most frequently cited characteristics of friendship are liking each other, mutual concern for the welfare of the other, understanding and trusting each other, engaging in activities together, and commitment. To be friends, two people must like each other and enjoy being with each other. Friends have a type of affection for each other that is not primarily a matter of duty or obligation. They find each other pleasant, interesting, amusing, or worthy of attention. The enjoyment of each other's company is the starting point for friendships and a continuing feature of it. People who enjoy being with each other tend to engage in more activities with each other, to come to know more about each other, and to develop some concern for the other's welfare. Established friends are interested in what is going on in their friend's life, even if they cannot spend much time together.

Friends are also concerned for each other's welfare. Each wants the other's life to go well, and is ready to do what she can to aid her friend. Friends look out for each other's interests. In this way, friends can be useful to each other, but their concern for each other is not simply the result of a selfish bargain. An agreement between selfish individuals for each to aid the other does not establish a friendship. A pact to which two people consent in order to obtain benefits just for themselves is not a friendship. A friend is concerned with the welfare of her friend independently of estimates of what benefits her friend will give her in return. She just cares about the good of her friend. A friend wants to help her friend for her friend's sake. She does not constantly calculate the returns she will get for this aid or make the aid conditional upon her receiving sufficient returns.

Friends understand and trust each other. They know each other's character. Each knows how the other tends to think, feel, evaluate, and act. Understanding how your friend tends to think, feel, evaluate, and act is the result both of spending time together and of your friend revealing himself to you. In spending time together, you observe your friend's reactions in different circumstances and emotional states. You also learn about your friend's psychological makeup through what he tells you. Friends confide in each other and seek each other's advice about difficult decisions. A certain amount of trust is necessary in order that someone reveal his thoughts and feelings to you. As friendships develop, each friend acquires more reason to trust the other with confidential information about himself. In knowing more about your friend's character and about his concern for your welfare, you know more about what he will do with the private information that you reveal to him.

The deepest friendships include commitment. Friends commit themselves to continue to be concerned for each other's welfare, even if they tend to drift apart later. Friends are supposed to be available to help each other, even when they do not particularly feel like doing so. Some friends commit themselves to maintain their friendship actively. They try to keep their friendship alive, rather than let it be pulled apart by external forces. They make an effort to keep in touch with each other and to find time to do things together.

ETHICAL IMPORTANCE OF FRIENDSHIP

Friendship has been considered to be an ethically important relationship both for its intrinsic features and for its influence on the moral character of friends.

Intrinsic Features

Friendship itself is an ethically valuable relationship mainly because it is nonselfish and concerned for the good of another person. Selfishness is the attitude in which you try to get things only for yourself (see chapter 2). Friends have affection for each other, are concerned for each other's welfare, understand and trust each other, and are committed to each other. A friend is not trying to get material goods, money, power, position, reputation, or security only for herself. She wants good things for her friend as well, and she may sacrifice some of her own benefits for the sake of her friend. A friend frequently uses her time, energy, money, influence, and material goods to help her friend accomplish his own goals. In the best friendships, a friend is not trying to get affection only for herself either, but also gives affection to her friend. You give to your friend something valuable—your affection, concern, and efforts to help—that benefits him. This is ethically good.

Another ethically good feature of friendship is the sensitivity to each other that friends have. They have some understanding of each other's moods, emotions, desires, and reactions, and they try to improve their understanding. You know more about what is likely to upset or depress your friend than you know about members of the general public. You may already know some ways to cheer up your friend when she is in a bad mood, and you are interested in finding out what other things might lift her spirits or upset her. Furthermore, friends are interested in each other's goals and standards. While friends normally share many values, interests, and perspectives, there are always some individual differences. A friend does not simply project his own ideas of what is important or valuable on to his friend. He tries to find out exactly what the other thinks and values. He tries to help his friend accomplish her own goals.

Friends also want to encourage each other to have good goals and standards. You want to interest your friend in some activity, form of art, or area of knowledge that you think is interesting, amusing, or important. You want to discourage your friend from activities, emotions, goals, and standards that you think are bad, stupid, immoral, or self-destructive. Friendship requires some balance between accepting your friend's goals and standards as they are, and trying to improve them in terms of your goals and standards. You want to improve your friend's life in terms of your conception of a good life, but you also want to respect your friend's goals and standards. You cannot simply impose your goals and values on your friend, and your friend cannot do this to you either. In the best friendships, each friend has some influence on the activities, emotions, goals, and standards of the other. The complex situation of each friend trying to improve the other while respecting the other's conceptions is ethically good. Each friend can benefit from the other's insights and experience, but not be dominated by the other's conceptions of what is good and valuable.

A final good feature of friendship is that it promotes self-knowledge. Your friend tries to understand your character—that is, how you tend to think, feel, evaluate, and act. Your friend may notice things about you of which you are unaware. For example, she may notice that you become nervous and irritable in certain types of circumstances, while you did not realize that those types of circumstances made you nervous or angry. Since friends tend to confide in each other, your friends are likely to tell you some things about yourself that you did not know. Their comments and reactions can greatly increase your understanding of your own character, because there are many psychological facts about a person that it is hard for the person himself to detect. Increased knowledge of your own tendencies is ethically good because it allows you to suppress and try to change bad tendencies and to try to increase good tendencies.

Influence on Moral Character

Friends treat each other well and develop tendencies, sensitivities, and abilities to treat each other well. You develop this type of character both in yourself and in your friend. You encourage her to have the right emotions toward you and to be disposed to treat you well. You also promote in yourself the right emotions toward her and dispositions to treat her well. The development of these traits of character need not be a conscious process. You do not have to plan to develop these tendencies, sensitivities, and abilities either in yourself or in your friend. These traits of character tend to be developed naturally without much thought about the matter. A person's psychological makeup tends to change automatically through the continuing interactions with her friend.

Some ethicists have considered friendship to provide a sort of training for dealing morally with people at large. Through interacting with your friend, you develop tendencies, sensitivities, and abilities that can generalize to other people. The same traits of character that dispose you to treat your friend well will also dispose you to treat other people well. According to this view, friendship will tend to change a person automatically so that he is more disposed to treat other people morally. For example, through friendship a person develops a sensitivity to other people's emotions, goals, and standards and learns to balance his own conceptions of goodness with other people's conceptions of goodness. This sensitivity to other people's emotions, goals, and standards is important for a moral outlook that is supposed to be concerned with the welfare of others. This sensitivity directs a person away from her own selfish concerns toward the concerns of members of the general public. Being disposed to balance your own conceptions of what is good with other people's conceptions is also important for a moral outlook. This directs you toward respect for other people as rational, goal-setting agents. It makes you inclined to pay attention to their views and not just to impose your ideas of goodness.

If friendship tends to change a person's character so that she is more disposed to treat other people morally, friendship would be very important for morality. Since some form of friendship exists in most human societies and having friends is widely recognized to be a good thing, there would be a natural source for treating other people morally. In being motivated to develop good friendships, a person would also develop a character that disposed her to treat all other people morally. Along with other nonselfish special relations with others, such as family love and the relation between parents and children, friendship would lead to and support a nonselfish and moral outlook toward others.

Possible Bad Effects

Some moral philosophers claim that friendship does not tend to change a person's character so that he is more disposed to treat other people morally. While recognizing that friends try to treat each other well, these thinkers point out that friends may not treat the general public well at all. A group of friends or even two friends can be concerned only about each other's welfare. As a group or unit, friends can be selfish. They may be so concerned for each other that they have little or no concern for outsiders. For example, a criminal gang may be united by friendship among its members and hostility toward everyone else. In this way friendship may not normally make people more moral, and may even make some people less moral toward the general public. The changes in their character that dispose them to treat their friends well may not generalize to cover people other than their friends. They may become so focused on their own group of friends that they treat outsiders less morally.

FRIENDSHIP AND MORAL DUTY

Friendship is a special relationship between people. Since friendship is a close, important, and long-lasting relationship that includes understanding another's personality, it has to be fairly selective. A person cannot be friends with everyone in the world or even with a large number of people. A person can have the special mutual understanding and concern of friendship only with a limited number of people. The exclusivity of friendship raises two main issues about moral duties. Does the special concern for your friends conflict directly with the moral attitude of concern for everyone? If friendship is compatible with morality, does friendship create special moral obligations toward your friends?

Special Concern and Universal Concern

Friendship requires preferential treatment of your friends. You devote your time, energy, personal concern, influence, and other things to your friends, rather than spreading these around equally to all people. These potentially beneficial things could be directed toward a larger public or all of humanity, but you direct them mainly toward your friends. You give your friends a larger share, even if you also devote your time, energy, personal concern, influence, and so on to the welfare of humanity. This special concern for your friends seems to conflict with many major traditions of morality. The Christian moral tradition of love for all people without distinction has been thought by some ethical thinkers to conflict with the special concern of friendship. If a Christian is supposed to love all people, even her enemies, because God loves all people, how can a Christian devote special concern to her friends? Doesn't Christian love and charity toward all—the Greek term for this love is *agape*—require that a Christian not give preference to her friends?

The Kantian moral tradition claims that reason, not passions, is the basis of morality, that moral principles have to be the same for all people, and that all rational agents are intrinsically valuable (see chapter 5). The preferential treatment of those people who are your friends seems to conflict with these basic ideas of Kantianism. Friendship is based mainly on affection and personal interests, not primarily on reason. Kantian morality seems to require treating all people impartially, but friendship seems to require that people not be impartial in deciding between their friends' welfare and other people's welfare. The special concern for your friends also seems to conflict with some basic ideas of utilitarianism. Act utilitarianism claims that whether an act is right or wrong depends upon whether it produces as much happiness as possible (see chapter 4). It seems likely that more overall happiness could sometimes be produced by giving your time, attention, and so on, not to your friends but to other people. For example, the twenty-dollar gift that you give to your friend might feed many starving people in underdeveloped countries (see chapter 11).

CHRISTIAN VIEWS

There are disagreements among Christian moral thinkers about the compatibility of friendship with Christian love and charity toward everyone. All of them think that love of friends is less important than Christian love of everyone (*agape*), so that they all want to limit the amount of preferential treatment that friends receive. However, some Christian moral theorists think that some preferential treatment of friends is permitted, while others think that it should be completely avoided. Those who advocate trying to overcome friendship, such as Kierkegaard in some of his religious writings, consider it to be entirely distinct from Christian love and in competition with it. They consider friendship to be based in natural affections that are not directed toward God and not subordinated to God's will. Those who would permit and even encourage a certain amount of friendship, such as Saint Augustine (354–430), either do not consider friendship to be distinct from Christian love or do not think that friendship need be in competition with love of everyone. Augustine thinks that love of friends should lead a person onward to love of God and thence to love of everyone else.

KANTIAN AND UTILITARIAN VIEWS

Kantian and utilitarian moral theorists have emphasized impersonal points of view for morally judging actions. These impersonal points of view do not give any special consideration to your own desires, emotions, goals, or happiness. Friendship raises questions for both of these moral theories, because it is not selfish but not impersonal either. You treat your friends better than people in general, because they are your friends. It is not because your friends are deserving of this preferential treatment from everyone. It is not because all people should treat your friends in this preferential way. You, but not everyone else, should treat them preferentially because of your special relationship with them.

Action based on friendship is not impersonal because friendship itself depends upon specific facts about you, such as your background, where you live and work, and what you like and value. You form friendships with people based on psychological factors, such as shared backgrounds, interests, and values, and on circumstantial factors, such as who happens to live next door or be in the same class at school. The preferential treatment of friends does not easily fit into Kantian or utilitarian accounts of moral action because of the reliance of friendship on specific facts about individual people. Most Kantian and utilitarian moral theorists do not want to condemn all forms of friendship, but they do think that preferential treatment of friends should be limited by other moral concerns. Kantians claim that morality requires that you never benefit your friend in such a way as to violate other people's rights. You may never treat anyone simply as a means to your friend's welfare. You must treat all rational agents, not just your friends, as ends in themselves.

Utilitarians similarly want to limit the preferential treatment of friends by considerations of general welfare. You may not benefit your friends in such a way as to reduce significantly the overall amount of happiness that is produced. Rule-utilitarians (see chapter 4) can allow for some amount of preferential treatment of friends, because friendship in general makes people happier. A system of rules that allows people to have friends and to treat them somewhat better than everyone else will produce more happiness than a system of rules that forbids friendship.

All moral theories place certain restrictions on the preferential treatment of friends. Anyone who holds an institutional position that requires him to be impartial should be impartial. In his official capacity, he cannot make exceptions or give preferential treatment to his friends. For example, a legal judge, a professor dealing with students, or a government official dealing with the public should not give preferential treatment to his friends.

Special Moral Obligations

Most people think that friendship creates special moral obligations to friends that do not exist toward the general public. Just as parents have special moral obligations toward their children, so friends have special duties to care for each other's welfare. Several features of friendship may contribute to the special moral obligations. One feature is the mutual build-up of expectations between friends. Friends have good reasons to expect more care and consideration from each other than from the general public. Friends are supposed to look out for each other's interests. By contributing to a person's belief that you are her friend, you encourage her to expect that you will be specially concerned about her welfare. This is like an implied promise. You lead her to think that you will be especially concerned about her welfare and to count on you. Your moral obligation to care for her welfare is at least partly a matter of doing what you have implicitly committed yourself to do. In many cases the commitment is stated explicitly, rather than being implicit. Friends literally promise to look out for each other's interests.

Another feature of friendship that contributes to special moral obligations is the trust that friends place in each other by revealing their thoughts and feelings to each other. A person reveals many private things about himself to his friends that he does not reveal to the general public. In knowing such personal things about your friends, you are in a special position to help or harm them. You would not be able to harm your friends in the same ways if they were just part of the general public. You are in a position to harm them in some ways because they have trusted you with their thoughts and feelings. This feature of friendship seems to create special obligations for you not to use against them the information with which they have trusted you. You have a duty to honor their trust in you.

Most people think that there is an essential nature of friendship that real relationships can approximate to a greater or lesser extent. The essential nature of friendship is to be a close, important, and long-lasting relationship, so that friendly relationships with acquaintances are friendships only to a limited degree. Being a friend of someone can be a one-sided or a mutual relationship. Most people think that mutual friendships are better than one-sided friendships, so that in trying to describe the best type of friendship, ethicists have described mutual friendships.

Friendship can be considered to be love between friends. Friends tend to share each other's views and to be affected by each other's values, interests, and outlook on the world. People frequently have many friends simultaneously, so that the influence of each friend is more limited than in the case of romantic love. Friends usually consider themselves to be equal with each other. Friends like each other, enjoy being with each other, and are concerned for each other's welfare. A friend wants to help her friend for her friend's sake, not for some return benefit. Friends understand each other's character and trust each other. The deepest friendships also include commitment.

Friendship has been considered to be an ethically important relationship both for its intrinsic features and for its influence on the moral character of friends. The most important ethically good intrinsic features are that friendship is nonselfish; concern for the good of another person; sensitive to another's moods, emotions, desires, and reactions; encouraging of good goals and standards in another; respectful of another's autonomy; and supportive of self-knowledge. Friendship has been considered to have a positive influence on moral character because friends develop tendencies, sensitivities, and abilities to treat each other well. These traits of character tend to be developed naturally without much thought about the matter. Some ethicists think that the same traits of character that dispose you to treat your friend well will also dispose you to treat other people well. According to this view, friendship will tend to change a person automatically so that she is more disposed to treat other people morally. Other ethicists point out that friends may not treat the general public well at all. A group of friends or even two friends may be so concerned for each other's welfare that they have little or no concern for outsiders.

A person can have only a limited number of friends. The exclusivity of friendship raises the question of whether the preferential treatment of your friends is compatible with the moral attitude of concern for everyone. The special concern for your friends seems to conflict with many major traditions of morality, such as Christian love for all people without distinction, Kantian rationality and impartiality in treating people, and the utilitarian emphasis on producing the greatest overall happiness. Christian moral thinkers disagree about the compatibility of friendship with Christian love and charity toward everyone. The preferential treatment of friends does not easily fit into Kantian or utilitarian accounts of moral action because of the reliance of friendship on specific facts about individual people. Most Kantian and utilitarian moral theorists do not want to condemn all forms of friendship, but they think that preferential treatment of friends should be limited by other moral concerns. All moral theories forbid preferential treatment of friends by officials whose position requires them to be impartial.

Most people think that friendship creates special moral obligations to friends that do not exist toward the general public. The mutual build-up of the expectation that your friend will look out for your welfare and the trust that friends place in each other by revealing their thoughts and feelings are two sources of special moral obligations.

Selected Readings

Aristotle. *Nicomachean Ethics, Books 8–9* (several good translations).

Badhwar, Neera. *Friendship: A Philosophical Reader.* Ithaca, NY: Cornell University Press, 1993.

Blum, Lawrence. *Friendship, Altruism, and Morality.* London: Routledge, 1980.

Meilaender, Gilbert. *Friendship.* Notre Dame, IN: Notre Dame University Press, 1981.

Pakaluk, Michael. *Other Selves: Philosophers on Friendship.* Indianapolis, IN: Hackett, 1991.

14

Animal Rights

To feed people, 3 billion chickens are killed every year in the United States. Cosmetics are tested by dropping them into the eyes of rabbits. Medical research takes the lives of millions of mice and other animals every year. In many Asian cultures, such use of animals is considered wrong. But most people in the United States eat meat, use cosmetics, and take drugs without ever considering the effect that these products have on animals. Recently animal-rights activists have argued that these practices are wrong.

HUMAN AND ANIMAL

"Human" refers to members of the species *homo sapiens*. Both authors and most readers of this book are paradigm humans. Paradigm humans are humans with the mental functions of normal adult humans. Nonparadigm humans are humans who lack the mental functions of normal adult humans. Human newborns, severely mentally handicapped humans, and humans in permanent comas are all nonparadigm humans. The distinction between paradigm and nonparadigm humans is important because nonparadigm humans are in many respects similar to animals. The word "animal" is used in two importantly different ways. Sometimes "animal" refers to any member of the biological kingdom *animalia*. Members of this kingdom typically have locomotion, rapid response to stimuli, and, unlike plants, cannot make their own food. On this definition of "animal," all humans are animals. On other occasions, "animal" refers to any *animalia* other than a human. On this definition, no humans are animals. For convenience, we will use the second definition of "animal."

FOUR CONTROVERSIES

There are four major areas in which the treatment of animals has raised controversy. The first is the use of animals in biomedical research. Animals are used in the development and testing of drugs that will be used on animals and humans as well as in scientific research intended to further our understanding of human and animal biology and psychology. Sometimes, as in research on the nature of pain, the research involves directly causing the animals pain and suffering. To study pain, one must have pain to study. In other experiments, animals are not directly caused pain, but they are given painful diseases. In the end, most of these animals are killed.

Another area of controversy is the raising and killing of animals for food. Humans do not require meat to live. Vegetarians must pay attention to their diet to be sure that they get all the necessary nutrients, but it is perfectly possible to live a normal, healthy life without ever eating meat. All eating of animals requires killing them, but it is possible to raise and kill the animals painlessly. Chickens can be given room to roam, scratch, and make nests. They can be killed in quick and painless ways. The same is true of cows, pigs, sheep, and all the other animals we eat. But many claim that in our society the animals we eat are not raised and killed painlessly. Many, if not most, veal calves, for example, are confined in dark stalls so small that they cannot even turn around. The stalls are dark and small because light and movement would cause the calf to produce iron, and this would color and flavor the meat. The calf would lick its own urine to retain what little iron it has, but the stalls are made so small that they cannot turn around to do this. The calves are also taken from their mothers and given iron-poor milk. Many cows are castrated, usually without anesthetic, to make them docile and improve the taste of their meat. Many chickens are raised in pens so packed with other chickens that they cannot move freely. The birds become frustrated and would peck each other to death except that their beaks are cut off to prevent them from doing this.

Another area of controversy is the use of animals in the production of cosmetics. The safety of most cosmetics is tested by dropping them into rabbits' eyes. This is very painful for the rabbits.

A final area of controversy is the use of animals in producing clothing. Animals are used in the production of fur, leather, and reptile-skin clothing. Some of these animals are trapped in the wild. Some of the traps crush the head of the animal so that it feels no pain. But many traps grab the leg of the animal so that it suffers enormous pain and slowly starves to death. Other animal clothing is made by raising animals on farms. Many of these farms use techniques similar to the ones mentioned in the previous paragraph.

SPECIESISM

Those who think that our treatment of animals is immoral often argue that this treatment is an example of speciesism. The term "speciesism" is chosen to draw a parallel between our treatment of animals and racism and sexism. Recall from chapter 9 that an act, practice, or attitude is sexist when it creates unjustified differences between the sexes or exploits irrelevant differences between the sexes. Similarly, an act, practice, or attitude is speciesist when it creates unjustified differences between species or exploits irrelevant differences between species. As with sexism, much of the debate on this issue turns on disagreement over what differences are unjustified and/or irrelevant. Most people who argue that our treatment of animals is speciesist think that the *mere* fact that one being is a member of one species and another being is a member of another species is not a relevant difference between the two beings. They argue that the differences between species, like differences between races and sexes, is nothing more than a difference in genetic code. Just as many argue that the mere fact that one has genes that makes one's skin black is morally irrelevant, animal-rights activists argue that the mere fact that a being has genes that make it have fur is morally irrelevant.

It is important to be clear about speciesism. Speciesism is the view that a difference of species, *without any other morally relevant difference*, is sufficient to justify differences in treatment. People often assume that differences in species are accompanied by morally relevant differences—such as having a soul, being able to feel pain, or being able to make choices. So someone, without thinking, might claim that all humans are able to feel pain. But when one remembers that some humans are in permanent comas, it is clear that this is not true. Suppose someone held that beings that feel pain are more morally important than beings that do not. Suppose further that this person thought that only humans can feel pain but that some nonparadigm humans do not feel pain. On these grounds, she then holds that killing animals and these nonparadigm humans is not wrong. Whatever the other merits of this view, it is not speciesist. (The merits of this view will be discussed below.) This person does not think the mere fact that one is human, is a member of the species *homo sapiens*, is morally important. Rather, she thinks that what is important is whether a being can feel pain or not. She then claims that it is a biological fact that only humans feel pain. This is compatible with there being some nonparadigm humans who do not feel pain. That this person is not speciesist is demonstrated by the fact that she thinks killing some nonparadigm humans is not wrong. What counts, according to this person, is ability to feel pain—not species. Suppose another person held that all humans, all being with the genetic code of *homo sapiens*, are morally more important than all other forms of life. He holds that a permanently comatose human is more important than any animal and more important than any possible space being—no matter how intelligent that being is. This is a speciesist view.

THE UTILITARIAN ARGUMENT

There are two different arguments for the view that we ought to stop eating meat and stop using animals for research, cosmetics, and clothing—the utilitarian argument and the rights argument. People who make the utilitarian argument are often referred to as "animal-rights activists," but they focus not on animal rights but on animal suffering. Recall from chapter 4 that according to classical act utilitarianism, an act is right if it maximizes happiness, and an act is wrong if it does not maximize happiness. (We will limit our discussion to this version of utilitarianism. You might want to review chapter 4 before proceeding.) Many utilitarians think that we ought to count the happiness of animals when we consider whether acts are right or wrong. These utilitarians hold that pleasure and pain are the morally important consequences and that animals feel pleasure and pain. Therefore, we ought to consider the happiness of animals in determining the moral status of eating meat and using animals for research, cosmetics, and clothing.

These utilitarians acknowledge that there are ways in which humans can suffer more than animals. Humans not only feel pain but dread the prospect of pain. Animals do not know that they will feel pain as often as humans do. Humans suffer in confinement and many animals do not. A human kept outside in a one-hundred-square-yard square area would suffer a great deal. A pig in that situation does not suffer at all. But these utilitarians also point out that there are way in which animals can suffer more than humans. Animals cannot be told that pain is for their long-term good. So an animal captured to be given an injection of a drug that will cure it of a disease is just as afraid as an animal captured to be killed. But humans can know that injections are going to make them feel better in the long run so they do not feel the terror that animals do when injected.

Many utilitarians argue that we would maximize happiness by not eating animals, not using them in research, and not using them to produce cosmetics and clothing. As noted above, eating animals is not necessary for humans to live a happy and healthy life. It is required only for the pleasures of taste. Cosmetics and animal clothing only serve the vanity of humans. They are clearly not necessary for us to live a happy life. If no one used cosmetics or animal clothing, they would not be missed. As for using animals in research, utilitarians argue that we can do research without using animals. These utilitarians argue that there would be a net increase in happiness if we stopped eating animals and stopped using them in research, cosmetics, and clothing. There would be a loss in human happiness, but this would be outweighed by a larger gain in animal happiness.

Animals Do Not Feel Pain

There are several objections to the utilitarian argument. Some, most notably the French philosopher Rene Descartes (1596–1650), have argued that animals do not feel pain or pleasure at all. Descartes thought that, while animals moved and acted in ways similar to humans, they do not feel anything. He thought that animals were unfeeling biological machines. They can be damaged, but not hurt. One who holds this view is not necessarily committed to the view that we may treat animals any way we please. First, some acts involving animals may hurt people. If you kick my cat, I might be upset. Second, doing acts that damage animals might have a psychological tendency to lead to acts that damage, and therefore hurt, humans. People who damage animals might tend to become people who damage humans.

Descartes's view of animals is no longer plausible. Given our current knowledge of biology, it is clear that animals feel pain. Our knowledge of animal pain comes from the same two sources as our knowledge that other humans feel pain. First, while you can feel your own pain and that is how you know that you can feel pain, you cannot feel another human's, say, Naomi's, pain. You know that Naomi feels pain because she reacts in ways very similar to the way you react when you feel pain. When you touch a hot stove you feel your own pain. You also scream and jump around. When Naomi touches a hot stove she screams and jumps around as you do. Second, you can be very sure that Naomi feels pain because biological investigation has revealed that her nervous system is very much like yours—nerve endings connected to neurons in the brain, and so forth. The same is true of a cat. If a cat touches a hot stove, it reacts in ways very similar to your and Naomi's reactions. Moreover, biological investigation has revealed that cats have nervous systems very similar to our own. Therefore, it is clear that most animals feel pain. There are some animals—oysters, for example—that might not. So the utilitarian argument may not apply to oysters.

Animal Research Maximizes Happiness

Another objection to the utilitarian argument for dramatically changing the way we treat animals is the claim that animal research does in fact maximize happiness. Those who make this objection argue that one consequence of using animals for research is a dramatic reduction in both human and animal suffering, as well as a dramatic increase in the number of human and animal lives saved. The research, they argue, either could not be done or could not be done nearly as fast without using animals. For example, cancer research is often done on mice. These mice suffer. But their suffering is outweighed, some claim, by the reduction in suffering that new cancer treatments bring. Therefore, they argue, we ought to do animal research. The pain caused to the animals used in research is outweighed by the happiness felt by the billions of people and animals who benefit from the products of that research.

Whether or not using animals in research maximizes happiness, the utilitarian seems to have a strong claim that the research on animals ought to be done in a way that minimizes the amount of pain they suffer. So animals used in research should be killed painlessly, they should be given painful disease only when necessary, and they should be kept in conditions that do not cause them to suffer.

Raising Animals for Food Maximizes Happiness

Just as some think that using animals for research maximizes happiness, some think that using animals for food maximizes happiness. They point out that people would be unhappy if they ate a vegetarian diet. They would want meat. They also argue that raising animals for food causes a great deal of animal pleasure. If we did not eat animals, we would not raise the vast majority of animals that we currently raise. Therefore, if we all became vegetarians, the pleasures felt by all the animals we eat would be lost. Those who make the utilitarian argument respond that people would not want to eat meat at all once they became used to a vegetarian diet. They point out that in many Asian cultures everyone is a vegetarian and that these people do not want to eat meat. They also argue that current food-raising practices mean that the animals we raise to eat have lives that contain more suffering than pleasure. So it would maximize happiness if we did not raise them at all.

Others argue that, while the utilitarian argument does show that we should not raise animals in ways that make their lives full of suffering, it does not show that we ought not to raise animals at all. First, many point out that it is not necessary to make animals suffer while raising them to be eaten. We do not have to castrate cows, keep chicken in small pens, or confine calves in dark stalls. Indeed, some cows, chickens, and calves are not raised this way. Animals raised for food while not being made to suffer are usually called free-range animals. For example, free-range chickens are chickens raised in pens large enough for them to walk around, scratch, and nest. Free-range meat is more expensive than the meat most of us currently eat. Second, those who make this objection to the utilitarian argument also claim that activists have anthropomorphized animals. In other words, they assert that activists have assumed that animals suffer when placed in situations that would cause humans to suffer. But, as we noted above, animals do not suffer in many situations that would cause humans to suffer. As we noted above, pigs do not suffer merely from being confined to a one-hundred-square-yard area, but humans do. Third, some argue that activists have exaggerated the frequency of the animal-raising procedures that cause animals to suffer. For these three reasons, many think that the utilitarian argument does not show that we ought to be vegetarians. It shows only that we ought to work to end animal-raising practices that cause animals to live lives full of suffering and not eat meat from animals raised in these ways.

Using Animals for Cosmetics and Clothing Maximizes Happiness

This objection parallels the previous two, so our discussion of it can be brief. Some argue that the pleasure humans get from cosmetics and animal clothing is greater than the pain caused animals in producing these things. This objection does not seem as strong as the previous two because there are ways to test cosmetics and make clothing that do not use animals. But some argue that as long as the animals used to test cosmetics and make clothing do not live lives of suffering, it maximizes happiness to use animals in this way. It is clearly possible to raise the animals used to make clothes without making them suffer. It may not be possible to use animals to test cosmetics without causing them to suffer. So the utilitarian argument may imply only that we ought to stop using animals to test cosmetics and raise the animals we use for clothing in ways that do not cause them to suffer.

THE RIGHTS ARGUMENT

Those who make the rights argument against eating meat and using animals for research, cosmetics, and clothing are animal-rights activists in the literal sense of that phrase—they think animals have rights. They often begin by asking people to consider the following situation. Suppose that by forcing a small group of paradigm humans to be medical research subjects we could make enormous strides in curing diseases like cancer and AIDS. Of course the members of the small group would suffer and some would die. But the progress we could make by using this small group of humans is so great that the happiness the research would bring to the millions cured of cancer and AIDS would outweigh the suffering caused to the small group of research subjects. Many think that even if all the facts are as we have outlined them here, it would still be very wrong to do the research. They argue that the research would violate the rights of the research subjects. In the terms we used in chapter 4, the research would have the intrinsic feature of violating the rights of the subjects. That is why, according to many, we ought not do this sort of research, even if it maximizes happiness.

Those who think animals have rights argue that the same is true when the research subjects are animals instead of humans. They argue that animals, like humans, have a right not to be used in this way. Therefore, they argue that using animals for food, in research, to test cosmetics or to make clothing is wrong. They claim that the rights of animals, like the rights of humans, are independent of whether they suffer or not. Suppose that we hooked the human research subjects to machines that gave them constant doses of a pleasure-inducing drug. Animal-rights activists and many others think that the research program would still violate the rights of the human subjects. Similarly, animal-rights activists claim that even if animals are raised in good conditions and die painlessly, their rights are still violated by using them for food, research, cosmetics, or clothing.

Those who think that animals have rights argue that animals (and humans) have rights because they have interests. Plants and inanimate objects like rocks do not have interests. To say that something has an interest in X means that not having X is bad for that thing. Humans have an interest in food because not having food is bad for humans. Animals also have an interest in food, and for the same reason. Plants and rocks have no interests because nothing can be bad *for them*. Destroying a rock or a plant might be bad for a human or an animal. The rock might have sentimental value for a human. The plant might be a necessary food source for the animal. But destroying a rock or plant cannot be bad for them because they have no experiences that could be good or bad. Suppose you are hit with a heavy object. You will have experiences—pain, throbbing sensation, itching as the wound heals. These experiences are unpleasant or bad. But if a rock or a plant is hit with a heavy object, it may be damaged but it will have no experiences. Rocks and plants do not experience anything. So they cannot have good or bad experiences.

Those who think that animals have rights argue that everything that has experiences has interests and rights. They admit that there are some animals who may have no interests, and so no rights. For example, some think that an investigation of their nervous systems reveals that oysters and other simple animals do not experience anything and therefore have no interests. If this is true, then on the rights argument, these animals have no rights and it is permissible to kill them for food, clothing, research, or cosmetics.

Animals Have No Interests

Some object to the rights argument on the grounds that animals have no experiences, no interests, and therefore no rights. This position is a version of the claim that animals do not feel pain. As we noted above, biological research and our own experiences with animals show that this view is false.

Natural to Kill Animals

Another objection to the rights argument is based on the claim that our desire to eat meat and use animals is natural. Some think that our desire to eat animals and use them for clothing is one of our natural instincts. They argue that it cannot be wrong to act on our natural instincts and so conclude that it is not wrong to kill animals for food and clothing. Notice that this objection does not apply to the use of animals in research and to make cosmetics. It seems implausible to claim that we have a natural instinct to do these things.

Those who defend the rights argument argue that an act can be wrong even if we have a natural instinct to do it. That an act is moral does not seem to follow from the fact that an act is instinctive. Suppose that 10 percent of humans were born with an instinctive desire to eat human flesh. It does not seem that it would be permissible for them to eat humans. The instinctive desires that a person has can be immoral, and in that case she ought not act on those desires.

God Has Given Us Animals to Use

According to the Bible, Genesis 9:3, God said: "Every moving thing that lives shall be food for you; and as I gave you the green plants, I give you everything." On the basis of this and other passages in the Bible, some object to the rights argument on the grounds that God has given animals to humans for human use. They claim that it is wrong to kill humans, not because it wrongs the humans, but because humans are God's property and killing them damages God's property. The animals were God's property, too, but he gave them to humans, so now all animals are the property of humans. Since all animals are the property of humans, humans may do anything they wish with them—including using them for food, research, cosmetics, or clothing. There is a slightly different version of this argument. Some think that God simply decreed that humans may use animals—without giving animals to humans as property. They claim that this decree means that there is nothing wrong with eating animals or using them for research, cosmetics, or clothing.

These arguments seem to have many problems, but most of them are beyond the scope of this chapter. Obviously they require that one believe in God. Many have argued that God does not exist. They also require that one believe that the Bible is an accurate account of what God has done. According to many Asian cultures, God has commanded us not to use animals, so one who makes this argument must be prepared to argue that the Bible is more authoritative than the texts of these other religions. It has proven very difficult to come up with such arguments. The arguments also require that one believe that God has the right to decide what lives and dies and that God can transfer this right to humans. Finally, the first of the two arguments moves from the claim that animals are the property of humans to the claim that humans may do anything with animals. Animal-rights activists deny this move. They claim that the mere fact that an animal is one's property does not mean that one may do anything one wants to it. They claim that your cat is definitely your property, but it would violate your cat's rights if you tortured it for fun.

Animals Are Not Part of the Moral Community

Some object to the rights argument on the grounds that animals are not part of the moral community. They point out that animals have no moral duties or moral responsibilities. They have no duties or responsibilities because they cannot understand what these things are. Suppose that a pack of wild dogs attacks a man who is hiking in Africa. We cannot say that these dogs have failed to do their duties or violated one of the man's rights. Because we cannot reason with the dogs and explain to them that they have a duty not to kill humans, they do not have such a duty. The case is very different if a woman is attacked by a group of humans. These humans can be told of their duty not to attack people, so they violate the woman's rights. According to this objection to the rights argument, if a being cannot violate rights, then that being cannot have rights. Since the dogs cannot violate the hiker's rights, they have no rights. This is what it means to be part of the moral community. A being is part of the moral community when it has rights and can violate rights.

Defenders of the rights argument agree that animals cannot violate rights. They agree that the dogs do not violate the hiker's rights. But they claim that one cannot conclude that a being does not have rights from the fact that the being cannot violate rights. Having rights and being able to violate rights are two different things. A being can have one without the other. They point out that human newborns cannot violate the rights of others for the same reason the wild dogs cannot—newborns cannot understand what it is to have moral duties. But the fact that human newborns cannot violate rights does not mean that human newborns have no rights.

So the defender of the rights argument thinks that the moral community is more complex than this objection assumes it is. There are beings, such as paradigm humans, that both have rights and can violate rights. These beings are full members of the moral community. There are beings, such as animals and human newborns, that have rights but cannot violate rights. These beings are partial members of the moral community. Finally, there are things, such as rocks, which neither have rights nor can violate rights. These things are not part of the moral community.

Animals Do Not Have the Right to Life

This objection to the rights argument and the next one are perhaps the most serious and most frequently raised. Those who argue that animals do not have the right to life begin by noting that the rights argument implies that a person who hunts squirrels for sport is the moral equivalent of one who hunts children for sport. They claim that this is implausible. Even if it is wrong to hunt squirrels, surely it is much worse to hunt children. Those who make this objection argue that the rights argument must be flawed because it implies that hunting squirrels and hunting children are morally equivalent. But what exactly is the problem with the rights argument?

THE SPECIFIC-INTERESTS ARGUMENT

Those who argue that animals have no right to life agree with those who make the rights argument that animals (and humans) have rights because they have interests. But, they continue, the rights argument's problem is the claim that a being that has one interest has the same rights as a being that has many interests. They think that the specific rights that a being has depend on the specific interests of the being. This is the first step in the specific interests argument. Squirrels have interests and so do children. But they do not have the same interests. To take an obvious example, a squirrel has an interest in being with squirrels, but a child does not. A child has an interest in going to school, but a squirrel does not. Different animals have different interests. A squirrel has no interest in flying south for the winter, but a wild goose does. Many argue that these differences in interests make a difference in the rights that squirrels, children, and geese have. They claim that a being can have a right to something only if that being has an interest in that thing. This does not mean that any time a being has an interest in something, it has a right to that thing. It means only that without an interest in something, a being cannot have a right to it. So squirrels and geese do not have a right to go to school because they have no interest in going to school. Children have no right to be with squirrels because they have no interest in being with squirrels.

Interests in the Future   The next step in the specific-interests argument is the claim that animals have no idea what the future is, and so they have no interests in the future. If they have no interests in the future, and a being can have a right to something only if that being has an interest in that thing, then it seems to follow that animals have no right to have a future. Another way to say that animals have no right to have a future is to say that they have no right to life. So while animals that can feel pain have an interest in not being in pain, and so can have a right not to be in pain, they do not have a right to life because they do not understand or have interests in the future. Both children and squirrels have an interest in not being in pain. But only children have a right to life. This explains why hunting squirrels and children is not morally equivalent.

SPECIFIC RIGHTS AND NONPARADIGM HUMANS

The specific-interests argument implies that the rights of beings will not follow the lines of species or biological kingdoms. Oysters and pigs are both animals, but if oysters cannot feel pain and pigs can, then, on this view, oysters cannot have a right not to be stuck with knives but pigs can. This view also implies that some nonparadigm humans do not have a right to life. Like animals, some nonparadigm humans (for example human newborns, humans with extremely severe mental problems and humans in permanent comas) do not understand or have interests in the future. Therefore, the specific-interests argument seems to imply that these nonparadigm humans do not have a right to life. This seems to be a serious problem with the argument.

Defenders of the specific-interests argument have two responses to this problem. The first is the claim that nonparadigm humans have all the rights that paradigm humans have just because they are members of the same species as paradigm humans. Those who make the rights argument respond that this is blatantly speciesist. If one claims that nonparadigm humans have rights merely because of their species, then one is claiming that differences in nothing but genetic code are morally important. This, as we saw above, seems to be parallel to the claim that humans with the genetic code that causes white skin are morally more important than humans with the genetic code that causes black skin.

Another response made by those who defend the specific-interests argument against the objection that their view implies that some nonparadigm humans do not have the right to life is to accept this consequence of their view. They agree that some nonparadigm humans do not have the right to life. They think it is perfectly plausible to hold, for example, that humans who have been in car accidents and whose brains were damaged to the point that they are in permanent comas do not have the right to life. It is permissible to kill them. They make a similar point about newborns born with brain defects so severe that they will be permanent newborns—never able to focus their eyes, control their bowels, walk, or talk.

Specific Interests and Newborns Defenders of the specific interests argument have a more difficult time when in comes to the subject of normal human newborns. While these newborns will in all probability become paradigm humans, they are currently not as intelligent as most cats. They certainly have no understanding of the future. So it seems that if a being can have a right to something only if that being has an interest in that thing, then human newborns do not have the right to life.

In defense of the view that normal human newborns, like animals, do not have a right to life, three points are often made. First, human newborns are usually loved by paradigm humans. So killing newborns may be wrong because it damages the interests of paradigm humans. The same would be true of animals that paradigm humans love. Second, a certain number of human newborns must survive if the species is to survive. So it may be wrong to kill human newborns because of the long-range effects on the species. Third, even if human newborns do not have the right to life, this does not mean that we do anything wrong by not killing them. While we have a moral duty not to kill beings with a right to life, it is morally permissible not to kill beings that do not have this right. Defenders of the rights arguments are unmoved by each of these three points. They argue that normal human newborns clearly have all the rights that paradigm humans have, and this shows that merely having a single interest in anything gives one the full protection of the right to life.

Interference with Nature

The final common objection to the rights argument is the claim that the argument implies that we ought to intervene in nature in massive ways. Suppose that you are walking in the woods with a ray gun that moves objects and stuns humans and animals. You see a person sleeping beside the path. There is a large boulder that is rolling toward the person. He will not awake and move out of the way in time, and so if you do nothing, he will be crushed to death. If you used it, your stun gun would deflect the boulder away from the sleeping person. It seems that you ought to use your stun gun. Suppose that the situation is the same, except that instead of a boulder rolling toward the sleeper, there is a person stalking him. The stalker will kill the sleeper unless you stun her with your gun. It seems that you ought to stun the stalker. Again, suppose that the situation is the same, except that instead of a person stalking the sleeper, it is a bear that is doing the stalking. Again, it seems that you ought to use your gun and stun the bear.

Now, suppose that instead of a sleeping human being stalked by a bear, you see a sleeping deer being stalked by a bear. Those who object to the rights argument think that if one asserts that animals have the same right to life that humans do, one is committed to the view that you ought to stun the bear so that the deer can escape. If animals and humans have the same right to life and if you ought to save the human from the bear, then you ought to save the deer from the bear. They take this to be one example of many possible situations in which people could do things to prevent wild animals from killing one another. Therefore, they think that the rights argument implies that we ought to intervene frequently in the many literal struggles for life that occur in nature. They take this to show that the argument is flawed.

"*H*uman" *refers to members of the species homo sapiens. Paradigm humans are humans with the mental functions of normal adult humans. Nonparadigm humans are humans who lack these mental functions. The word "animal" is used in two different ways. Sometimes "animal" refers to any member of the biological kingdom animalia. On this definition, all humans are animals. On other occasions, "animal" refers to any animalia other than a human. In this chapter we have used the second definition of "animal."*

There are four major areas in which the treatment of animals has raised controversy. The first is the use of animals in biomedical research. In this research, animals are directly caused to suffer or are given painful diseases. In the end, most of these animals are killed. The second is the raising and killing of animals for food. Humans do not require meat to live.

All eating of animals requires killing them, but it is possible to raise and kill the animals painlessly. But many claim that in our society the animals we eat are not raised and killed painlessly. The third area of controversy is the use of animals in cosmetics. The safety of most cosmetics is tested by dropping them into rabbits' eyes. A final area of controversy is the use of animals in producing clothing. Animals are used in the production of fur, leather, and reptile-skin clothing. Some of these animals are trapped in the wild, while others are raised on farms.

The term "speciesism" is chosen to draw a parallel between our treatment of animals and racism and sexism. An act, practice, or attitude is speciesist when it creates unjustified differences between species or exploits irrelevant differences between species. Most people who argue that our treatment of animals is speciesist think that the mere fact that one being is a member of one species and another being is a member of another species is not a relevant difference between the two beings. They argue that the differences between species, like differences between races and sexes, is nothing more than a difference in genetic code.

There are two arguments for the view that we ought to stop eating meat, stop animal research, and stop using animals for cosmetics and clothing—the utilitarian argument and the rights argument. Many utilitarians argue that we would maximize happiness by not eating animals and not using them for research, cosmetics, and clothing. Eating animals is not necessary for humans to live a happy and healthy life. Cosmetics and animal clothing only serve the vanity of humans. Utilitarians argue that we can do research without using animals. In response, some have argued that animals do not feel pain or pleasure at all. Biological research and our own experiences with animals show that this view is false. Others argue that the total effect of animal research and raising animals for food is to maximize happiness. They stress the benefits of the knowledge gain in animal research and the fact that if we did not raise animals for food, many animals would never come into existence. Many argue that the utilitarian argument only shows that we ought not to raise animals in ways that cause them to suffer—not that we ought not to raise animals for research or food at all.

The rights argument asserts that animals have rights because they have interests. To say that something has an interest in X means that not having X is bad for that thing. Those who make the rights argument think that animals have rights that are violated if we use them in research, for food, for cosmetics, or for clothing. Some object to the rights argument on the grounds that we have a natural instinct to kill animals and it cannot be wrong to act on our natural instincts. But those who defend the rights argument claim that one cannot conclude that an act is moral from the fact that it is instinctive. Others object to the rights argument because they think that animals have no duties and that a being cannot have rights unless it has duties. Defenders of the rights argument claim that a being can have rights even if it has no duties. Still others object to the rights argument on the grounds that, while animals have some rights, they do not have the right to life because they do not understand what the future is. Some respond that this implies that normal human newborns do not have a right to life. Finally, some object to the rights argument because they think it implies that we ought to try to keep wild animals from killing on another.

Selected Readings

Feinberg, Joel. *Rights, Justice, and the Bounds of Liberty*. Princeton, NJ: Princeton University Press, 1980.

Frey, R. G. *Interests and Rights: The Case Against Animals*. Oxford: Oxford University Press, 1980.

Regan, Tom. *The Case for Animal Rights*. Berkeley, CA: University of California Press, 1983.

Regan, Tom and Peter Singer (eds). *Animal Rights and Human Obligations*, 2nd ed. Englewood Cliffs, NJ: Prentice-Hall, 1989.

Sechzer, Jeri. *The Role of Animals in Biomedical Research*. New York: New York Academy of Sciences, 1983.

Singer, Peter. *Animal Liberation*, 2nd ed. New York: New York Review, 1990.

Glossary

Abortion The ending of a pregnancy before live birth.

Absurdity In existential philosophy, the frightening sense that there is no rational world order and no meaning to life.

Absolute Standards Moral standards that are objective and universal.

Act Utilitarianism The view that an act is right if it maximizes happiness and that otherwise it is wrong. See *Classical Act Utilitarianism* and *Average Act Utilitarianism*.

Action-Based Ethics A family of moral theories which focus primarily on the moral evaluation of acts, not persons. The view that we ought to begin moral theory with a theory of right action and then define virtue in terms of right action.

Active Nondiscrimination Programs Programs which do not explicitly use sex-race in hiring and admissions but instead make an active effort to ensure that all current hiring and admissions are completely sex-race blind, find those who perform sexist-racist acts, and severely punish these people. See *Affirmative Action Programs*.

Affirmative Action Programs Programs which explicitly use sex and/or race in hiring and admissions in order to reduce the effect of past and current sexism and/or racism. See *Active Nondiscrimination Programs*.

Agape Christian love and charity toward all people.

Animal Either (1) a member of the biological kingdom *animalia* or (2) any *animalia* other than a human.

Anxiety In existential philosophy, the mood of uncertainty that accompanies existential freedom.

Applied ethics The study of specific ethical issues that are controversial, such as whether abortion should be permitted.

Average Act Utilitarianism The view that an act is right if it maximizes average happiness and that otherwise it is wrong.

Authenticity In existential philosophy, being your own person by being responsible for your values and worldview.

Average Rule Utilitarianism The view that an act is right if the system of rules which would, if followed by everyone, maximize average happiness includes a rule which states that the act is right.

Bad Faith In Sartre's existentialism, self-deception that is designed to avoid freedom and responsibility for yourself.

The Basic Argument for Equal Treatment The argument that: Unless there is a relevant difference between two groups of people, they ought to be treated in the same way. There are no relevant differences between women and men and/or people of different races. Therefore, women and men and/or people of different races ought to be treated in the same way. See *The Revised Argument for Equal Treatment.*

Categorical Imperative   A command or requirement that applies to someone without conditions. According to Kant, there is one general unconditional moral requirement that underlies all morality. See *Formula of Universal Law and Formula of the End in Itself.*

Censorship   Governmental prohibition of the distribution of pictures or descriptions.

Character   The sum total of a person's tendencies to feel, think, and act in specific ways.

Classical Act Utilitarianism   The view that an act is right if it maximizes total happiness and that otherwise the act is wrong.

Classical Rule Utilitarianism   The view that an act is right if the system of rules which would, if followed by everyone, maximize total happiness includes a rule which states that the act is right.

Clinically Sexually Explicit   Sexually explicit materials which are neither obscene nor sexually interesting. See *Obscene, Sexually Explicit and Erotica.*

Consequentialism   The view that whether an act is right or wrong is determined, directly or indirectly, by the act's consequences and not by its intrinsic features.

Covert Racism   Racism which occurs when an act, practice, or attitude does not explicitly use race but is nevertheless designed with the intent to create unjustified differences between the races or to exploit irrelevant differences between the races. See *Racism, Overt Racism,* and *Unintentional Racism.*

Divine Command   The theory that God is the source of morality and that God requires people to be moral.

Developmentalism   The view that rich people in rich countries have strong and extensive moral obligations to give to poor people in poor countries. See *Neo-Malthusianism.*

The Doctrine of the Mean   Aristotle's claim that for every virtue there are two vices—a vice of excess and a vice of lack.

The Direct Compensation Principle   The moral principle that people who do immoral actions ought to be punished and made to compensate those hurt by these actions. See *The Indirect Compensation Principle.*

Egoistic Hedonism   The view that the best way to live is to pursue pleasurable experiences and anything that will contribute to your own favorable balance of pleasure over pain.

Emotivism   A subjectivist theory that moral judgments in language are expressions of emotional reactions to worldly events and attempts to influence other people's behavior.

Erotica   Sexually explicit, but not obscene, pictures or descriptions which are sexually interesting. See *Clinically Sexually Explicit, Sexually Explicit, Pornography and Obscene.*

Ethics   The part of philosophy that rationally studies how to live, what sort of person to be, how to treat other people, and how to judge other people.

Existential Freedom   A person's power to choose and be responsible for her own values, way of living, and worldview.

Existentialism A type of philosophy that focuses on questions about individual freedom, the meaning of life, and personal relationships.

Expected Happiness A property of actions. It is the sum of the happiness produced by every possible outcome of the action times the probability that the action will produce that outcome.

Egoistic Ethical Hedonism The view that an act by a person is right if it produces the most pleasure for that person. See *Egoistic Hedonism.*

Extreme poverty The poverty experienced by those in the bottom twenty percent of the world's wealth.

Formula of the End in Itself One formulation of Kant's Categorical Imperative: Act in such a way that you treat humanity, whether in your own person or in the person of another, always at the same time as an end in itself and never simply as a means.

Formula of Universal Law One formulation of Kant's Categorical Imperative: Act only according to that maxim whereby you can, at the same time, will that it should become a universal law.

The Function Argument An argument central to Aristotle's theory of virtue. The function of something is what it does better than anything else. The thing humans do better than anything else is reason. So, the function of humans is to reason. A good person is a person who performs the function of persons well. Therefore, a good person is a person who reasons well.

Gender The differences between women and men which are sociological in origin. See *Sex.*

Good Will In Kant's philosophy, intending to do what is morally good because it is morally good.

The Harm Principle States that the government may prohibit an act if it is an act in which one person harms another.

Hedonism The view that the only good in life is pleasure.

Hypothetical Imperative A command or requirement that applies to someone only under certain conditions, such as that he has certain desires or emotions.

I-Thou In Buber's philosophy, a reciprocal relationship with another person that is not shaped by preconceptions or purposes.

The Indirect Compensation Principle The moral principle that people who benefit from the immoral actions of others ought to compensate those hurt by these actions. See *The Direct Compensation Principle.*

Interests What a being has when something can be good or bad for that being.

Intrinsic Features Features of an act that are not part of the act's consequences.

Intuition See *Moral Intuition.*

Legal Moralism The principle that the government may prohibit an act if it is an act which, while it harms or offends no one, is immoral.

Legal Paternalism The principle that the government may prohibit an act if it is an act in which one person harms herself.

Legally obscene Material that (1) the average person, applying contemporary community standards, would find, taken as a whole, appeals to the prurient interest and (2) depicts or describes, in a patently offensive way, sexual conduct that is specifically defined by law and, (3) taken as a whole, lacks serious literary, artistic, political or scientific value.

Maximizing Consequentialism Any version of consequentialism which holds that we ought to produce as much happiness as possible. See *Consequentialism.*

Moral Intuition A special mental sense which can detect which actions and results of actions are objectively good or evil.

Moral Philosophy In its broader meaning, it is the same thing as ethics. In its narrower meaning, moral philosophy is the investigation of the basic principles and underlying ideas of Western morality.

Moral Relativism The position that different moral standards govern people in different cultures or different historical periods so that no moral standards are universal or absolute.

Moral Subjectivism The view that moral standards are always a matter of personal opinion, individual emotions, or societal customs, and so are not objective.

Mutual Relationship A relationship in which one person's attitude toward another, such as Manuel being a friend to Julius, is the same as the other person's attitude toward him (Julius is also a friend to Manuel).

Natural Law The moral theory that claims that there are naturally good and naturally bad ways for people to live.

Neo-Malthusianism The view that, in many countries, population growth will outpace economic growth and lead to extreme poverty and that, therefore, rich countries ought not aid these countries. See *Developmentalism*.

Nihilism The position that nothing is objectively good, so that any action is as good as any other.

Non-Maximizing Consequentialism Any version of consequentialism which holds that we ought not produce as much happiness as possible. See *Maximizing Consequentialism*.

Noumenal World In Kant's philosophy, the ultimately real world which is not spatial, temporal, or subject to natural causation.

Objective Standards Moral standards that are independent of people's beliefs, emotions, or customs.

Obscene Something extraordinarily offensive, indecent or repulsive. See *Legally Obscene, Sexually Explicit, Clinically Sexually Explicit, Pornography,* and *Erotica*.

The Offense Principle States that the government may prohibit an act if it is an act in which one person offends another.

Overt Racism Racism which occurs when a racist act, practice, or attitude explicitly uses race. See *Racism, Cover Racism,* and *Unintentional Racism*.

Paradigm Humans Humans with the mental functions of normal adult humans.

Photographic Child Pornography Sexually explicit and obscene photographs of children engaged in sexual conduct.

Pornography Material that is sexually explicit and obscene. See *Sexually Explicit, Obscene, Erotica,* and *Clinically Sexually Explicit*.

Potentiality to be a Person A fetus's capability of developing into a baby and a self-conscious person. In moral disputes about abortion, this potentiality is sometimes used to support a fetus's right to life.

Preferential Treatment Programs A type of affirmative action program in which a school or firm either considers all applicants from all sexes-races for all positions but gives a certain amount of preference to applicants of a certain race, or sets aside a certain number of positions for members of a certain sex-race. See *Affirmative Action Program*.

Psychological Hedonism The theory that it is a psychological fact about people that they pursue only what they think will bring them pleasure and that they avoid only what they think will bring them pain.

Racial Conservative One who thinks that there are many relevant natural differences between people of different races and that these differences imply that some races ought to be subordinate to others. See *Racial Liberal, Racial Progressive,* and *Racial Radical.*

Racial Liberal One who thinks that there are no natural and relevant differences between people of different races. See *Racial Conservative, Racial Progressive,* and *Racial Radical.*

Racial Progressive One who thinks that there are many relevant natural differences between people of different races and that these differences do not imply that some races ought to be subordinate to others. See *Racial Conservative, Racial Liberal,* and *Racial Radical.*

Racial Radical One who thinks that there are many relevant natural differences between people of different races and that we ought to use technology to remove the natural disabilities of inferior races. See *Racial Conservative, Racial Liberal,* and *Racial Progressive.*

Racism The view that racist acts, practices, or attitudes ought to be encouraged. An act, practice, or attitude is racist when it creates unjustified differences between the races or exploits irrelevant differences between the races. People are racist when they knowingly perform a racist act, support a racist practice, or have a racist attitude. See *Sexism.*

Rational World Order An intrinsic unity, reasonableness, and purpose to the universe that is frequently traced to a divine plan.

Relative Standards Moral standards that exist only for some type of people, or only for some historical periods, or only for some environmental or cultural conditions.

The Revised Argument for Equal Treatment The argument that: Unless there is a relevant natural difference between two groups of people, they ought to be treated in the same way. There are no relevant natural differences between women and men and/or people of different races. Therefore, women and men and/or people of different races ought to be treated in the same way. See *The Basic Argument for Equal Treatment.*

Rule Utilitarianism The view that an act is right if the system of rules which would, if followed by everyone, maximize happiness includes a rule which states that the act is right. See *Classical Rule Utilitarianism* and *Average Rule Utilitarianism.*

Self-development The view that the best way to live is to develop your talents and abilities to their fullest extent.

Self-effacing A view is self-effacing when the view implies that people should not believe the view.

Self-interest The view that the best way to live is to promote your own interests, whether these interests are selfish or not.

Selfishness The view that the best way to live is to care only for yourself.

Selfish Hedonism See *Egoistic Hedonism.*

Sex The differences between women and men which are biological in origin. See *Gender.*

Sex Correlations Differences in the number of a particular sex that succeed at a particular task which are the result of natural differences between the sexes—not sexual socialization. See *Sex Roles.*

Sex Roles Differences in the number of a particular sex that succeed at a particular task which are the result of sexual socialization. See *Sex Correlations.*

Sexism The view that sexist acts, practices or attitudes ought to be encouraged. An act, practice or attitude is sexist when it creates unjustified differences between the sexes or exploits irrelevant differences between the sexes. People are sexist when they knowingly perform a sexist act, support a sexist practice, or have a sexist attitude. See *Racism*.

Sexual Socialization The process by which people come to embody the attitudes, beliefs and characteristics associated with their sex in their society. See *Socialization*.

Sexual Conservative One who thinks that there are many relevant natural differences between women and men and that these differences imply that women ought to be subordinate to men. See *Sexual Liberal, Sexual Progressive*, and *Sexual Radical*.

Sexual Liberal One who thinks that there are no natural and relevant differences between the sexes. See *Sexual Conservative, Sexual Progressive*, and *Sexual Radical*.

Sexual Progressive One who thinks that there are many relevant natural differences between women and men and that these differences do not imply that women ought to be subordinate to men. See *Sexual Conservative, Sexual Liberal*, and *Sexual Radical*.

Sexual Radical One who thinks that there are many relevant natural differences between women and men and that we ought to use technology to remove the natural disabilities of women. See *Sexual Conservative, Sexual Liberal*, and *Sexual Progressive*.

Sexually Blind Society A possible ideal society. In a sexually blind society people are indifferent to whether someone is a man or a woman. See *Sexually Stratified Society* and *Sexually Diverse Society*.

Sexually Diverse Society A possible ideal society. In a sexually diverse society people care about the differences between men and women, neither sex is subordinate to the other, and everyone regards the differences between the sexes as something to be celebrated. See *Sexually Blind Society* and *Sexually Stratified Society*.

Sexually Explicit Pictures or descriptions which contain detailed or graphic depictions or descriptions of sexual acts or organs. See *Obscene, Clinically Sexually Explicit, Pornography,* and *Erotica*.

Sexually Stratified Society A possible ideal society. In a sexually stratified society people care about the differences between women and men and one sex occupies a place subordinate to the other. See *Sexually Blind Society* and *Sexually Diverse Society*.

Slippery-Slope Arguments Arguments in which one argues that if we do some seemingly appropriate act, then we will inevitably do some other clearly inappropriate act.

Social and Political Philosophy The study of the fundamental principles of society and the state, including what form of government and economic system is best.

Social Contract The theory that morality and the authority of government derives from an agreement or contract between people to give up some of their powers in exchange for the benefits of law, order, and a civilized society.

Socialization The process by which people come to accept and embody attitudes, beliefs and characteristics of their society. See *Sexual Socialization*.

Speciesism The view that speciesist acts, practices or attitudes ought to be encouraged. An act, practice or attitude is speciesist when it creates unjustified differences between species or exploits irrelevant differences between species. Also, the view that a difference of species, without any other morally relevant difference, is sufficient to justify treating animals and humans differently.

Strong Virtue Ethics Ethical theories which hold that action-based ethics are not only incomplete but seriously flawed because they have ignored the virtues. The view that we ought to begin moral theory with a theory of virtue and then define right action in terms of virtue. See *Virtue Ethics* and *Weak Virtue Ethics.*

Subjective Standards Moral standards that are only a matter of personal opinion, individual emotions, or societal customs.

Triage The practice of sorting wounded soldiers (or countries) into three groups—those that will survive (or develop) without aid, those that will survive (or develop) only if given aid and those that will not survive (or develop) even if given aid—and giving aid only to the second group.

True Self An inner nature that is different from a person's everyday understanding of herself. Many moral theories are based on the idea that people have a true self that should be developed.

Unintentional Racism Racism which occurs when an act, practice, or attitude has the effect of creating unjustified differences between the races or of exploiting irrelevant differences between the races, but the people involved in the act, practice or attitude do not intend (or perhaps even realize) this effect. See *Racism, Overt Racism,* and *Covert Racism.*

Universal Standards Moral standards that apply to all people at all times in all conditions.

Universalistic Consequentialism Any version of consequentialism which holds that everyone is equal in moral importance. See *Consequentialism.*

Universalization The requirement that a moral principle must apply in the same way to all people who are in similar circumstances.

Utilitarianism A version of consequentialism. See *Classical Act Utilitarianism, Average Act Utilitarianism, Classical Rule Utilitarianism,* and *Average Rule Utilitarianism.*

Viability The ability of a fetus to survive outside the mother's womb.

Vice A bad quality of people, an undesirable disposition of people.

Virtue A good quality of people, a desirable disposition of people.

Virtue Ethics A family of moral theories which focus primarily on the moral evaluation of persons, not acts.

Weak Virtue Ethics Ethical theories which hold that, while action-based approaches are correct and useful, they are incomplete because they fail to give the virtues the analysis they deserve. See *Virtue Ethics* and *Strong Virtue Ethics.*

Will to Power In Nietzsche's philosophy, the natural drive in living things to control other things.

Index